What Is Christianity?

What Is Christianity?

An Introduction
to the Christian Religion

Gail Ramshaw

Fortress Press

Minneapolis

WHAT IS CHRISTIANITY?
An Introduction to the Christian Religion

Cover image: Catholic mosaic on the Basilica of the Rosary in Lourdes © Shutterstock.com / Idambies. Bad district. Vandalism. Graffity on a wall. Kiev, Ukraine © Shutterstock.com / Sergey Kamshylin. Marble statue of the crucifixion of Jesus with a colorful out of focus background © Shutterstock.com / Kamira. Shadow of a cross on a wall © Shutterstock.com / Taigi. Medieval style door in Grenoble, France © Shutterstock.com / TeeraPhoto. Stained glass window of Jesus Christ carrying the cross © Shutterstock.com / Nancy Bauer. Statue of Christ © Shutterstock.com / chiakto. Old wooden cross depicting crucifixion of Jesus Christ © Shutterstock.com / CURAphotography
Cover design: Alisha Lofgren
Book design: PerfecType, Nashville, TN

Library of Congress Cataloging-in-Publication Data
ISBN: 978-0-8006-9819-5

Manufactured in the U.S.A.

CONTENTS

ACKNOWLEDGMENTS

As I complete the writing of this textbook, I acknowledge help from many people, and I offer them my thanks. Thanks to the 1960s theology faculty of Valparaiso University, where I learned more about my Lutheran heritage. Thanks to my graduate professors, especially Russian Orthodox Alexander Schmemann, Roman Catholic Raymond E. Brown, and Anglican Cyril Richardson: their vast learning inspired my life of scholarship. At La Salle University, where I taught Christianity for twenty-two years, my thanks to the administration, for supporting my teaching and granting me leaves; to the chairs of the Religion Department, especially David Efroymson, Geffrey Kelly, and Margaret McGuinness; to the director for many years of the Honors Program, John Grady; and to my colleagues, for years of helpful conversation. I learned about undergraduates from the 3900 students who wanted, or did not want, to take my courses. I am grateful to the authors of the many textbooks I used over the years, from which I learned much about Christianity and the ways it can be presented. As a scholar of liturgical language, I collaborated with and learned from Christians of many denominations. My gratitude to my colleagues in the ecumenical North American Academy of Liturgy and to my hosts in North America, Europe, and Asia, who taught me more than books can about world Christianity as a lived experience. My thanks to Fortress Press, first to Michael West for the suggestion to write this textbook, and now to publisher and managing director Will Bergkamp for his support. Special gratitude to project manager Marissa Wold and to copyeditor David Cottingham for their gracious assistance. Thanks to Esther Diley for securing permission on the use of the images. Prior to and during the writing, dear friends prodded my thinking on the many related topics. To my sister Elaine Ramshaw, thanks for help with the films. Finally, from beginning to end, more than gratitude to Gordon Lathrop, who read and commented on each draft with mind and heart.

The preparation of this textbook was completed in 2013 on June 29, the date on which the apostles Peter and Paul are commemorated, without whom there would be no Christianity as we know it.

Gail Ramshaw

Introduction:
Why study Christianity?

Fig. Intro. 1. This crucifix, crafted by an unknown twentieth-century El Salvadorian La Palma artisan, depicts the cross of Christ as the tree of life. The dove represents the Holy Spirit.

Why study religion?

Most humans dead and alive have been and are to some small or great degree religious. In past and present, people have lived within a community in which one or several religions determine the worldview, influence thoughts, and guide behavior. Twenty thousand years ago, enormous effort went into painting religious imagery far inside caves in present-day France and Spain, and scholars now can only speculate about the meaning of these works of art. Understanding centuries of human history requires consideration of the religious attitudes of the people involved. Currently, daily news items include sometimes comforting and sometimes horrific evidence that religion continues to inspire humankind. Thus like it or not, the human species is connected to religion. An educated person ought to know something about the ways that religion establishes values and creates psychological and social order for its adherents. Such study will help a twenty-first-century person understand world events and may also assist in one's personal relationship to religion.

religion = a communal worldview about ultimate reality enacted in rituals and expressed through ethics

One way to study religion is to read primary religious texts. For centuries, persons engaged in religious practice have written down their understanding of the meaning and effect of their religion. Official religious documents indicate how the community's leaders hoped that religion would function for and by the people. On the other hand, individuals' accounts of religious experience are instructive, since not only do they indicate the power of religion in people's lives, but often individuals describe their religion in a way other than how their leaders taught it.

Given the universality of religion, the magnitude of effort, time, and resources consumed in religious behavior, and the persistence of religion over tens or hundreds of thousands of years, cultural ecologists argue that there must have been important adaptive advantages to religion during our evolution.—Brian Hayden[1]

For about 150 years, scholars have attempted an objective study of the phenomenon of religion. These phenomenologists analyze a religion, oftentimes other than their own, to understand why humans engage in such behavior and what good or ill comes from its **practice**. What do people believe? What is their ethical system? What are their collective and personal rituals? How does this system form a community? A well-known example of such a theory is the one identified with Karl Marx, who believed that religion is a fraud invented by the rich to keep the poor content in their position of subservience. Other theorists proposed far more benign theories about what religion is and how it functions.

Why study Christianity?

In the twenty-first century, approximately one-third of the human race identifies as Christian. To be aware of what all Christians mean by what they say and do, a student of Christianity will need to learn something about what its leaders claim about that meaning, both what is universally accepted and what is hotly debated, as well as about the historical development of the religion and the lived experience of its practitioners.

Studying Christianity is not simple. Like an interstate highway, the road called Christian is extremely broad. Some cars are traveling fast, others slow. Some are obeying the traffic regulations, while others are pushing the limits or ignoring

to practice a religion = to participate regularly in its activities

Christianity = a worldwide religion based on **faith** in the **resurrection** of **Jesus Christ**

faith = a communal worldview appropriated by an individual that guides one's life; confidence in a saving **God**

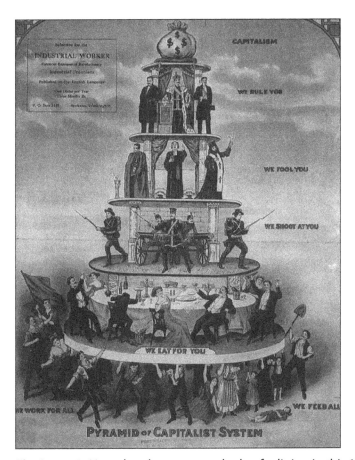

Fig. Intro. 2. Note the placement and role of religion in this 1911 poster depicting the Marxist Pyramid of Capitalist System.

God = (uppercase *G*) the supreme being

Jesus = the standard English spelling of Yeshua, the given name of a first-century Jewish preacher and healer

Christ = the anointed one, from the Greek **christos**, rendering the Hebrew **moshiach**, messiah

resurrection, being risen from the dead = a transformed human existence after death

theology = the systematic study of God and related topics

Trinity = the Christian mystery of one God as three, named Father, Son, and Holy Spirit

some of the rules entirely. There are shoulders alongside the roadway: Are the shoulders part of the roadway? There is, however, an edge where the pavement stops, so that everyone agrees that if you are driving through the adjacent cornfield, you are no longer on the highway. So it is that Christians over the centuries and around the world have practiced their faith in many and diverse ways.

An example of this diversity is another book titled *What Is Christianity?* In 1899, the historian Adolf von Harnack published a set of lectures that he had delivered at the University of Berlin, Germany, in which he argued that nearly all Christian teachings and practices were seriously in error.[2] Christians, Harnack said, are to imitate Jesus by living in the love of God and toward the neighbor—and that's all there is to it. Harnack argued that nearly everything said in **theology** about Jesus and God, for example the teaching that God is a **Trinity**, was wrong and ought to be abandoned. Why Harnack's answer to the question "What Is Christianity?" is so interesting is that, despite his fame as a theological thinker, nearly all teachers and believers of the religion reject his claims.

Fig. Intro. 3. What do you know about Christianity that could help you interpret this eighteenth-century painting?

Many different kinds of students take a course in Christianity. Some students are practicing Christians, some of whom are well versed in their own **branch** or **denomination**, some of whom know about the religion as a whole, and others who have only a rudimentary idea of what Christianity is all about. For some practicing Christians, the academic study of a wide range of Christian beliefs and practices may feel liberating, and for others it may be disturbing. For yet other students,

branch = one of the four major divisions within Christianity: Eastern Orthodoxy, Roman Catholicism, Protestantism, Pentecostalism

denomination = a subdivision of a branch of Christianity, with a distinctive pattern of belief and practice

Fig. Intro. 4. What do you know about Christianity that could help you interpret this image? The man and the woman are not Jesus and his mother Mary.

Christianity is wholly unfamiliar, or their small knowledge of the religion may have been shaped by popular culture, for example by movies in which Christianity may be erroneously depicted. This textbook attempts to serve all these varied students by objectively describing commonalities and at least some of the differences within the religion.

How is this textbook set up?

Rather than a narrative history of the development of Christianity or a systematic study of theology, this textbook looks at the lived experience of the Christian **church**. Each of the twelve chapters addresses an issue that is fundamental to the Christian religion, and each chapter is subdivided into specific smaller questions. Each chapter includes:

church = any assembly of Christians; a building used for worship; a service of worship; also, a non-Christian religious organization; Church = part of the official title of an international, national, or local Christian organization

1. A depiction of the **crucifix**, the primary symbol of Christianity, that is particularly appropriate to the topic, along with some information about the image
2. "An Answer from a scholar," a short section in which one of the renowned scholars of religion answers the chapter's question theoretically
3. "Answers from the churches," an essay summarizing the Christian responses to the question in past and present, focusing on dominant agreement, yet with some reference to minority positions

crucifix = the body of Jesus affixed to a cross, recalling his crucifixion, a method of execution in which the tortured victim was affixed to an upright stake and died of asphyxiation

4. In the sidebar, definitions of Christian terms that occur in boldface in the text
5. In the sidebar, quotations related to the text
6. Pictures to instigate discussion
7. Suggestions that include
   a. A list of required vocabulary
   b. Questions for further study
   c. A topic for debate
   d. A subject for a personal essay
   e. A biblical passage, a short story, a novel, and a film that enhance consideration of the chapter's question
   f. A list of several books for further reading.

The textbook concludes with a chronology of Christian history and a book list.

Instructors can find useful additional information about the textbook's images and suggestions in a Teachers Aid provided on the product website.

Welcome, then, to this textbook and to its questions: *What Is Christianity?*

Suggestions

1. Review the Introduction's vocabulary: branch, Christ, Christianity, church/Church, crucifix, denomination, faith, God, Jesus, practice, religion, resurrection, theology, Trinity.
2. Compare the definition of Christianity given in this Introduction with other definitions in dictionaries and online, and present arguments for and against each.
3. Access and discuss a pie chart of the current global distribution of Christianity.
4. Discuss a current news item concerning some aspect of the Christian church. Do you understand the details that have been reported? What more information is needed?
5. Write a personal essay describing your connections with or knowledge of Christianity.
6. In the Bible, look up Acts 9:2 and Acts 11:26. Comment on the difference.
7. View and discuss the 1985 film *Agnes of God*, in which each of the three major characters holds a different understanding of Christianity.

For Further Reading

Micklethwait, John, and Adrian Wooldridge. *God Is Back: How the Global Revival of Faith Is Changing the World.* New York: Penguin, 2009.

Pals, Daniel L. *Eight Theories of Religion.* 2nd ed. New York: Oxford University Press, 2006.

Putnam, Robert D., and David E. Campbell. *American Grace: How Religion Divides and Unites Us.* New York: Simon & Schuster, 2010.

Why is the Bible central to Christianity?

1

Fig. 1.1. A page from a fifteenth-century blockbook called a *Biblia Pauperum*. Because the meaning of Jesus relates to the Old Testament, the crucifixion is flanked by two Old Testament stories: God saving Isaac from child sacrifice (Gen. 22:1-14), and Moses displaying a bronze serpent to cure Israelites from snakebite (Num. 21:4-9).

◇ An answer from a scholar

Mircea Eliade (1907–1986) was a Romanian historian of religion renowned for his analyses of religious experience. In his 1963 book *Myth and Reality*[1] Eliade described **myths** as traditional stories that narrate sacred history. By relating what occurred at the origin of life or at the beginning of a society, a myth indicates the highest cultural values; it provides answers to the question of the origin of evil, offers a model for exemplary behavior, and explains and interprets death. Such myths are true, not in the sense that they are factually accurate, but rather in the sense that they convey essential values. Myths are told through the generations to maintain communal identity from parents to children, to pass down a particular vision of how to achieve the good life, and to elevate human life by connection with the **divine**.

Eliade taught that groups rehearse these myths during communal **rituals**. By celebrating the myth in a festival with storytelling, feasting, singing, performance, and games, the community renews its communal bonds, experiences something of the power of the first creation, and instills yet again the positive values celebrated in the story. Without the communal repetition of myths, humans are less than they might be, since these cultural stories of beginnings and endings, struggles and victories, villains and heroes give layers of meaning to individual and communal existence. Prayers also refer to the myths; for example, to heal a sick person now, the deity is asked to re-create a perfect world. It is as if telling the **sacred** story renews the life of the believer, who can be transformed by primordial powers. According to Eliade, all religions have myths. Although one religion may judge the myths of another religion to be false tales, the believing community honors its sacred stories as religiously true and conveying extraordinary power for them.

Using Eliade, one can say that Christianity finds its treasured myths in the **Bible**. Eliade described various types of myths, all of which can be found in the Bible. Cosmological myths tell about the origin of the universe; Genesis 1, Genesis 2, Job 38-39, Psalm 104, Proverbs 8, and John 1 describe

---

myth = a traditional story told to convey cultural values

divine = an extraordinary power beyond what is human

For the man of the archaic societies, the essential thing is to know the myths. It is essential not only because myths provide him with an explanation of the World and his own mode of being in the World, but above all because, by recollecting the myths, by re-enacting them, he is able to repeat what the Gods, the Heroes, of the Ancestors did *ab origine*. To know the myths is to learn not only how things came into existence but also where to find them and how to make them reappear when they disappear.—Mircea Eliade[2]

in different ways the creation of the world. Etiological myths describe how something came to be; for example, in Gen. 9:13, the phenomenon of the rainbow is explained as God's bow (as in bow and arrow) placed in the sky to become a sign of promise, rather than a threatening weapon. Eschatological myths describe how the world will come to its end; Mark 13 and the Book of Revelation are examples of biblical descriptions of the end of all things. Transformation myths illustrate how persons survive disasters and are changed into something better than they were: the long narrative in Exodus tells how a group of slaves became a free nation, and Scripture includes many transformational tales in which Jesus healed people who were sick, maimed, demon-possessed, and even dead. Both happy and sad historical memories, for example the remembrance of the **martyrs**, are connected with the transformative power of Jesus.

A summary of the contents of the Bible
    Old Testament / Hebrew Scriptures:
        5 books of Moses and the law, the "Pentateuch"
        12 books of history, about the years
            1150–500 BCE
        17 books about and oracles from preachers,
            "the prophets"
        5 books of maxims and poetry, called "Wisdom
            writings"
Some churches add:
    7 books from 300–100 BCE, "the apocrypha,"
        "deuterocanonical"
New Testament
    4 Gospels
    1 history
    21 letters, often called epistles
    1 book of visions

Biblical references use a numbering system that was made up by Stephen Langton in the thirteenth century. For example, "John 3:16" means the Gospel according to John, the third chapter, the sixteenth verse.

ritual = a repeated symbolic communal activity

sacred = embodying and conveying divine power

martyr = a person killed because of religious conviction

Bible/Scripture = a compilation of some seventy books held to be sacred and authoritative in Christianity

Gospel/gospel = (uppercase G) a biblical book that narrates the meaning of the life of Jesus; (lowercase g) the good news that God saves the world through Jesus; a style of American religious music characterized by simple melody and harmony and rigorous beat

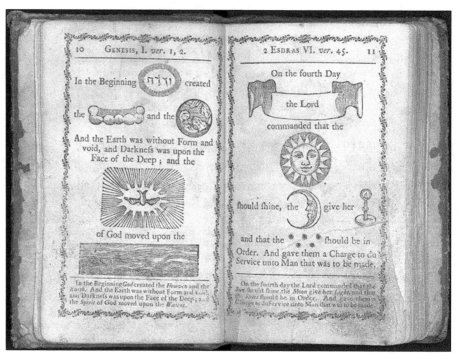

Fig. 1.2. *Hieroglyphick* Bibles, such as this one printed in 1788 by Isaiah Thomas, were popular in early America for teaching children Bible stories.

Christians focus on whichever biblical myths best instill their own values. For many centuries, the most significant cosmological myth for Christians was in Genesis 2. The well-known story tells how God shaped a male out of the dirt of the ground (the Hebrew word *adamah* means soil), and because the man was lonely, God created the animals, but finally created a female out of the male's rib. Instructed by Eliade, one can say that this myth stressed the following values: males are superior to females; the female belongs to the male; and at death humans return to the earth. Whether or not persons think of this story as factual, its values might be maintained as true. However, recently Christians have focused on the cosmological myth in Genesis 1. In this telling, after all the animals are created, God creates males and females at the same time. Both bear what is called "the image of God," and God blesses them simultaneously. This myth suggests gender equality, and it stresses humans' connection with God, rather than with the soil. Eliade stressed that whichever are the treasured myths, so will be the values of that religious community.

◈ Answers from the churches

Christian churches teach that the Bible is of primary importance. The reading of Scripture is one of the main components of all Christian **worship**. Proclaiming the Bible instructs the community in its faith. Scripture is a major source for theological reflection. Meditation on Scripture is a foundation for personal devotion. Memorized Bible passages become daily prayers. So what are the contents of the Bible, and how is Scripture interpreted?

worship = a ritual by which believers honor God and unite their community

What are the contents of the Old Testament?

The Christian Bible began at least 2500 years ago when the Hebrews, an ancient Near Eastern ethnic and religious community, told its memories and recorded its worldview first orally, and then in written form. Later in history, the Hebrews were called Israelites, and still later **Jews**. Over the centuries of living in the Near and Middle East, this group eventually compiled its most treasured stories into the Hebrew Scriptures, called by Christians the Old Testament. These Scriptures include: stories of their origin as descendants of Abraham and Sarah, who lived about 1800 BCE; their escape from Egyptian slavery in perhaps 1250 BCE; their occupation of Canaan, the lands east of the Mediterranean Sea; the establishment of a kingdom that was most successful under King David in 1000 BCE; their final military defeat by 587 BCE; their deportation to the enemy lands; and their eventual return to their land. Important in Israelite memory are God's **covenant** of care for the people, a law of commands given by God, ritual worship centered in the temple in Jerusalem, and instruction and oracles preached by the **prophets**. The various written texts, although composed over a millennium, share a primary theme—that God is to be worshiped as the giver of life who expects moral behavior, yet is perpetually forgiving. God is both just and merciful.

Jews = the descendants of Judah, a great-grandson of Abraham, as ethnic identity or religious community

covenant = the mutual commitment between God and the people

prophet = a person speaking for God about present behavior and future outcomes

Many scholars agree that much of the work by which the Jews compiled their stories into an authorized sacred book took place after 600 BCE when, the Jews having been deported and with no access to the temple in Jerusalem, they needed to clarify what their religious community was all about. This editing effort is apparent in the story of the flood in Gen. 6:9–9:17. The content of Gen. 6:5-8, which refers to God as "the LORD" (in Hebrew, *YHWH*), is repeated in 6:11-13, which refers to

God as "God" (in Hebrew, *Elohim*). In the God story (see 6:19), there is one pair of each animal, and in the LORD story (7:2), there are seven pairs of ritually clean animals and one pair of ritually unclean animals. Many biblical scholars conclude that two different versions of the flood story were interleaved into one account, and this editing was organized by rabbis hoping to secure their traditional memories, without which their identity might be lost. For the last two hundred years, scholars have worked to trace four main sources that were compiled into the current text of the Hebrew Scriptures, to date these different sources, and to understand the similarities and differences between them.

By the first century of the Common Era, the Roman Empire controlled all the land surrounding the Mediterranean, including the eastern shore lands in which many Jews resided. In the year 70, squelching attempts of Jewish revolutionaries to regain their independence, the Roman armies destroyed the city of Jerusalem, and in about 90, responding to this situation of devastation, Jewish rabbis authorized the final form of their Scriptures for religious use. Today, when Jews gather in synagogues, they read from and comment upon this **canon**, referred to with the acronym Tanakh: the T refers to the books of the law, the Torah; the N to the books of the prophets (in Hebrew, *Nebiim*); and the K the books of songs and poetic writings (in Hebrew, *Kethubim*). When the New Testament mentions "the Scriptures," it means the Tanakh.

What are the contents of the New Testament?

canon = the approved and authorized list of biblical books

Many Jews expected that God would keep the promise to send a leader who, like Moses, would save them from enemy domination. One person who aroused considerable interest in this regard was a first-century itinerant preacher and healer named Jesus from Nazareth. All the first-century accounts of Jesus that have survived into our century were written by his followers. Many questions that contemporary people have regarding Jesus are not answered in these early accounts.

These accounts do say that he traveled throughout the eastern shore lands of the Mediterranean, preaching about the arrival of what is termed "**the kingdom of God**." Jesus both taught traditional Jewish beliefs and challenged some current religious practices. He told **parables**, healed the sick, and acted in countercultural ways, for example by eating with disreputable persons and by welcoming women into his circle. His **disciples** believed him to be the Christ, the one anointed by God

the kingdom of God = a complex biblical term that refers to the realm of divine authority, not merely spatial nor temporal; also called "the kingdom of heaven"

to save the Jews, and they said that his **miracles** proved that he demonstrated divine power. Yet he was convicted in a religious court of blasphemy and in a Roman civil trial of sedition, and he was executed by crucifixion in about 30 CE. After his burial, his followers claimed that God had raised him from death to a new and transformed life, and that this future was open to all who believed in him. People in the Jesus movement spoke to others about their faith in his resurrection, and within several decades people began to write out their memories and interpretations of Jesus. Thus began the New Testament.

The earliest books in the New Testament, which were composed in Greek, the primary written language of the Roman Empire, are letters that Paul and anonymous church leaders wrote to other Christians to clarify **doctrine** and to counsel them about controversies.

Scholars judge that these letters were written between 50 and the early second century. Some of the letters follow a first-century pattern in which a student wrote in the name of the teacher: what is now called plagiarism was considered honor to the teacher. Thus some New Testament writings, written under the name of Paul or Peter, may have been written after their deaths by their followers. Because these letters and essays are the earliest Christian writings, they were and remain extremely significant for the church. Although the letters agree about some beliefs, the twenty-one essays differ from one another on other issues, and so through the centuries church leaders have debated the relative value of various passages of these letters.

Paul taught that humans need to be connected with God; that because of **sin** humans cannot achieve this on their own; that the gospel proclaims to the world that Jesus' death and resurrection **reconciles** humankind to God; that believers are now **justified** before the judgment of God; that Christ grants an extraordinary existence to all participants in the community of believers, both Jews and **Gentiles**, who receive his Spirit; and that finally through the life, death, and resurrection of Christ, death itself is conquered. Paul, originally a devout practicing Jew, taught that through Jesus Christ, God's promises in the Hebrew Scriptures were realized and were available now to all

parable = a short anecdote with a surprising religious message

disciple = a follower of Jesus; sometimes referring to an inner circle of twelve men

miracle = an extraordinary event beyond nature, caused by divine intervention

doctrine = the authoritative belief of an association

Blessed Lord, which has caused all holy Scriptures to be written for our learning; grant us that we may in such wise hear them, read, mark, learn, and inwardly digest them; that by patience and comfort of thy holy word, we may embrace, and ever hold fast the blessed hope of everlasting life, which thou hast given us in our savior Jesus Christ.—Thomas Cranmer, *The Book of Common Prayer*, 1549

sin = the human situation of distance from God and disobedience of divine commands

to reconcile = to restore peace in a situation of conflict

to justify = to make right before the law

Gentile = a person who is not Jewish

peoples of the world. Some historians claim that Christianity owes more to Paul's writings than it does to memories about Jesus.

Although not composed first, the four Gospels are placed first in the New Testament. Most biblical scholars agree that the Gospels were written three to eight decades after the life of Jesus and after a period of the oral transmission of stories. Although many people know the four Gospels somehow blended together or imaginatively amplified through feature

Fig. 1.3. The crucifix in a Roman Catholic Church in China. Most Christian artists depict Jesus as resembling those believers who see the image. Here Jesus wears a traditional Chinese topknot.

films, each Gospel is like a theological painting of the meaning of Jesus, in some ways similar and in interesting ways different from the other Gospels. In all four, the last two days of Jesus' life are covered in great detail. The writers did not sign their work: the names Matthew, Mark, Luke, and John are the names that tradition has given to the texts. None of the four **evangelists** claims to have known Jesus or been part of the original Jesus movement. Yet all four describe Jesus in ultimate terms, as the one from God who gives life to the world and who changes the self and the community utterly.

Most scholars agree that Mark was the earliest full Gospel. Written in about 70 perhaps at Rome, the Gospel records the faith of Christians who for nearly forty years had believed that Jesus, the messiah sent by God, had to suffer and die in order to save humankind (8:27–9:50). In Mark, Jesus preaches the coming of the kingdom of God, although the term is not defined. Mark includes no birth narratives, and the original text of Mark had no resurrection appearances. That Jesus is the Christ, and in a mysterious way God, remains a secret. God gives to the community of believers, who now face persecution, a share in the life given to the world through Jesus, who was himself persecuted to death. In Mark, Jesus is the hidden messiah.

evangelist = the author of a Christian gospel; also, a preacher to the unchurched

Most scholars agree that about ten years later, the author of Matthew expanded on Mark for an especially Jewish audience. Repeatedly the evangelist quotes a Greek translation of the Hebrew Scriptures, to prove that Jesus is the messiah that some Jews sought. According to Matthew's **Christology**, Jesus is like Moses, a great lawgiver and intermediary who conveys God's will to the people, with his Sermon on the Mount (chapters 5–7) a parallel to the words of Moses from Mount Sinai. Like the greatest prophets, Jesus can perform miracles, and through his death, God set up a new covenant, by which believers encounter God as both just and merciful. Matthew includes several stories about Jesus' infancy and two post-resurrection appearances. For Matthew, Jesus is the new Moses.

Perhaps a decade after Matthew, Luke penned his Gospel. In his introduction (1:1-4) he describes his "investigating everything carefully from the very first."[3] Only Luke includes many well-known stories about Jesus: for example, the angel coming to Mary, Jesus' birth in Bethlehem, parables like the **Good Samaritan** (10:25-37), and Jesus forgiving the thief crucified next to him (23:41-43). Luke, writing especially for a Gentile audience, describes Jesus as the Savior, a term familiar in Roman paganism. Meal clubs were popular in the Roman Empire, and Luke tells many

Christology = a theory explaining what it means that Jesus is the Christ

> Our Father in heaven,
> hallowed be your name,
> your kingdom come,
> your will be done on earth as in heaven.
> Give us today our daily bread.
> Forgive us our sins as we forgive those who sin against us.
> Save us from the time of trial
> and deliver us from evil.
> For the kingdom, the power and the glory are yours,
> now and forever. Amen
>
> —the 1988 version by the English Language
> Liturgical Consultation of the slightly different
> texts in Matt. 6:9-13 and Luke 11:2-4

the Good Samaritan = in a parable of Jesus, the hated outsider who cares for the man in need

ascension = Jesus' return to the realm of God and thus no longer being visible on earth

apostle = a prominent Christian preacher

synoptics = the Gospels of Matthew, Mark, and Luke, similar in content and order

stories of Jesus eating with both followers and public sinners. Luke stresses Jesus' compassion in healing the sick and forgiving sinners. For Luke, Jesus is the loving Savior. The only evangelist who describes Jesus' **ascension**, Luke also wrote the Acts of the **Apostles**, a book included in the Bible about the early Christian church. Because of the similarity of Matthew, Mark, and Luke, they are grouped together as the **synoptics**.

Perhaps ten to twenty years later, the fourth evangelist edited the theology of his community. In John's Gospel, Jesus is unequivocally divine, the presence of God on earth. In place of any birth narratives, John's opening poem borrows from Greek philosophy to call Jesus *Logos*, the Word of God from before the creation of the world. In John, Jesus delivers lengthy poetic speeches that develop "I am" metaphors, for example, "I am the bread of life" (6:35), "I am the gate for the sheep" (10:7): the hearer is expected to know that one translation of the Hebrew name of God, *YHWH*, is "I am who I am" (Exod. 3:14). In the synoptics, Jesus' last supper was a celebration of the Jewish feast of Passover, but in John, Jesus was crucified the day before Passover, while the lambs were being slaughtered for the feast. Only in John is Jesus buried in a garden. After the crucifixion, John describes the risen Christ appearing to his followers on the first day of the week. For John, Jesus is God.

Fig. 1.4. A page from the *Book of Kells*, which contains the four Gospels, handwritten and illustrated in Ireland in the seventh century. The winged man stands for Matthew, the lion for Mark, the ox for Luke, and the eagle for John: see Rev. 4:6-7.

Several of the New Testament letters that were written late in the first century and early in the second century dealt with emerging issues of church organization and behavior. These general writings, sometimes called "**catholic**," addressed the tensions arising between Christians and the wider culture. Since the world had not yet come to an end, Christians had to develop rules for the church, such as who could serve as **bishops**, and codes of conduct that included even details about what clothing women were to wear. Revelation, the final book of the New Testament, describes a detailed vision of the end of the world. Scholars disagree about its

Logos = Greek for "word," a title used in Greek philosophy for the emanation of God on earth and important in early Christologies catholic = (lowercase c) pertaining to all Christians universally; Catholic = (uppercase C) part of the name of one church

bishop = overseer of a geographical grouping of churches

theologian = a person learned in the study of God

meanings, and **theologians** differ concerning its significance. Some churches attend closely to its symbolic language about the future, and other churches judge the book unhelpful for contemporary believers and seldom read or interpret it.

How did all these books become the Bible?

In the second century, two different proposals attempted to simplify Scripture for Christians. A man named Marcion suggested that Christians no longer needed the Old Testament. This would radically shorten the sacred text. But he was condemned by church leaders who instead judged that the New Testament continued and amplified the Old Testament, and that without knowing the Hebrew Scriptures, readers could not understand the vocabulary used by the New Testament authors. Another man named Tatian thought that having four Gospels was confusing. Knowing that in some ways their content was mutually contradictory, Tatian compiled the four into one account and omitted the passages that seemed not to fit. But his proposal too was rejected by church leaders, who valued the four different Christologies of the Gospels. An influential second-century bishop named Irenaeus argued that some Christians had developed false doctrines because they had focused on only one of the four Gospels to the exclusion of the others.

Originally, each of the books in both Old and New Testament was handwritten on its own scroll. But already in the second century the four Gospels and the letters of Paul were handwritten on sheets of animal skins or papyrus and, for easy reference in worship and study, were bound together in what were called codexes, what are now called books. During the second and third centuries, theologians and bishops discussed which writings were authoritative enough that they could be read aloud when the community gathered for worship. It was not until 367, at a meeting of bishops, that one prominent bishop named Athanasius proposed what is the current list of Christian books—which would be added to the Hebrew Scriptures as the full canon for Christians.

The main criterion used in deciding which books were worthy of canonization was their closeness to the testimony of the apostles. Theologians rejected other accounts of the life of Jesus that they judged fanciful, for example the Gospel of Peter, in which the cross of Jesus itself talks. Athanasius's proposal was accepted. Although no church **council** has ever decreed that the Bible is a closed collection of books and should not be added to, in fact no other books have been added to the list since the fourth century, and churches have taught

Fig. 1.5. A page from the fourth-century manuscript *Codex Sinaiticus*. Note that in the Greek, there are no spaces between words.

that all other religious books have far less authority than those on the fourth-century list. Recently some scholars have studied the noncanonical books from the second and third centuries with great interest, hoping to learn about the many variations within early Christianity. Yet believers tend to trust that God led the early theologians to make the right decisions, and that the Bible as it is will continue to serve the church well.

council = a meeting of bishops to decide on controversial issues

How have Christians interpreted the Bible?

What has replaced other books being added to the Bible is the perpetual interpretation of the Scripture. Anyone who reads the whole Bible sees its complexity. Composed over about a thousand years by many authors in different life situations, the books carry a dominant theme but through many permutations. The texts themselves indicate that their authors and editors were choosing what and how to write. Yet throughout Christian history, believers have maintained that Scripture is the word of God. This metaphoric term suggests that God has a mouth and was literally talking in some language. To explain this term, most churches teach that God inspired the authors, and that everything necessary for faith is conveyed through this word of God, even though this word arose from different writers over many centuries. An alternate interpretation is that God miraculously dictated the Bible and that thus, at least in its original form, it is **inerrant**.

inerrant = having no errors

Interpretation of the Christian message began even before the New Testament was written down. Jesus and his movement spoke Aramaic, a language similar to Hebrew; yet Jesus' words are recorded in Greek. Anyone who speaks several languages knows that translations cannot be absolutely precise, since grammar differs and vocabulary reflects a specific worldview. All translation involves interpretation to some degree. Thus although some Christians prefer Bibles that have Jesus' words printed in red, other Christians consider that at best these words are English translations of Greek translations of what Jesus may have said in Aramaic.

The task of translation continued. Although in some religions the sacred text is never to be translated but rather memorized in its original language, no Christian churches have required believers to learn first-century Greek in order to read the Bible. In Greek-speaking communities, New Testament Greek is maintained, although of course in Greece the language developed and changed through the centuries. The first famous full translation of the Hebrew and Greek of the Bible into the language of the common people of the western half of Europe was completed by a biblical scholar named Jerome in 405. This translation of the Bible into Latin is called the **Vulgate** (think of the "vulgar" people!), and this translation was officially used by the Roman Catholic Church until the 1960s.

Vulgate = the fifth-century Latin translation of the Hebrew and Greek of the Bible

Throughout Christian history, innumerable unofficial translations of at least the Gospels into other languages were made. With the printing press introduced in Europe in 1450 and literacy newly important in society, Christians in several countries translated the entire Bible into their vernacular language. An early famous translation into German was published by Martin Luther in 1534, and its popularity was instrumental in bringing about a split in the European church into Roman Catholics, who maintained their use of the Vulgate, and Protestants, who protested for the availability of the Bible in their language. By 1536 William Tyndale had

In Anglo-Saxon, the English language of the year 700: "Aelc thara the thas min word gehierth, and tha wyrcth, bith gelic thaem wisan were, se his hus ofer stan getimbrode." For help in reading this, check Matt. 7:24.

Fig. 1.6. In this Eastern Orthodox image, Christ is holding a Bible open to Matt. 9:28, "Come to me."

translated most of the Bible into English, but he was burned at the stake for his work, and Miles Coverdale completed the effort. That biblical translators could be martyred indicates how important the Bible was, both to those undertaking the massive task of translation and to those who forbade vernacular translations. Over the last 1500 years, many of the world's oral languages have been given written alphabets by Christian **missionaries** and linguists in order that the Bible could be rendered into this speech. By the early twenty-first century, over one-third of the world's 6,900 languages have at least part of the Bible translated into their tongue, and this covers about 98 percent of the world's population.

missionary = a person preaching Christianity in a foreign location

KJV = the 1611 translation into English of the Hebrew and Greek of the Bible

The most famous English translation is called the **KJV**, the 1611 King James Version. James, the king of England from 1603 to 1625, authorized a translation for use in the Church of England, and still today some Protestants prefer its beautiful, albeit archaic, speech. It is interesting that when the KJV was completed, the use of "thou, thine, thee" for "you, your, you" was already passing out of the vernacular, but the committee decided to retain this old-fashioned way to address one's beloved family, friends, and God, as a way to lend a tone of tradition to the new translation.

In the twentieth century, many biblical translations were published. Some attempt to keep the translation as close as possible to the wording and syntax of the Hebrew and Greek. Others try to make the sense of the passage readily available to contemporary readers. So, for example, some translations render what the Greek calls "the third hour of the day" as "nine o'clock in the morning." Some churches approve one translation as most appropriate for use in worship. A translation preferred by a scholar may be different from the one chosen to accompany daily devotion.

Yet translation is only one of the techniques used in biblical interpretation. Each week at public Christian worship, just as in the Jewish synagogue, the leader of the community is expected to comment upon the biblical text that was read aloud, explaining what it means for the contemporary community. Many **clergy** wrote out their **sermons**, and one can read 1900 years of such homilies to discover how the Bible was being interpreted. Over the centuries various methods of training preachers have developed, so that clergy can be experts on the Bible and the history of doctrine and interpretation. Some churches require their clergy to learn Hebrew and Greek, in order that they can study the original text.

clergy = trained and designated leaders of a Christian community; variously called father, minister, mother, pastor, preacher, teaching elder

Another vehicle for biblical interpretation involves the very choices of which Scripture to proclaim in public worship. The Bible is a hugely long book, and most Christian teachers have judged that much of it, although interesting to study, is not important enough for believers that it ought to be read aloud and commented on in worship. For example, churches do not read aloud the instructions on what to do with a building if its walls have leprosy (Leviticus 14). In some churches, the preacher can choose which part of the Bible to read and

sermon/homily = an explanation of the meaning of a biblical text

John 3:16 in several translations:

For God louede so the world that he yaf his oon bigetun sone, that ech man that beliueth

in him perische not, but haue euerlastynge llijf.—John Wyclif, 1384

For God so loveth the world, that he hath given his only son, that none that believe in

him, should perish, but should have everlasting life.—Tyndale-Coverdale, 1535

For this is how God loved the world: he gave his only Son, so that everyone who believes

in him may not perish but may have eternal life.—New Jerusalem Bible, 1985

For God so loved the world that he gave his only Son, so that everyone who believes in

him may not perish but may have eternal life.—New Revised Standard Version, 1991

This is how much God loved the world: he gave his Son, his one and only Son. And this is why: so that no one need be destroyed; by believing in him, anyone can have a whole

and lasting life.—Eugene H. Peterson, *The Message*, 1993

comment upon. Other churches have prepared and authorized a **lectionary** that their clergy are expected to adhere to. Most likely, churches that differ with regard to which passages are read aloud and which are omitted from worship also differ in their opinion about which passages are applicable to contemporary Christian belief. Some churches stress passages that describe eternal punishment, and others do not. In places that maintained slaves, clergy used verses such as Ephesians 6:5-9 as a biblical defense of slavery, and in the twentieth century, churches that opposed women's equality preached on those passages that taught male superiority (for example, Eph.

lectionary = the list of biblical selections appointed for worship; the volume in which these selections are printed sequentially

A long, stupid sermon from that insufferable bore, Mr Garie, gave me a dreadful head ache. He repeated everything at least three times, until I was wild with irritated nerves and impatience. Invariably, the most beautiful passages of the bible, those I cry over alone, appear absurd from his lips.—Sarah Morgan, 1862[4]

5:22-30), while those who sought women's rights preached about women's role in early Christianity (especially excerpts from Luke).

Two opposite **hermeneutical** directions that assist preachers for their weekly task have been evident throughout the church since the second century. The theologians in Antioch (in current Turkey) preferred a literal approach, stressing the historical accuracy of the biblical stories, and the theologians in Alexandria, Egypt, preferred a more allegorical approach, by which metaphoric passages are important for the faith. Thus some preachers taught that it is most important to believe that Jesus miraculously raised Lazarus from the dead (John 11:1-44), while others stressed the meaning of this story, that through Christ all believers are given new life. The preeminent Christian theologian Augustine wrote in his autobiography that he first took the Christian religion seriously when he heard the preaching of Ambrose, the bishop of Milan, because Ambrose gave "spiritual" interpretations of biblical texts, rather than the more common literal ones.[5] During the sixteenth century, Roman Catholics, early Protestant followers of Martin Luther, and later Protestant

hermeneutics = a method of interpretation

Fig. 1.7. A nineteenth-century drawing depicting the 1801 Revival in Cane Ridge, Kentucky, a famous six-day-long camp meeting that included preaching to the 12,000 people present.

followers of Ulrich Zwingli engaged in bitter battles, and their governments even martyred persons of the opposite position, about whether "this is my body," the words of Jesus spoken at a meal with his disciples before his death, were more literal or more metaphoric.

From the nineteenth century on, these two methods of biblical interpretation became more oppositional. The more literal believers came to be called **fundamentalists**. For these churches and believers, the Bible is inerrant, and biblical stories are accepted as factually correct. The idea is that, for example, if God did not create the world in six days, as Genesis 1 says, then there is no reason for people to believe that Jesus rose from the dead, since, if the reliability of one claim in Scripture is questioned, then the reliability of the whole is in doubt. On the other hand, churches that adopt the more allegorical approach are less concerned about the historicity of biblical accounts, since they value religious metaphors, and they are not troubled when searching for a contemporary application of the Bible's ancient worldview.

During the twentieth century, other new hermeneutical approaches became well known, either accepted or rejected. Christian feminists raised many questions about the male dominance in the biblical texts themselves. For example, in Luke 8:1-3, why are only twelve men highlighted, although several women are so important to Jesus' work that they are named here? Such questions have encouraged some churches to alter their inherited patterns of male dominance. Christians who have dark skin color have challenged the biblical language pattern in which light is good and dark is evil. Pastoral counselors question especially parts of the Psalms in which sickness is viewed as divine punishment for sin. Because Christians take the Bible so seriously, they continue to struggle with its difficult passages, even while accepting its basic truth in their lives.

Another method of biblical interpretation has become increasingly important in Christianity. When printed Bibles became available to Christians who were not trained in the history of biblical interpretation, personal interpretation of Scripture became popular. One example is the method developed in the sixteenth century by Ignatius of Loyola, a Roman

> Not one statement has ever been disproved by any real facts of science or history, and God will surely honor and bless the faith and witness of anyone who fully believes and obeys His Word. —Henry M. Morris and Martin E. Clark, *The Bible Has the Answer*[6]

fundamentalism = a method of religious conservatism that holds to literal scriptural interpretation and absolute trust in church authority

> Metaphors and metaphorical narratives can be profoundly true even if they are not literally or factually true. Being a Christian is not about believing in the Bible or about believing in Christianity. Rather, it is about a deepening relationship with the God to whom the Bible points. —Marcus J. Borg, *Reading the Bible Again for the First Time*[7]

Catholic who encouraged Christians to use their own imagination to enter into the biblical stories, so that for example they see themselves walking with Jesus. In those places where church authority was challenged, private interpretations could be preferred over official teaching. Christians resided for decades on the American frontier before churches were built, and their religious faith was nurtured as individuals read the Bible and undoubtedly interpreted it according to their own lights.

Scripture still sometimes leaves me breathless. I see such honesty, such beauty, such profundity, such ultimacy. A grand cosmic tragedy with innumerable small scenes, but magnificent new life emerging out of it all.—Miriam Adeney[8]

Fig. 1.8. Many different editions of the same Bible translation are available. Most include scholarly notes that are not part of the biblical text itself. This edition focuses on ecological concerns.

To conclude this chapter, a biblical verse: "Now Jesus did many other signs in the presence of his disciples, which are not written in this book. But these are written so that you may come to believe that Jesus is the Messiah, the Son of God, and that through believing you may have life in his name" (John 20:30-31). This passage suggests that the Bible does not contain everything that believers may wish for. Many readers are disappointed to discover what issues Scripture does not cover and what questions it does not answer. But according to John, the Bible was written so that people may come to faith and life in Jesus, and the church teaches that this is enough. So the Bible is read daily, proclaimed weekly at worship, and interpreted over and over in different ways, century after century.

> Scripture is not just a holy book from which we extract teaching and biblical principles. Rather, it is a story in which we participate. Scripture speaks to us because Scripture speaks about us. We need to allow Scripture to become the interpreter of who we are in the specific concrete sense.—Kwame Bediako[9]

Suggestions

1. Review the chapter's vocabulary: apostle, ascension, Bible, bishop, canon, catholic/Catholic, Christology, clergy, council, covenant, disciple, divine, doctrine, evangelist, fundamentalism, Gentile, Good Samaritan, Gospel/gospel, hermeneutics, homily, inerrant, Jew, justify, kingdom of God / of heaven, KJV, lectionary, *Logos*, martyr, miracle, missionary, myth, parable, prophet, reconcile, ritual, sacred, Scripture, sermon, sin, synoptics, theologian, Vulgate, worship.

2. Identify the myths of our society and the role they play in forming identity.

3. Present arguments for and against citing the Bible in a discussion of whether there are miracles in today's world.

4. Compare the biblical accounts of Christ's resurrection: 1 Cor. 15:3-11; Mark 16:1-8; Matt. 28:1-10; Luke 24:1-12; and John 20:1-18.

5. Write a personal essay in which you describe a book that has been important to you, and explain why.

6. In 1 Cor. 10:4, Paul interprets for Christians the story of the Israelites getting water from the rock (Exod. 17:1-7). Discuss Paul's hermeneutic.

7. Read and discuss the short story "God's Goodness" by Marjorie Kemper.[10] A Christian caregiver and a dying teenage boy reflect on the biblical book of Job. To understand the story, an acquaintance with the Book of Job is helpful.

8. For a major project, read and write a report on the 1953 novel *Go Tell It on the Mountain* by James Baldwin. The characters think and speak in biblical terms. Use a King James Version concordance (an index of words in the Bible) to locate all the biblical sources in a paragraph or page.

9. View and discuss the 1995 movie *Dead Man Walking*. Citing the Bible is important to the religious sister who is counseling the man on death row, to the convict himself, and to both the supporters and the critics of capital punishment.

For Further Reading

De Hamel, Christopher. *The Book: A History of the Bible*. London: Phaidon, 2001.

Greenman, Jeffrey P., Timothy Larsen, and Stephen R. Spencer, eds. *The Sermon on the Mount through the Centuries: From the Early Church to John Paul II*. Grand Rapids: Brazos, 2007.

Sumney, Jerry L. *The Bible: An Introduction*. Minneapolis: Fortress Press, 2010.

What do Christians believe about God?

2

Fig. 2.1. Frans Floris's 1562 painting *Allegory of the Trinity* depicts God as a white, old, bearded man; the crucified Christ; and the dove of the Spirit. God's care for the people is like that of a mother hen and her chicks (Matt. 23:37).

◈ An answer from a scholar

Rudolf Otto (1869–1937) was a German theologian who reacted against the eighteenth-century European and American focus on the priority of human rationality and science. Otto began his *The Idea of the Holy* by asserting that readers who had never had a religious experience and could not recall any personal religious feelings should not bother reading his book, because they would not know what he was talking about. Otto stressed that the religious person experienced something Wholly Other.

numinous = possessing and conveying supernatural mystery

mystery = supernatural essence or experience, beyond understanding; for some Christians, a term for their central religious rituals and beliefs

The consciousness of a "wholly other" evades precise formulation in words, and we have to employ symbolic phrases which seem sometimes sheer paradox, that is, irrational, not merely non-rational, in import. The object of religious awe or reverence cannot be fully determined conceptually: it is non-rational, as is the beauty of a musical composition, which no less eludes complete conceptual analysis.—Rudolf Otto[2]

This Other was a nonrational human perception. Being religious was primarily experiencing this Otherness, this Beyond-the-Rational, and Otto coined a word to describe this Wholly Other: the **numinous**. Religion is about this **mystery**, this beyond-ness, this unique sensation. Like the thinkers of the Romantic movement of the nineteenth century, Otto stressed religion's feelings, not its doctrines or requirements. Otto said that unfortunately religious traditions tend to take the mystery out of religious experience until it is "simply rolled out so thin and flat as to be finally eliminated altogether."[1] The feelings that people experience in the face of the Holy constitute genuine religion, and without such overwhelming experiences, religion does not in fact exist. Thus for Otto, if what is presented is dull and boring, it is not religion.

Otto claimed that rationality separates and fragments, but religious experience unites. This is seen in the related words "whole" and "holy," different spellings of the same word. To focus the word "holy" on only moral perfection shrinks religion into something less than it means to be. Calling a splendid church building a "holy space" means not that the room is morally excellent, but that when people are in the room, they are awestruck by feelings of both humility and grandeur. From their experience of this Other, people receive energy and a positively transformed identity.

All humans, Otto said, seek this deeper essence, this quality of spirit that is beyond what is seen and readily analyzed. Otto wrote that when faced with the Holy, humans experience two opposite feelings: first, they are repelled by the Holy. Because they are stunned to encounter something so beyond human rationality, they back away, and religions are filled with stories

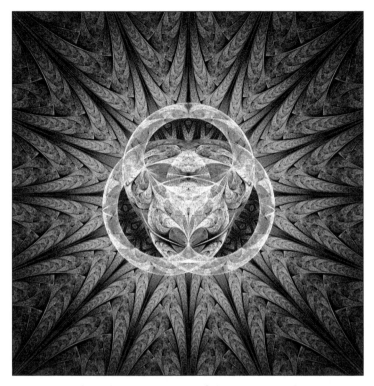

Fig. 2.2. A digital art depiction of the triune God by Lyle Hatch

of people fleeing from God, hiding from the Holy, or requiring the professional clergy to represent them in the face of the divine.

However, thousands of years of art, architecture, literature, and celebration prove that many humans, saddened by the knowledge of their own limitations and fragmentation, seek this Whole, the Holy, the Other. They choose to participate in religious activities that approach the mystery, and some persons seek as many and as lengthy religious experiences as possible. If some persons have not been both unnerved and fascinated by what is truly religious, their deprivation does not lessen the power of those who have.

Otto compares religion to music. Many people have had profound, even overwhelming experiences listening to music. Yet they cannot explain these experiences in rational terms, and a description of music is nowhere near the experience of music. Because a deaf person has not heard music does not diminish the feelings of those who love music and eagerly

> God's being is my life. If my life is God's being, then God's existence must be my existence and God's is-ness is my is-ness, neither less nor more.—Meister Eckhart, c. 1320[3]

listen to it. However, Otto laments that too often a description of religion replaces the experience of religion. Otto hopes that even modern people can experience transformative religion, without which human life is radically diminished.

mercy = undeserved kindness and acceptance

Using Rudolf Otto, one can say that in Christianity, the Wholly Other is called the triune God. The centuries of stories recall persons both repelled by God's divine judgment and yet attracted to God's divine **mercy**. Unfortunately, especially when the church has taught that the Holy is only about morality, the experience of this Other has been substantially shrunken. For Christianity to function as an effective religion, the community must again experience the numinous. That is, Christians must be open to the complex experience of the Wholly Other when they imagine, discuss, and approach the being they call God.

Si comprehendis non est Deus. If you comprehend what you are saying, what you have comprehended is not God.—Augustine, c. 400[4]

◈ Answers from the churches

What are the sources of Christian belief in God?

One source of the Christian beliefs about God is the Jewish religious tradition. For example, the Hebrew Scriptures say that one cannot look on the face of God and survive. Thus Moses is chosen to meet with God, so that the terrified people need not. However, this awesome God is also the gracious God who saved the people from slavery and miraculously fed them while they were nomads. God both repels and attracts. During the early centuries of the churches, Christians maintained the Jewish principle never to draw or sculpt God in any way, since God as **spirit** can never be adequately depicted.

Spirit = (uppercase S) one of the names of God; spirit = (lowercase s) a being or essence that has no body

A second-century Christian **heresy** proposed that the God of the Old Testament was a bad god and the God of the New Testament was the good god, and versions of this idea are still around today. Yet all Christian theologians have denied any such distinction, teaching instead that the God of the Moses stories is the God of the Jesus movement and the God of the Christian faith. Christianity is a **monotheistic** religion, and the English language capitalizes the noun *God*.

heresy = a teaching about a fundamental item of faith judged contrary to authorized belief

In the Hebrew Scriptures, God has a divine name. The Hebrew language, originally written without any vowels, represented God's name with four consonants, *YHWH*. Most

monotheism = the belief that only one deity exists

scholars say that *YHWH* means "I am who I am," thus referring both to God's unknowability and to God's presence with the people. A tradition developed that the **tetragrammaton** was too sacred to pronounce. Thus when a Jew reads a biblical selection in Hebrew aloud in the synagogue, if the passage includes *YHWH*, the reader substitutes a different word, *Adonai*, meaning master, Lord. Most English-language Bibles represent *YHWH* with four capital letters, "LORD," and *Adonai* with "Lord," and this double use of the title *Lord* became central to Christian theology. Sometimes the Hebrew refers to God as **YHWH Sabaoth**, which is usually rendered in English as "LORD of hosts" or "God of power and might."

A second root of Christianity was the religious mix within the Roman Empire at the time of the life of Jesus. Many students know something of this polytheism through their study of Greek and Roman myths. These myths were the religious stories revered by many of the residents of the Roman Empire. In these stories, gods and goddesses were immortal, but very like human beings in their loves and hates, devotions and deceits, and they were described as having human-like bodies. During the first century, the Roman emperors claimed that after death, and perhaps even during their life, they too were divine and must be worshiped as such. Since by the year 100 more Christians had been raised as pagans than were Jewish, Christians had to distinguish their God from these gods. However, when the region's polytheism declined, Christians adopted its practice of painting and sculpting deities, first with symbolic depictions of Jesus, and later also images of God, who was made to resemble Jupiter. Yet in 1667 the Eastern Orthodox churches condemned anthropomorphic depictions of God as "exceedingly absurd and unseemly."[5]

Greek philosophers had taught about a perfect being who was the great creator God. For Aristotle, this Prime Mover is eternal and unchangeable, omnipotent and omniscient, a being who was the highest and the most and the best of all that is desired and good. Christian theologians in the early centuries of the churches blended together a Greek philosophically perfect being with Hebrew biblical accounts of a just and merciful deity to describe the Wholly Other Christian God.

A third root of Christianity was the Jesus movement. As the New Testament writings indicate, during Jesus' life a

tetragrammaton = YHWH, the four consonants of the Hebrew name of God

YHWH Sabaoth = a Hebrew designation of God, perhaps meaning Yahweh of the army hosts of heaven

Once multiple divinities are discarded, along with their rivalries and conflicting powers, religion is concerned with just two poles: the human and the divine. Religious events take place not on Mount Olympus or in some imagined godly castle, but in the earthly realm. Religious history becomes fully part of human history. And the telling of the history, along with commentary and reinterpretation, becomes an aspect of the religion itself. These faiths are historical faiths.—Edward Rothstein[6]

What is God? God is a Spirit, infinite, eternal, and unchangeable in his being, wisdom, power, holiness, justice, goodness, and truth.—the Westminster Catechism, 1640s

incarnation = the embodiment of God in the human being Jesus

movement arose that claimed that he was the messiah whom God had sent to save the people. He was Lord, that is, he was their master. Yet also in the first century, some of those who attested to the power of the Jesus movement claimed that Jesus was divine. That is, when meeting Jesus, people encountered God. Thus, miraculously, Jesus was LORD, that is, the same being as *YHWH*. The technical term for Jesus being God is **incarnation**, the putting into flesh (*carne*: think carnivorous) something that has no flesh. Thus for Christians, God was (1) the just and merciful God of the Jewish past, (2) the philosophically perfect being described by Greek philosophers, and (3) the one who as Jesus suffered with and for the world and granted the people eternal life.

Jesus was not the religious figure that many people sought. He had broken religious regulations and had eaten with disreputable persons. He had not established a politically independent nation. Most horrific, however, was that Jesus, God's messiah, had been executed by crucifixion. The Roman Empire used this mode of torture and execution for the lowest of the low, and the Scriptures had said that even God cursed anyone who had been hanged on a tree. Thus one could well be repelled by Jesus.

Yet people were attracted to Jesus. The Gospels report that while he lived, people left their homes and livelihood and joined his itinerant ministry of preaching and healing. This attraction intensified after his death. His followers said that he was alive again, and he continues to give life beyond human expectation and description. As Paul wrote, Christ is for believers "wisdom from God, and **righteousness** and **sanctification** and **redemption**" (1 Cor. 1:30), and believers accept the God of the crucified and risen Christ as the deity worthy of worship.

righteousness = being morally acquitted before God

sanctification = being made holy

redemption = returning to God what had been under the power of evil, like buying back something that was wrongly purchased

Why did these sources develop into a religion?

All of this experiencing of God could function only on the level of the individual, and throughout the Christian traditions, some believers have relished the personal nature of such experiences. From the fourth century on, individual hermits and **monastic** groups designed a pattern of living that maximized time for private meditation on God. Sometimes this took the form of study of and contemplation on the Bible.

At other times some **mystics** had extraordinary **visions** of God. In the nineteenth century, American thinkers like Ralph Waldo Emerson came to advocate only a personal relationship with God, believing that the Wholly Other God was accessible in each person's heart while walking in the woods and usually became misrepresented by the Christian religion.

The Bible records the story of Moses seeing God in a burning bush and of Mary Magdalene encountering the risen Christ. In both stories, the individual is sent back to share with the community. A community gathered around the accounts of the personal experience, authenticated it, meditated on its meanings, and shared it with others, who also hoped to experience the divine. Books were written, and rituals celebrated. At least for the Christian religion, the development of theology was and remains paramount. In a much-quoted passage of the New Testament, Jesus asks his disciples, "Who do people say that I am?" (Mark 8:27). As if perpetually attempting to give this question a fuller answer, theologians have constructed systems of thought that describe God, the meaning of the incarnation, and its effect on the believer, and the various churches have adopted some theologies while rejecting others. Although some children have been taught that they are not to think about the faith, but only to believe, theologians say that this suggestion radically misrepresents the Christian religion, which is thinking all the time: Who is God? What did Christ achieve, and why? What difference does that make in human life? What is to be avoided, and what embraced, and why?

Throughout history it has not been easy for churches to balance the experience of dread with the experience of joy. Many churches and **cathedrals** built in Europe a thousand years ago displayed as their primary piece of art an enormous Last Judgment, with monsters and demons hauling people down to eternal punishment. Christ stood in the place of God as a stern judge who was ready to punish evildoers. Thus confronting God was an experience of terror, and much Christian ritual sought to appease an angry God. Some denominations today continue to stress human sinfulness and the just judgment of the Almighty. On the other hand, other churches preach a gentle God, a kind grandfather who loves people just as they are and will welcome nearly

monasticism = life in single-sex communities (male monk or friar, female nun or sister) in which individuals' vows of for example poverty, chastity, obedience, and stability encourage focus on God

mysticism = the personal direct experience of God, apart from the usual religious methods of worship

vision = a personal sensory experience of the supernatural

What is the divine darkness? Trinity! Higher than any being, any divinity, any goodness! Guide of Christians in the wisdom of heaven! Lead us up beyond unknowing and light, up to the farthest, highest peak of mystic scripture, where the mysteries of God's Word lie simple, absolute and unchangeable in the brilliant darkness of a hidden silence.—Pseudo-Dionysius, c. 600[7]

cathedral = the main city church that houses the chair (cathedra = chair in Greek) of the bishop; also, a large church building

everyone into everlasting bliss. Yet whether churches stress moral perfection or joyous freedom, or try to balance the two, both descriptions are deemed Christian.

Christianity has constructed at least five different avenues along which the community travels so that God can be made available to everyone who believes. The first avenue has been discussed in chapter 1: the Bible was written to record both individual and communal interactions with God. The Scriptures continue to serve as the primary resource for Christian accessibility to God, with individual churches choosing which parts of the Bible to teach and how they are to be interpreted.

The second avenue is tradition. Because the Bible is so complex, theologians and preachers had to interpret it, so that its meaning could be made current and alive for the people of each generation. Naturally, in different cultures, in many languages, and over the centuries, there come to be not one narrow tradition, but many traditions, and always there is the question whether one's

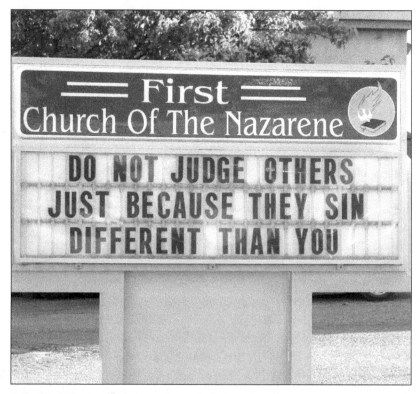

Fig. 2.3. An advertisement for a Christian church

tradition has developed in the right way. These traditions will be discussed especially in chapter 5.

One of the tasks of the church was to organize biblical teachings into **creeds**. Two creeds in particular have been accepted by Christian churches throughout the ages and around the globe. For this reason, they are called the **ecumenical** creeds. In some churches, the worshipers recite these creeds in unison, each week or at special celebrations. The most commonly used is called the Apostles' Creed, not because the apostles wrote it, but because when it was crafted in the fifth century, the church leaders said that it presented the teaching of the apostles. This creed developed out of questions that a person was asked at the time of **baptism**. Imagine the fourth-century priest asking, Do you believe in God? Yes, I believe in God, the Father almighty, creator of heaven of earth, and so on, through the entire creed. A longer creed, called the Nicene Creed, was developed to add more philosophical language to the statement about Jesus.

A third avenue is worship. Most Christians throughout time have received most of their information about their religion and many of their experiences of it while attending the authorized worship services of their community. Thus what happened at worship was of highest significance, because through it the community stood before God, facing divine judgment and receiving divine mercy. Worship will be discussed in chapter 5.

A fourth avenue is reason. Mystics agree with Rudolf Otto that one's experience of God is beyond reason, and since the scientific revolution in the eighteenth century, some Christians have stressed that faith in God is totally

creed = a statement of belief

ecumenical = applicable to all Christians worldwide

baptism = the ritual of washing employed when one becomes a Christian

Fig. 2.4. Calvin contemplates the mystery of Santa Claus.

I know only enough of God to want to worship him, by any means ready to hand. . . . There is one church here, so I go to it. Once, in the middle of the long pastoral prayer of intercession for the whole world—for the gift of wisdom to its leaders, for hope and mercy to the grieving and pained, succor to the oppressed, and God's grace to all—in the middle of this he stopped, and burst out, "Lord, we bring you these same petitions every week." After a shocked pause, he continued reading the prayer. Because of this, I like him very much.—Annie Dillard[8]

opposite the discoveries of rational scientific study. Yet especially beginning in the thirteenth century, the Christian church in Western Europe stressed that rationality helped humans understand the things of God. Since God gave uniquely to humans the ability to reason, it made no sense that this gift from God might lead humans away from God. The great theologians of the second millennium assumed that a rational approach to the faith was essential. Reason will be discussed in chapters 7 and 11.

A fifth avenue, personal experience, brings the route full circle. Experience was at the outset, prior to the formation of the religion, but especially in the last two hundred years, experience is again held up as central for genuine religion. If persons are told something by an outside authority that directly contradicts or calls invalid what they have personally experienced, they may well trust their own experience rather than the teaching of the outsider. Currently, some church leaders worry that personal experience has become too important for many Christians, who may not be sufficiently formed in Scriptures, tradition, creed, worship, and reason for their experience to fit into Christianity: theologians assert that although the Christian highway is broad, there are curbs on each edge.

What is the Trinity?

In some religions, the creator god is only one of many deities and is no longer involved in human life. Christianity rejected these claims, teaching that God is one, yet God is three; God continually creates; and the good creator God daily nurtures the universe, humankind, and each individual. This one God is over all peoples around the world. The worship of other deities is understood either as a serious sin or a sad error, because these other constructions are not divine and cannot give the worshipers the life they seek. Churches have taught that no matter where on earth one lived, no matter what language one spoke, the one God was accessible there. At various times in history, Christians persecuted and even executed persons who worshiped other gods, the idea being that such people were dangerous to the civic order and must be eliminated so that believers could live in peace. However, most Christians today agree that persecution of other religions is wrong, and some teach that in most systems of belief, the one true God can be found.

I believe in God, the Father almighty,
creator of heaven and earth.
I believe in Jesus Christ, God's only Son, our Lord,
who was conceived by the Holy Spirit,
born of the Virgin Mary,
suffered under Pontius Pilate,
was crucified, died, and was buried;
he descended to the dead.
On the third day he rose again;
he ascended into heaven,
he is seated at the right hand of the Father,
and he will come to judge the living and the dead.
I believe in the Holy Spirit,
the holy catholic church,
the communion of saints,
the forgiveness of sins,
the resurrection of the body,
and the life everlasting. Amen

—the 1988 translation by the English Language Liturgical
Consultation of the Apostles' Creed

Christians described God in fundamentally different ways from the one God of the other two world monotheisms, Judaism and Islam. For Christians, the one God is not a monad, a single and total Oneness. Beginning already in the late first century, many people who interacted with Jesus and who later believed in him as the single divine incarnation came to speak of Jesus as God. And then a third phenomenon was experienced: Jesus was not dead, but his divine Spirit was alive and well, transforming individuals and inspiring the community. It took theologians about three hundred years of meditating on various passages in what was being affirmed as the Bible, but by the fourth century there was agreement that the one God is three. God is triune.

To affirm faith in the Trinity means that Christians believe in a single God who is in itself a complex loving interrelationship. This interrelationship existed from before human time. For early Christian teachers, the poem in Genesis 1 describing the creation of the world was evidence of the triune God, for God spoke a word (later embodied in Jesus) and breathed a spirit (later

SAINT ENLIGHTENER PATRICK OF IRELAND

Fig. 2.5. Patrick, who preached Christianity in Ireland in the fifth century, taught that the Trinity is like a shamrock—three nodes in one leaf.

called the Holy Spirit). The Gospels' description of the baptism of Jesus was another example of the presence of the Trinity: the voice of God was heard from heaven, Jesus was standing in the Jordan River, and a dove alighted on his head. One of the few biblical passages that explicitly speaks of the three (Matt. 28:19) describes baptism "in the name of the Father and of the Son and of the Holy Spirit." This triune God, sometimes ridiculed by outsiders as bizarre, is defended by Christians as one of the most brilliant proposals of the faith: that God, the Wholly Other, is in past, present, and future, before everything, in Christ, and within the believing community.

The most common category used to refer to these Three is derived from the Latin word *persona*. For modern speakers of English, a "person" is an independent human consciousness, but this is not what theologians mean by God having three persons. Rather, *persona* meant something more like manifestation or mode of expression. The one God was three, and because even theologians admitted that it is impossible to state in human language the mystery of the Trinity, centuries of theologians refined what has been said about the Three-in-One, agreeing with some past theologians, but proposing their own understanding.

In another use of the word "person," Christians say that God is personal. When calling God personal, Christians mean that a human can relate to God, and God to humans, in a way similar to how humans relate to one another. Many contemporary Christians are so accustomed to this idea that it may be surprising that some religions do not imagine that there can be a personal relationship between the divine and the human. But most churches have taught that although humans are not equal to God, God and humans can and do meet one another in a mutual and meaningful way.

Theologians have understood the triune God in two different ways. One way was to describe how this Trinity is God within God's own self. Some early theologians thought and wrote in Latin, others in Greek, but both came to agree that using the biblical terms of Father, Son, and Holy Spirit was the best way to indicate the mystery of the one God. The Son is the son of the Father; the Spirit is the spirit of the Father's son. The language indicates God's inner self, God's life within God. Other theologians focused more on how God is triune for believers. Thus God the Father has sent the Son to save the world, and the Spirit is God's continuing gift of life for the world. But whether the language hopes to describe God as God or God for us, the primary terms used are Father, Son, and Spirit. For the Spirit, some churches continue to use the noun Ghost, an older English translation of the biblical Greek word *pneuma*.

Beginning already in the fifth century but especially an issue in the twentieth and twenty-first centuries is the problem that arises from using anthropomorphic terms for God. Especially the biblical book of the Psalms includes many metaphors for God: God is likened to a shield, shepherd, rock, king, light, warrior, fortress, judge, stronghold, cup, hiding place, sun, deliverer, dwelling place. Some medieval mystics preferred the metaphor of lover; others meditated on God as

I shall clothe myself in your eternal will, and by this light I shall come to know that you, eternal Trinity, and table and food and waiter for us. You are the table that offers us as food the Lamb, your only-begotten Son. He is the most exquisite of foods for us. And the Holy Spirit is indeed a waiter for us who serves us charity for our neighbors.—Catherine of Siena, 1379[9]

Fig. 2.6. In this contemporary church window, the symbols avoid a male father and son, yet include a human hand.

mother. Ought the church use only biblical language, or ought it expand its language to describe God in new ways? The question of how to name and imagine the Trinity remains an extremely controversial issue. Yet all Christians agree that when referring in English to the Trinity, "they" is not the appropriate pronoun, since God is one.

Just as with the balancing of the opposite feelings of dread and joy, it has been a challenge for churches to balance the life of the Father, of the Son, and of the Holy Spirit. Usually a branch or denomination of the church focuses on one or another. In the seventh century the Christians in Western Europe, in order to stress that salvation comes through

filioque = "and the Son," a phrase in the Western Nicene Creed affirming that the Holy Spirit proceeds from the Son as well as from the Father

the Son, added a phrase to the Nicene Creed, to indicate that even the Holy Spirit proceeds from the Son. However, the Christians in the East rejected the addition of the *filioque*, asserting that the Spirit comes only from the Father. This seemingly narrow doctrinal controversy had considerable effect in later centuries.

During the last century, a fourth branch of Christianity called Pentecostalism has arisen and spread around the world, and it stresses, not the work of the Son, but rather the power of the Holy Spirit. The worship of these churches includes repeated prayers to the Spirit and healings that are credited to the Spirit. Worshipers are encouraged to participate in intense celebration of the power of the Spirit to inspire and strengthen believers in the joy of communion with God. Yet some Christians are skeptical of the experiences of the Spirit's visitation, and they organize worship in such a way as to discourage any such intervention of the Spirit.

> We humans have a hard time holding irreconcilable concepts in perfect balance. One way to sort out which church best suits you is to see if their Trinity affinity matches yours.—Carmen Renee Berry[10]

How is God creator, and of what?

Christians believe that the triune God is the creator of the world and that God's power to create continues throughout time. At the beginning of time, God brought life into being. Some early theologians proposed that God had merely given order to what was an original chaos. But the dominant teaching became that God had made everything out of nothing, in Latin *ex nihilo*. This idea affirmed that God had complete priority and absolute power over everything. In previous centuries, before the scientific revolution, the question of how God created the world was far less an issue than it has become today. Some theologians were glad to speak in literalist ways, and others wrote that the biblical accounts used ancient worldviews and poetic metaphors. The debates over the last two hundred years about the method God used in creation will be discussed in chapter 11.

A central teaching that followed from the belief that God created the world was that the universe was good. This idea rejected a pagan religious idea common in Europe during the first several centuries of the Common Era, which proposed that of the many gods, the creator was something of a trickster, or at least semi-competent. This helped account for all the evil in

> Our feeling of ignorance, vanity, want, weakness, in short, depravity and corruption, reminds us that in the Lord, and none but he, dwell the true light of wisdom, solid virtue, exuberant goodness. Every person, on coming to the knowledge of himself, is not only urged to seek God, but is also led as by the hand to find him.—John Calvin, 1559[11]

the world, but it sometimes urged religious persons to distance themselves as much as they could from the things of nature. Being religious was about getting as far away as one could from a bad earth. Much of Christianity taught the contrary, that the one good God created a good earth, and God loved the world so much that God joined human life in the incarnation.

But the **theodicy** question continues to occupy the minds of theologians: How can a religion claim that God and God's creation are good, considering all the world's evils and the suffering of the innocent? Christians have proposed several answers to the theodicy question, but none has received universal approval. Some claim that suffering is divine punishment for sin. Others claim that God allows evil as a test of believers' trust in Christ. Others suggest that God sends evil to strengthen and improve one's character. Others point out that humans are always seeking independence from God, and so they then cannot expect God to intervene to prohibit evil and sorrow. Some take comfort in the idea that God shares the sufferings of the human race.

> theodicy = the challenge of justifying the goodness of God in the face of human suffering

Still others suggest that the Greek philosophical idea that God is almighty is in fact wrong: God is not almighty and so cannot to be blamed for the existence of suffering. Christian Science, a religion that is an offshoot of Christianity, developed into its central thesis an earlier idea that evil does not actually exist outside the mind, since only the good of God exists. The Bible includes many passages that touch on this age-old human question, but Scripture presents no single fully developed doctrine. Most famously, the Book of Job, which addresses the theodicy question, concludes with no answer to the question. Thus the theological questioning continues.

An influential belief during the eighteenth century was Deism, the idea that although God did create the world, God has done nothing since. God was like a watchmaker, designing a system that now ran on its own. This proposal was rejected by Christians, who teach that God is constantly the creator. Every occasion of life comes from God. In the last decades of the twentieth century, this teaching became important for two quite different groups of believers: liberal Christians interested in an ecologically responsible Green religion, and conservative Christians who opposed abortions. Each group understands that human behavior must reflect that God is continually creating. Some theology has claimed that humans are a sort of emissary of God on earth and can exert authority over the rest of the created order.

Especially in the nineteenth century, some theologians developed what is called **natural theology**, suggesting that the observation of a wondrous nature

Fig. 2.7. Christian theologians offer various proposals on the question of suffering.

shows forth the being of its creator God. But much contemporary study of nature is less open to an easy connection between the violent earth and a gracious divinity.

An important idea in the Scripture and throughout the tradition was God's creation of a people. In the Old Testament, the Jews express their conviction that God formed Israel as an especially beloved people, and the New Testament adapts that idea in the claim that thanks to the death and resurrection of Christ, believers have been formed into a new communal identity. Sometimes this teaching has meant that churches assumed that God cared only for Christians: yet the famous Bible verse from John 3:16 says that God so loved, not the church, but the world, and many contemporary churches teach that all people are children of God. Perhaps the most cherished belief that evolved from the claim that God is creator is that human

natural theology = the connection between a good Creator God and the observable life of the universe

How wonderful the Three-in-One,
whose energies of dancing light
are undivided, pure and good,
communing love in shared delight.
How wonderful the Living God:
Divine Beloved, Empow'ring Friend,
Eternal Love, Three-in-One,
our hopes' beginning, way and end.—Brian Wren, 1988[12]

beings are an especially beloved creation of God. In different ways, both of the two stories in Genesis make humans the apex of creation. Chapter 11 will deal with the dilemma of how Christians, given scientific evolutionary discoveries, can maintain the belief that humans are somehow unique in the eyes of God.

Just as God is the creator in past and present, so Christians claim that God will be the creator in the future. The Bible speaks in many passages and diverse ways about a violent end of this world, which will be followed by God's creation of a new, perfected world. During the first century of Christianity, it was assumed that this end of the world was imminent and that Christ would return to usher in a new creation. Some churches give considerable focus to this second creation. In an optimistic version, God is helping the world to get better and better, until Christ returns to establish a new creation. In the more common pessimistic version, evil is making the world worse and worse, and there will have to be a monumental battle in which evil is conquered, after which Christ will establish a new earth. Some proposals speak of a millennium of a thousand years somewhere along the way, during the time of evil or the time of bliss. However, some churches have paid little attention to the idea of God's new creation at the end of the world, except to affirm that after one's death each person will be re-created by the continuing creating God to be with God.

Whether one has interest in or sympathy with predictions of the end of the world, one can understand how these develop from the belief in God's continuing creation. Christians claim that God creates at the beginning of time, each day, and even after everything comes to its end. God continuously brings life into being, and it is this belief that impels Christians to pray that the triune God will each day conquer evil, renew nature, establish justice, heal the sick, and in yet other ways be Creator.

Suggestions

1. Review the chapter's vocabulary: baptism, cathedral, creed, ecumenical, *filioque*, heresy, incarnation, mercy, monasticism, monotheism, mystery, mysticism, natural theology, numinous, redemption, righteousness, sanctification, Spirit/spirit, tetragrammaton, theodicy, vision, *YHWH Sabaoth*.

2. Discuss any situations in which simultaneously you have been overwhelmed by what Otto describes as the dual experiences of terror and fascination.

3. Present arguments for and against monotheism as the best religious belief. Contrast it with atheism and polytheism.

4. Select which artistic depictions of the triune God in this chapter appeal to you. Do you find any of them religiously unhelpful or even offensive?

5. Write a personal essay in which you discuss the theodicy question: How can a good God exist, considering the suffering of the innocent?

6. Analyze Psalm 18, discussing its names and metaphors for God.

7. Read and discuss the short story "A Father's Story" by Andre Dubus.[13] A devout Roman Catholic man contrasts his way of loving his daughter with God the Father's treatment of the Son.

8. For a major project, read and write a report on the 2007 bestselling novel *The Shack* by William P. Young. A grieving father, distraught by the murder of his daughter, is met by the Trinity, who, appearing to him as an African American woman, a Middle Eastern laborer, and a shimmering Asian female, teach him about the Trinity's relationships of love and the gift of human freedom. What do you think about depicting the Trinity this way?

9. View and discuss the 2011 movie *The Tree of Life*, which explores the being of God using the Christian theological categories of nature and grace. Many of the film's voice-overs are prayers. Compare the God of this film with the contents of this chapter.

For Further Reading

Armstrong, Karen. *A History of God: The 4,000-Year Quest of Judaism, Christianity and Islam*. New York: Ballantine, 1993.

Moltmann, Jürgen. *God in Creation*. Minneapolis: Fortress Press, 1993.

O'Collins, Gerald, SJ. *The Tripersonal God: Understanding and Interpreting the Trinity*. Mahwah, NJ: Paulist, 1999.

What do Christians believe about Jesus? | 3

Fig. 3.1. Matthias Grünewald (1455–1528), who painted this crucifix for a hospital chapel during an epidemic of ergotism, a severe skin disease, depicted Jesus as having ergotism. The lamb symbolizes the death of Christ.

◇ An answer from a scholar

The eminent psychiatrist Carl G. Jung (1875–1961) taught that the human psyche has many layers; that humans are not conscious of most of these layers; and yet that the layers of **the unconscious** influence or even determine human behavior. Jung theorized that the least significant part of this unconscious was the personal unconscious, which had developed from one's individual experiences. The most powerful part of the unconscious psyche, Jung conjectured, had instead been passed down through heredity over the millennia, in a process that approximated the way that natural instincts are instilled in the newborn. Jung believed that this collective unconscious was more or less universal throughout humanity, and it bonded humans together by a kind of primordial language of images.[1] Such universality accounted for the similarities in the art, the myths, and even the dreams recorded over centuries. Jung spoke positively about the role of religion to make these images available to the conscious mind through sacred stories and religious rituals.

the unconscious = the part of the human psyche that strongly influences human behavior yet does not ordinarily enter into one's awareness

Jung proposed that this collective unconscious is composed of classic symbols that he called **archetypes**.[3] Jung listed some of these archetypes as the hero, the child, the mother, the wise old man, the trickster, birth, transformation, sacrifice, the self. When people speak of their "inner child," they are describing

archetype = an inherited mode of human thought; a symbol recurring throughout human minds and cultures

The personality is seldom, in the beginning, what it will be later on. For this reason the possibility of enlarging it exists, at least during the first half of life. If some great idea takes hold of us from outside, we must understand that it takes hold of us only because something in us responds to it and goes out to meet it. Real increase of personality means consciousness of an enlargement that flows from inner sources. A classic example of enlargement is St. Paul, who, on his way to Damascus, was suddenly confronted by Christ. True though it may be that this Christ of St. Paul's would hardly have been possible without the historical Jesus, the apparition of Christ came to St. Paul not from the historical Jesus but from the depths of his own unconscious. Christ himself is the perfect symbol of the hidden immortal within the mortal man.—C. G. Jung, 1940[2]

the archetype of the child that exists in the unconscious, which a healthy adult should access as an aid toward wholeness. Important for Jung's theories was the idea that in every male there is the anima, the archetype of the female, and in every female there is the animus, the archetype of the male. Both sexes ought to find ways to express the archetype of the other, toward fullness of their person.

To Jung, the archetype of the hero, more powerful than an idea, more universal than a cultural pattern, is found in all human psyches. This hero is an expression of the human desire to conquer difficulties, and Jung proposed that an individual can draw on the hero in daily life. Even if one's personal life is

Fig. 3.2. Raphael's painting *St. George and the Dragon*, 1506. A Jungian sees in the legend of this saint the archetype of the hero.

marked by failures, the hero is an interior prod to empower a person to courageous living. Current society celebrates the hero through films, in which a few poorly equipped good guys overcome massive evil armies. Jung described how religions celebrate the hero archetype. For example, in Judaism, the hero Moses led the Israelites through countless hardships away from slavery into freedom, and the religious practice of Judaism celebrates this archetype, helping persons access it in their own unconscious and embody it in their own lives.

Jung called the goal of human life individuation: that is, each individual ought to become, over the decades of living, the sum of as many as possible of these archetypes. As people mature towards individuation, they call up into their active lives more of the richness of the ancient symbols. People who do not access these archetypes grow stunted. Dreams, art, story, film, religion: these provide a kind of mental therapy. Jung called the archetype of the individuated person the self, a totality that is similar to how monotheism imagines God to be.

Using Jung, one can claim that the story of Christ exemplifies the archetype of the hero. Jesus healed people of disease, alone he went bravely into death, and he conquered the power of evil. Attention to the birth of Jesus, celebrated at Christmas, awakens people to the innocence of the child. The archetype of transformation is epitomized by the story of Christ's rising from the dead and by Christianity's hope that believers can be brought from death into life. The mythic symbol of **sacrifice**, evident in many religious systems, is apparent in the crucifixion of Christ, who sacrificed himself, dying so that others will live. For Jung, access to the archetype of sacrifice can inspire believers to copy the selfless lifestyle of Jesus. Christian mystics expressed the archetype of the anima/animus when they wrote about Christ as the beloved one who enters them, and in response they enter Christ. That Christians describe Christ as both human and divine exemplified for Jung the archetype of the self, in which the human is whole and complete. For the Jungian, any historicity of Jesus is beside the point: images have their greatest value as psychological symbols, not as historical records.

to sacrifice = to give one's self, or a representation of one's being, to help the other; originally, to kill something so as to give it to God

◈ Answers from the churches

Chapter 1 described how the New Testament includes both memories of and interpretations about Jesus of Nazareth. Chapter 2 explained that the primary difference between the Christian understanding of God and that of Judaism and Islam is that for Christians, the triune God became incarnate in Jesus of

Nazareth. Chapter 3 will deal with why Christians elevate Jesus into the being of God and can proclaim his unique role in the **salvation** of all humanity.

salvation = being saved from death, eternal punishment, or some type of misery

Why is there a need for Christ?

A common Christian teaching is that God cares especially for humankind. Genesis 1:27 conveys this idea by stating that male and female humans, the epitome of creation, were both made in the **image of God**. Both Jews and Christians have long debated what this image is. Theologians rejected the suggestion that it means that humans look like God, since God does not have a body.

Lord, you are my lover, my longing, my flowing stream, my sun, and I am your reflection.—Mechthild of Magdeburg, 1265[4]

Rather, theologians identified this image with the aspect of human nature that they most admired. Some theologians suggested that it means for humans to have inherited from God a unique power within the universe. The philosophical theologians of the Middle Ages said that since God was Reason, this image was rationality. Later theologians who doubted the capabilities of human rationality described this divine image as the ability to maintain a profoundly loving relationship. Another proposal is that God can create; thus, the image of God is the human ability to put things together in new ways and so create a more diverse and complex world. Yet another proposal borrowed from Greek philosophy is that the image of God is immortality. God is eternal, and God gave humans an eternal **soul** that will never die. So, whether "the image of God" is power, reason, love, creativity, or **immortality**, this image signified the perfection of creation and the special connection between God and humankind.

the image of God = an enigmatic description in Genesis 1 of some aspect of the human being

soul = a nonmaterial and perhaps immortal aspect of human beings

immortality = the quality of not being subject to death

Genesis 2–3, probably written down about three hundred years earlier than Genesis 1, does not use the phrase "the image of God." Instead, its narrative tells of the first man and first woman disobeying a divine command. The tree with the forbidden fruit is called "the tree of knowledge of good and evil." (The idea that it was an apple tree was popularized by Western Christians who saw the similarity in Latin between the words "evil," *m lum*, and "apple," *m lum*.) The serpent promises that if woman eats the fruit, she will "be like God, knowing good and evil" (Gen. 3:4-5). After eating, the couple realizes that they are naked. It is impossible to overstate how much Christian

Fig. 3.3. Calvin contemplates evil.

thought has been given to what this story says about God, humans, sin, gender, and sexual relationships.

In some ways the two Genesis accounts are opposite each other. In chapter 1, humans are somehow like God, and in chapters 2–3, to be like God is somehow a sin. Yet Christian theologians saw a similarity in the biblical accounts. Whether by losing or marring the image of God or by disobeying a divine command, humans are not what God intended. Theology summarizes this teaching with the simple term **the Fall**, as if humans are now lower than God had intended them to be. Most Christian theologians described this Fall as the human alienation from God. The fundamental task is for humans to get the relationship with God restored, and only God can effect this. Some theologians taught that even if people live moral lives, they were still not relating to God. People needed to be saved from this situation and returned to God, and only God has the power to do this.

> the Fall = the loss of an original human perfection

Most Christians have learned that this Fall led to human sins, and this sin has been described in various ways. Some churches stress the Ten Commandments as recorded in both Exodus and Deuteronomy. The first sins listed are against God: idolatry, image-adoration, swearing, and violating the Sabbath. The later commandments forbid dishonoring of one's parents, murdering, committing adultery, stealing, lying in court, and coveting the neighbor's property. Matthew intensified these commandments by saying that being angry is like murder and thinking lustfully is like adultery (5:21-30). Paul's list of sins includes fornication, impurity, licentiousness, idolatry, sorcery, enmities, strife, jealousy, anger, quarrels, dissensions, factions, envy, drunkenness, carousing, and "things like these" (Gal. 5:19-21). From the fourth century it became common to describe Seven Deadly Sins: anger, greed, sloth, pride, lust, envy, and gluttony. Some twentieth-century theologians and preachers emphasized social sins, chronic systemic injustices, such as racism or sexism, and although individuals try to deny personal responsibility for such pervasive evils, everyone is implicated in these sins. Others teach that sin is also not doing good, being less than God asks and denying the image of God in one's self. If persons assert that they are not very sinful, it was usual for clergy over the centuries to call them to deeper self-awareness: everyone sins, often.

Sin has ramifications. An early Christian understanding was that God punished sin by condemning humans to die. Those who were saved by Jesus Christ will conquer death at the end of time, when like Jesus himself, all believers will be raised from the dead. This hope is cited in both the Apostles' and the Nicene Creeds, which list among the articles of faith "the resurrection of the body." In some miraculous way, the dead will be given a new body, as Jesus had, and in their new body Christians will enjoy a life with God in a new earth.

The more common Christian belief comes from Greek philosophy. According to this idea, all humans have an immortal soul. This divine soul cannot die, and after the body dies, the souls of all sinners who have not been forgiven by God will spend eternity in **hell**. For countless people, fearing hell has been a powerful incentive to accept the disciplines of Christianity. Many medieval churches have their interior walls painted with pictures of the damned who are suffering in hell, even being cooked in huge pots over flames tended by demons.

So, whether it is the soul alone or the soul reconnected with the body, the usual teaching was that only those who believe in Christ or who have lived faithful Christian lives (perhaps only members of one certain denomination) will go immediately to **heaven**. For some centuries and locales, no other religious option was available, so this teaching functioned as a confirmation of the community's self-identity and a psychological protection against what is alien. Many Christians connected the immortality of the soul and the resurrection of the body, anticipating that at the end of time, a raised body will be reconnected with the immortal soul. Some twentieth-century Christians

> Sin is the ruin and misery of the soul; it is destructive in its nature; and if God should leave it without restraint, there would need nothing else to make the soul perfectly miserable. The corruption of the heart of man is a thing that is immoderate and boundless in its fury; and as the heart is now a sink of sin, so, if sin was not restrained, it would immediately turn the soul into a fiery oven, or a furnace of fire and brimstone.— Jonathan Edwards, 1741[5]

hell = the totally evil existence apart from God; often, a literal place of everlasting punishment by fire

heaven = the perfect existence filled with God; often, a literal place where God is and where believers will live after death

applied the theory of relativity to these doctrines and assert that the reception of the soul into heaven and the resurrection of the body at the end of time occur simultaneously.

Why do people sin? Are they so under the power of the **devil** that they cannot live rightly, or can people save themselves? The fourth century witnessed a famous debate on these issues that continues today. One position was taught by Pelagius, an English monk, who said that since God had created humans with the divine image, they were capable of pleasing God and avoiding sin. Humans were simply lazy and selfish, always straying from the straight and narrow pathway, but Christians try to live according to the divine image God gave them. Christ offered both forgiveness for their sins and an example of the moral life.

> devil = a supernatural being who personifies and perpetuates evil; also called Satan

Pelagius was opposed by a bishop who is now recognized as one of the most influential theologians in Christian history. Augustine, the bishop in Hippo in what is now Algeria, taught that the Fall had shattered the relationship between God and humankind. Augustine suggested that this alteration of the human species had been passed down, almost genetically, perhaps even through sexual intercourse, to every human. To describe this, Augustine coined the term **original sin**. People were not to blame Eve and Adam, nor those around them, nor even the devil, for leading them into sin. Rather, each person is to blame for disobeying God from birth on. In his autobiography—a genre that many historians say Augustine invented—Augustine wrote that even the infant crying for milk is sinning, for the infant cares nothing about God or the mother, but sees itself as the only important thing in the universe.[6] Thus, taught Augustine, even infants need to be baptized. Only God could reconstitute the human person, and God had sent Christ to be this re-creation of humankind.

> original sin = the sin of Adam and Eve passed down to make all humans sinful

> Western churches = those church bodies originally located in what was the western part of the Roman Empire, with its capital in Rome; usually now comprising the Roman Catholic and Protestant churches

In 417, a council of bishops condemned Pelagius's position, and especially the **Western churches** adopted Augustine's position as the primary understanding of the human condition. Augustine is not so prized in the **Eastern churches**, and throughout history and across different groups of believers, some Christians have continued to lean toward Pelagius and others toward Augustine, with sin either as small or great mistakes or as the condition of absolute alienation from God. Sin

> Eastern churches = those church bodies originally located in what was the eastern part of the Roman Empire, with its capital in Constantinople (now Istanbul); usually now comprising the national Orthodox churches

Fig. 3.4. Compare the faces of the serpent and of Eve in this depiction of the Fall from the workshop of Giovanni della Robbia in 1515.

is of course not the only human problem. Other problems are disease, and injustice, and the psychic distress of meaninglessness. However, the simplest Christian answer to the question "Why is there a need for Christ?" is: because humans sin.

How does Christ meet human need?

To explain how Christ meets human need, theologians begin with the Bible. Since the four Gospels present different details about Jesus' life, historians

Historical Jesus = what can be said about the biography of Jesus of Nazareth apart from religious faith

have searched for what has been called the **Historical Jesus**, that is, what secular historians can agree about the life of Jesus of Nazareth.[7] Some historians suggest that it is most accurate to see Jesus as rabbi, a teacher of the Torah. Yet churches have asserted that Jesus was more than a rabbi—a rabbi can teach but not save.

Throughout the New Testament, the key to Jesus' salvation is his resurrection, which theologians teach was both in history and beyond time. The many titles that Christians have given Jesus indicate **orthodox** answers to the question of how Jesus saves. For each title, Christians borrowed a term from their religious past or their secular society and altered its meaning so as to express their faith in Christ. Thus each title expresses a worldview altered by the believers' experience of the resurrection.

orthodox = officially approved; Orthodox = part of a name of a church

Jesus is called Christ, meaning the one whom God has anointed as king to save and rule the people. Some first-century Jews believed that God would send a messiah to save the people from domination by the Roman Empire. At his trial, Jesus was convicted in the Roman court of sedition, that is, of working to overthrow the government. The Gospels record that the Roman governor Pontius Pilate posted this charge on the cross: "This is the king of the Jews." So how does Jesus as Christ meet human need? When believers, who for centuries have abbreviated "Christ" with its opening Greek letters *Chi Rho*, called Jesus Christ, they meant that he conquered not the Roman Empire, but evil and sin throughout the world. Humans need to be freed from the rule of evil in their lives, to become as citizens in the reign of God. In recent centuries, some Christians have also taught that Jesus as messiah liberates oppressed peoples, leading African American slaves to freedom and shaping a just society for the poor. Especially Eastern churches include in the ritual of baptism an **anointing** with oil, as a symbol that the Christian has now joined with Christ as one chosen by God to live in freedom and goodness.

anointing = making the sign of the cross on the body with scented oil

Jesus is called God's Word (uppercase *W*) because he embodies the word (lowercase *w*) of God. In Greek philosophy, God, who held together all things, was utterly beyond this world, yet God could be known by divine *logos*, an emanation from the divine, something like the rays from the sun. In English, *logos* is translated as "word." The Gospel of John speaks of God's revelation as the Logos: Jesus emanated from God and held all things together. So how does Jesus as the Word of God save? Humans need to receive God's revelation of life, and God sends out truth and wholeness through the Logos. Humans need to hear the good words of God, that is, they need to receive Jesus, the Word. To be filled with this Word is to be filled with God.

Jesus is the **Son of Man.** This title, important in the New Testament, derives from the several centuries before the birth of Jesus, when the political situation of the Jewish people under the domination of foreign powers looked hopeless. Perhaps the world was so evil that God would have to destroy it and start all over again. This **apocalyptic** idea of a tumultuous destruction of the earth included the appearance of a powerful mysterious figure, called the Son of Man, somewhat human, somewhat divine, who would bring judgment upon sin. The Gospel of Mark identifies Jesus as this Son of Man, the judge who would appear soon in the skies to condemn evil and establish a new world in which God reigned. The famous fresco by Michelangelo on the front wall of the Sistine Chapel in Rome depicts Christ as this Son of Man. Some churches continue to stress the imminent end of the world when Christ will come to judge the earth. Other churches have transferred much of this idea to the individual, who at death will meet and be judged by the Son of Man.

One of the most common titles for Jesus is Savior. The Hebrew Scriptures assert that only God can save. The common Jewish name Yeshua, which English translates as Jesus, means "God saves." In Greek and Roman religions, many gods and goddesses assisted humans with divine power, and religious rituals appealed to these saviors for aid. When Christians claimed that Jesus was the savior, they were using language familiar in their polytheistic society. Especially the Gospel of Luke utilized the title Savior. So, if Jesus is Savior, what are humans saved from? This question has been answered in many ways. Jesus saves people from alienation from God; from an eternity in hell; from the power of the devil; from living with the guilt of their sins; from meaningless lives. The original source of the verb "to save" related to physical health: a savior was a healer. Thus many Christians, even when relying on modern medicine, thank Christ for healing.

The title most important to theologians articulating the mystery of Trinity was that Jesus is **the Son of God** (in English, uppercase *S*). Israelites and other Near Eastern religions called their kings a son of God, thus conferring divine

---

Works done to benefit the poor and needy identify Jesus as the Messiah. The alleviation of the suffering of some of the poor in the time of Jesus is a sure promise that the good news of the reign of God is being proclaimed to all the poor of history. Hostility did not arise because the teaching of the Messiah was political (which it clearly was not, particularly in the strict sense of the term), but precisely because it was a religious teaching that affected all human existence. To believe in Christ is also to assume his practice.—Gustavo Gutiérrez, OP[8]

Son of Man = title identifying Jesus Christ as the supernatural judge at the end of time

apocalypticism = the belief that with cosmic catastrophes God will destroy the evil world in order to establish a new one

The second article of the Nicene Creed, 1988 translation:
We believe in one Lord, Jesus Christ,
the only Son of God,
eternally begotten of the Father,
God from God, Light from Light,
true God from true God,
begotten, not made,
of one Being with the Father;
through him all things were made.
For us and for our salvation
he came down from heaven,
was incarnate of the Holy Spirit and the Virgin Mary
and became truly human.
For our sake he was crucified under Pontius Pilate;
he suffered death and was buried.
On the third day he rose again
in accordance with the Scriptures;
he ascended into heaven
and is seated at the right hand of the Father.
He will come again in glory to judge the living and the dead,
and his kingdom will have no end.

authorization on their monarch. King David was referred to as the son of God. The polytheism popular in the Roman Empire had plenty of sons of God, demi-gods with extraordinary powers, since the male deities impregnated goddesses and human women, who then bore the god offspring. Yet theologians have always taught that the term does not mean that God had sexual intercourse with Mary. In the New Testament the title Son of God points to Jesus' unique relationship with God, one likened to that between a son and his father. The Gospel of Mark says that Jesus called God **Abba** in prayer. So, if Jesus is the Son of God, how does that save? Through faith, believers can live in the same relationship with God that Jesus had. Rather than being estranged from God because of sin, believers have been adopted to live within God the Father's **grace**. In many churches, the baptism ritual calls the newly baptized a son or a daughter of God.

abba = first-century Aramaic title probably meaning papa

grace = the undeserved love from God

The Christian tradition has employed metaphors that illumine some aspect of Christ's work of salvation. For several centuries before the birth of Christ, Jewish poets writing in Greek described the wisdom of God in creating the world and in administering justice as if wisdom was a mighty woman in the sky named **Sophia**, the Greek noun for wisdom. Many cultures share this poetic tradition: even the United States Supreme Court building displays a statue of such a Wise Woman. Some Christian hymns and prayers likened Christ to Sophia in the skies.

Sophia = female personification of divine wisdom

The metaphor of Jesus as mother was especially beloved by the fourteenth-century woman Julian of Norwich. Some mystics likened the blood of Christ to the postpartum blood of a mother and the wine of **Communion** to mother's milk.

Communion = a central Christian ritual, in which the people eat bread and drink wine (see chapter 6); to commune = to participate in the ritual meal

Fig. 3.5. The earliest extant depiction of Christ, painted on the wall of a catacomb in Rome, likens Jesus to a loving shepherd who tends the flock of believers.

priest = a religious functionary who mediates between God and the people; a title some churches give to their clergy

A metaphor for Christ important especially in the New Testament book of Hebrews is **priest**. In the Old Testament, priests led the temple rituals, slaughtering animals to be symbolic gifts to God. The animals' blood was an especially significant sign of life. The Jewish temple was destroyed by the Roman armies in 70 CE, thus ending the system of priests offering such sacrifices. But Roman paganism was filled with sacrifices, altars for sacrifice in temples, public spaces, and private homes. Early Christians used this practice as a metaphor for the work of Jesus. He was like

Fig. 3.6. The fourteenth-century icon by Sergius of Radonezh depicts Christ dressed as an Eastern Orthodox priest. The crown is the type of headdress worn by Orthodox bishops.

a priest making an offering to God, and his own blood connected God and the worshiper.

A popular animal metaphor especially during times of persecution was that Jesus is the fish. An acronym formed by the Greek phrase "Jesus Christ, God's Son, Savior," spells out *ichthus*, the Greek noun for fish. Inspired also by New Testament stories that connected Jesus with fish, Christians used the fish as a secret sign of their allegiance, and in recent decades this fish has appeared as a Christian identification on automobiles. Perhaps the most common animal image of Jesus is the lamb. Like the lambs sacrificed in Jewish religious ritual, Jesus was killed so as to connect God's life with the life of believers. They live, but he, the lamb of God, died. Jesus is also the butterfly, who at the resurrection emerges out of the tomb as if flying from the chrysalis. Jesus is also the pelican, who according to an error in scientific observation, was thought to pierce her own breast and feed her dying young with her own blood. Jesus is the phoenix, who, according to myths, burned itself up and then came newly to life out of the ashes of the fire. Popular medieval legends of a unicorn that is tamed by a virgin woman led to Christian art in which, depicted in a lush garden, Christ as the unicorn has laid its horn over the lap of the virgin Mary.

A theologically important title for Jesus is **Lord.** In New Testament Greek, an honored male was called *kyrios*, which English can translate as lord, master, or sir, and in Spanish as *señor*. One's husband was *kyrios*, the emperor was *kyrios*. Jesus' followers called him *kyrios*. Jesus saves because he is lord and master, the authority in believers' lives. However, when the Hebrew Scriptures were translated into Greek, *kyrios* was used to render *Adonai*, the circumlocution for *YHWH*. Thus for early Christians of Jewish background, calling Jesus *kyrios* meant both that Jesus was their master and that Jesus bore the name of God. Jesus saves because he is of God.

The ultimate title that Christians give to Jesus is God. In the New Testament, when the disciples are on a boat during a severe storm, and Jesus comes walking to them on the water, with the power of God he calms the winds, and he says in Greek, "*Ego eimi*," which can be translated as either "It is I" or "I AM," which is the name of God (Mark 6:50). When Thomas meets the risen Christ, he calls out, "My Lord and my God!" (John 20:28). In monotheism, only God can save, and Jesus saves because he is God.

During the early centuries of the church, salvation was usually understood as a communal experience. The members of a church were participants with

O Divine Word! You are the Adored Eagle whom I love and who alone attracts me. Coming into this land of exile, You willed to suffer and to die in order to draw souls to the bosom of the Eternal Fire of the Blessed Trinity.— Thérèse of Lisieux, 1899[9]

Lord = master; LORD = an English rendering of YHWH, the Hebrew name of God

others in worship and the moral life. Many times what in English Bibles is translated "you" is a plural pronoun in Hebrew and Greek. In recent centuries, especially some Western churches have stressed salvation as intended primarily for the individual. These churches emphasize the individual's choosing to believe in Christ and thus going to heaven after death.

A second difference in understanding salvation is that for some churches, the goal of salvation, whether communal or individual, is achieved after death in heaven. For other Christians, the utopia that is called heaven will come to this earth when God destroys this evil world and forms a new one. Yet other Christians teach that the salvation promised by God is a condition that is realized during one's life. One lives by trusting God, being at peace with the neighbor, and helping those in need, and such a life is better than one spent in doubt, resentment, and selfishness. For these Christians, it is as if Christ saves you from yourself.

A third variation in defining salvation has to do with the public or private nature of the saved life. Some churches assume that the lifestyle of believers will be far different from that of the wider culture. For some of these churches, the world is so evil that it is best to be as separated from it as possible. In other churches, Christians are called to transform the world to be a better place. These churches stress political action, so as to make the society more clearly reflect divine goodness.

Other variations in defining salvation exist among the churches. Some churches stress the necessity for believers to live a holy life, while other churches stress the action of God to forgive. Each of these churches cites passages of the Bible to support their emphasis. So, whether to the group or the individual, whether after death or during life, whether publicly or privately, and whether with required participation or by free gift, Christians claim that what they need in life comes from God because of Jesus, who is Christ, Word of God, Son of Man, Savior, Son of God, Lord, and God, the second person of the Trinity, who can be likened to a shepherd, Sophia, mother, priest, lamb, fish, pelican, phoenix, unicorn, eagle.

What is meant by the two natures of Christ?

The implications of calling Jesus both a human and God came to fruition in the fourth and fifth centuries as theologians laid out the doctrine of the Trinity. One of the two major proposals came from Arius, a clergyman in Alexandria, Egypt. Arius used logic to demonstrate that Jesus was divine, but was not God. God had created Christ, and Christians ought to venerate Jesus, but since God is one, the Son cannot also be God. His opponent, Athanasius, bishop in Alexandria, Egypt, taught the opposite: Jesus was God, who lived as a human but was God throughout time. Citing the poem at the beginning of the Gospel of John in his defense, Athanasius appealed to divine mystery in his argument.

To bring an end to the controversies, the Roman Emperor Constantine, who by that time supported Christianity, funded a council of bishops to assemble in 325 in Nicea, a city in what is now Turkey. He hoped to get the church's authorities, some of whom thought and spoke in Latin and others in Greek, to preach in unity. Eventually the teachings of Arius were condemned, and those of Athanasius accepted. A later council, convened in 431 in Ephesus, also in present-day Turkey, adopted the phrase "the two natures of Christ" as the best way to articulate how the New Testament speaks of Jesus: Jesus Christ is both fully human and fully divine. This mystery cannot be fully understood, but must be accepted by faith. The Nicene Creed reflects the work of these councils: the Son of God, who was born and died, was "of one Being" with God the Father. Especially in the West, theologians dedicated considerable time and energy into probing the meaning of this mystery.

In the decades after Nicea, theological debate about how to articulate the mystery of God intensified. How could God be both one and three? A trio of theologians, Basil, his brother Gregory of Nyssa, and a friend Gregory of Nazianzus, proposed categories that looked promising: the Greek word *ousia*, in Latin *substantia*, meaning one substance, referred to the one Godhead, and the Greek word *hypostaseis*, in Latin *persona*, meaning a being, referred to the Father, the Son, and the Spirit. At a bishops' council held in Chalcedon, a city in the same region, in 451, agreement was finally reached: God was one substance and three persons, one *ousia* and three hypostases. The Roman Emperor declared the edicts of the Council of Chalcedon to be imperial law.[10]

Although there has been ostensible agreement about the nature of Christ and the Godhead since the fifth century, most churches lean in one direction or another. What is sometimes called a lower Christology stresses Christ's humanity, teaching that Jesus is a model for life. What is referred to as a higher Christology stresses his divinity; Christ is God on earth, embodying divine power. Some churches teach believers to pray to God as Father, which suggests that the Father has priority over the Son. Other churches teach that the Son is fully God, that God is and always was triune, and that no one person of the Trinity has priority over the other two. Generally one can say that some Protestants maintain the lowest Christology and the least attention to God as triune, and the Orthodox churches the highest Christology and the greatest emphasis on the Trinity. Especially the Eastern churches teach that God became human in

divinization/deification = becoming totally identified with and filled by God

Jesus so that humans can become God. By their term **divinization** (or **deification**) they mean that, thanks to the miracle of the incarnation, believers can become caught up into the life of God, as if absorbed into God and being transformed into what God had first intended.

When did Christ accomplish salvation?

theory of atonement = a theological proposal explaining how through Christ God and humankind became reconciled

Theologians have offered at least five different answers as to when and how Jesus saved humankind. These **theories of atonement** propose precisely how God and humans were brought once again to be "at-one" with each other. The earliest theory of atonement focused on Christ's resurrection and borrowed its language from warfare. God and the devil are perpetually embattled, and the devil holds people captive in the power of evil. Jesus had to pay the devil a ransom to free humankind; the ransom was his life. When Christ died, it seemed as if the devil had won, but Christ rose from the dead on Easter and conquered death and the devil. Art inspired by this theory shows Christ standing up inside a sarcophagus and holding a victory standard, as if he has conquered the enemy in a battle. The early Christians called Resurrection Day **Pascha**, that is, Passover. At Passover, Jews celebrate that Moses led the people to safety away from slavery and the Egyptian army. In a similar way in his resurrection, Christ saved his people from death and the devil. Christian funeral rites usually affirm that because of Christ's resurrection, death has been overcome.

"It means," said Aslan, "that though the Witch knew the Deep Magic, there is a magic deeper still which she did not know. Her knowledge goes back only to the dawn of Time. But if she could have looked a little further back, into the stillness and the darkness before Time dawned, she would have read there a different incantation. She would have known that when a willing victim who had committed no treachery was killed in a traitor's stead, the Table would crack and Death itself would start working backwards."—C. S. Lewis, *The Lion, the Witch, and the Wardrobe.*[11]

Over the next centuries, especially Eastern theologians thought about Holy Saturday, the day that Christ was dead and descended into Hades, the underground realm that housed the dead. Christ then brought up to God all the righteous who had died, and this event came to symbolize Christ's salvation of all people. A beloved image of the resurrection in Orthodox churches shows Christ standing on the smashed doors of Hades as he pulls Adam and Eve up to heaven. This theory of atonement is called Christ's "**harrowing of hell.**"

The most pervasive theory of atonement in the Western churches was delineated in the eleventh century by Anselm, who served as **archbishop** of Canterbury, England.

Employing medieval ideas of legal rights, Anselm proposed that since God is total righteousness, God demands human obedience; yet there is no way that sinful humans can satisfy God's honor. Only the sinless Jesus could appease the anger of the divine judge and pay the debt owed, and this was achieved when he sacrificed himself by dying on the cross on what is called in English Good Friday. Every Roman Catholic church displays artwork called the **Stations of the Cross**, pictures of each step along the way of Jesus' arrest, trials, sufferings, and death, to remind worshipers how much Jesus

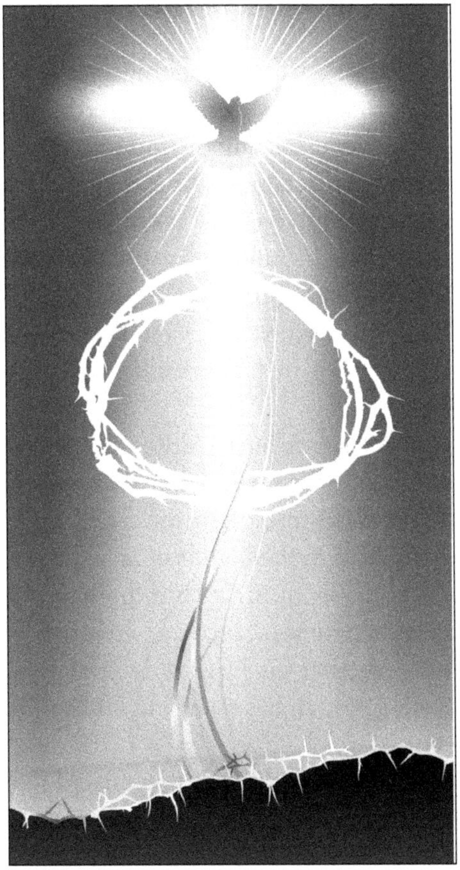

Pascha = the original title for the annual celebration of Christ's resurrection; also called Easter; the Christian Passover from death to life

the harrowing of hell = Christ plundering hell of all the righteous dead and bringing them to God

archbishop = a bishop, usually located in a major city, with oversight over other bishops or local churches

Stations of the Cross = artistic representations of fourteen incidents from Jesus' arrest to his death

Fig. 3.7. Some Christians heed the commandment never to make images of the divine (Exod. 20:4). This Easter cross includes symbols for the Trinity and for Christ's death and resurrection.

suffered to appease God's anger over sin. Many Christians have been encouraged to join in Christ's sacrifice by being willing to suffer for sins. The question "Are you saved?" is asking whether the individual has accepted the forgiveness offered through the death of Christ, and this acceptance implies that humans by themselves are unable to please God.

For centuries some Christians have symbolized the goodness of the cross by depicting the cross as the tree of life, on which Christ's death brought life to the world. Recently some theologians have proposed that in his death Christ joins all of suffering humanity and transforms human sufferings with the power of his loving presence. These theories retain a focus on Jesus' death, but replace the medieval emphasis on God's righteous judgment with a psychological sense of comfort and the hope for life.

One of Anselm's students, Peter Abelard, who became an influential professor of theology, shifted attention away from God's justice to God's love. Throughout his life, Christ personified divine love, healing the sick and teaching mercy, and this love makes God and humankind at-one. The cross of Christ was God's ultimate expression of divine love and forgiveness, and it intends to change the hearts of believers, so that they love God and one another. As the Gospel of John describes, on the night before Jesus' arrest and death, he symbolized extraordinary love by washing their feet, as a servant would (13:1-20). Church art that depicts Jesus as a loving teacher or metaphorically as a caring shepherd suggests this theory of atonement.

Another theory moves atonement back to Christ's birth. Although the first three centuries of Christians did not celebrate Jesus' birth in any way, during recent centuries some Christians have made Christmas their most important religious festival. The infant born in the stable at Bethlehem becomes the primary image of salvation, because as God becomes incarnate as a human, the entire human race is renewed and restored. The importance of Christmas in the churches and the omnipresence of art depicting the birth of Jesus suggest that the idea of God laid in an animal feeding trough has enduring fascination for believers.

Another emphasis is usually combined with one of the famous five. Here the final victory that Jesus achieves, the ultimate atonement, will occur at the end of time. Only when the **eschaton** comes, will Christ finally destroy all that is evil and vindicate all that is good. Over the centuries some Christians have predicted the precise moment of the eschaton and awaited its arrival. The extraordinary popularity of the novels of the Left Behind series[12] suggests the high interest among some Christians for speculating about the

eschaton = the end of the world, the conclusion of all things human

eschaton—when it will come, how long it will take, who will be saved through it, and who will be damned.

The theories of atonement attend to the birth, life, death, entombment, resurrection, and second coming of Jesus Christ. Each theory cites biblical passages in its defense. In many churches, these theories overlap. A preacher may emphasize one, the art in the church another, and the hymns a third. Theologians continue the debates, currently aware of how language, culture, and even the personalities of the prominent figures have influenced historical decisions. As if to start and to conclude all such discussions, the church continues to refer to Jesus Christ as did the last chapter of the Bible (Rev. 22:13), with the first and last letters of the Greek alphabet: Jesus is Alpha and Omega, the beginning and the end.

Suggestions

1. Review the chapter's vocabulary: Abba, anointing, apocalyptic, archbishop, archetype, Communion, deification, devil, divinization, Eastern churches, eschaton, the Fall, grace, harrowing of hell, heaven, hell, Historical Jesus, image of God, immortality, Lord/LORD, original sin, orthodox/Orthodox, Pascha, priest, sacrifice, salvation, Son of Man, Sophia, soul, Stations of the Cross, theory of atonement, the unconscious, Western churches.
2. Do a Jungian analysis of the *Lord of the Rings* trilogy.
3. Present arguments for and against the existence of a literal hell.
4. Choose one of the Councils at which the doctrine about Christ was developed—Nicea, Constantinople, Ephesus, or Chalcedon—and report in detail on the issues it addressed.
5. Write a personal essay in which you describe the Jesus that you have been exposed to.
6. In the Bible, Colossians 1:15-20 is a late first-century description of the meaning of Jesus. Analyze it in the light of the categories in this chapter.
7. Read and discuss the 1999 short story "The Deacon" by Mary Gordon.[13] In Roman Catholicism, a deacon assists the clergy at and outside worship. Where is Jesus in this story?
8. For a major project, read and report on the classic 1897 novel *In His Steps*, the source of the popular question "What would Jesus do?" For Rev. Henry Maxwell, a primary thing Jesus would do was to close all saloons. Compare the Christological understanding of Maxwell's followers with the contents of this chapter.

9. View and discuss the film *Jesus of Montreal*, in which a group of actors presents an updated passion play about the death of Jesus. What does this "Jesus" accomplish?

For Further Reading

Borg, Marcus J., ed. *Jesus at 2000*. Boulder, CO: Westview, 1997.

Kärkkäinen, Veli-Matti. *Christology: A Global Introduction*. Grand Rapids: Baker, 2003.

O'Collins, Gerald, SJ. *Christology: A Biblical, Historical, and Systematic Study of Jesus*. New York: Oxford University Press, 2009.

Pelikan, Jaroslav. *Jesus through the Centuries: His Place in the History of Culture*. New Haven: Yale University Press, 1985.

What do Christians believe about the Spirit and the church?

4

Fig. 4.1. This 1998 *Crucifixion* by the Chinese Christian artist He Qi sets the cross of Christ under the dove of the Holy Spirit and surrounded by the church of suffering humanity.

◈ An answer from a scholar

Émile Durkheim (1858–1917) was a French scholar who throughout his career sought to understand what holds society together. His basic presupposition was that human individuals are in the first place social beings, with their state of mind and behavior shaped by and within the collective. Thus to understand the individual, one needs first to study social phenomena. Although he admitted that a totally objective study of society is impossible, Durkheim modeled the attempt, and he thereby invented and made intellectually respectable the field of sociology.

social fact = a way of acting within a collective that provides an external restraint on the behavior of its individuals

Durkheim considered the power of what he called **social facts**, those beliefs and practices within societies that influence their individuals. Society to a great degree determines those individuals within it. Language, thought patterns, sense of identity, social worth, morals: Durkheim said that all these derive from one's social setting. The more of these social facts that might be removed, the less human its persons would become; and within a different society, an individual would be a different person.

Durkheim was descended from a long line of rabbis, yet was himself not a religious Jew. However, it was perhaps this aspect of his biography that accounts for the intense focus he gave to religion. In his 1912 book *The Elemental Forms of Religious Life*, he highlighted religion as a primary social fact. Religion, he claimed, is the most fundamental social institution among human communities, giving birth to all that is essential for the human being, and is historically the primary source of camaraderie, solidarity, and morality within the species. Durkheim wrote that, for example, the human phenomenon of maintaining a calendar was a social fact that organized individuals to fit into the patterns of the collective, and that contemporary calendars had evolved from ancient religion. Religion holds individuals together into a group because they share a common idea about what is sacred, they share beliefs and practices issuing from those ideas of the sacred, and they agree to a consequent morality. Durkheim wrote about the lessening of the role of religion in twentieth-century Europe and wondered what would replace its formative role in uniting and focusing human society.

Durkheim analyzed rates of suicide and proposed that the lesser the role of religion in a society, the higher the suicide rate. This illustrated for him that religion bonded the individual into the whole, and with less religion, an individual could more easily exit from being human, that is, could commit suicide. In his later work, Durkheim studied **totemism**, the phenomenon of

totem = a sacred object or creature that serves as a collective emblem for the group holy symbols in an ancient form of Australian religion. The community upheld the totem, which was a symbolic center for the people, and it in turn upheld the community. Durkheim saw that as a kind of totem Christianity had God the Father, "the guardian of physical order as well as the legislator and judge of human conduct."[1]

Durkheim wrote about "spirit," that which has authority to organize and perpetuate a social order within the religious community. By enacting that spirit, the community considered itself in some way holy. In what was perhaps his most distinctive phrase, Durkheim defined religion as society worshiping itself: that is, religion is the community honoring its own values and ethics and shaping its participants to share in and perpetuate those values and ethics. Worship activities are important because they organize the individuals into a collective group, without which they would be less than human.

Using Durkheim, one can say that Christianity is an example of the human phenomenon of religion, in which the communal identification of spirit has brought about beliefs about what is sacred, practices that maintain these values, and a fundamental code of morality. The communal agreement on spirit is

Fig. 4.2. According to Durkheim, these Senegalese monks praying before they eat are enacting a social fact: the individuals are bonded together before a god who provides the food. The depiction of Christ eating with his disciples functions as a totem.

Religion is above all a system of notions by which individuals imagine the society to which they belong and their obscure yet intimate relations with that society. . . . We can be sure that acts of worship, whatever they might be, are not futile or meaningless gestures. By seeming to strengthen the ties between the worshipper and his god, they really strengthen the ties that bind the individual to his society, since god is merely the symbolic expression of society.—Émile Durkheim[2]

enacted within the society that is called church. Durkheim's proposals illumine why Paul, in the earliest Christian writings, tells the members of the Christian community that they need not circumcise their sons or keep kosher diets, since circumcision and kosher are two of the primary identity markers only in Judaism. For Paul, it is the Holy Spirit that binds the community into one church, forms their values, guides their behavior, and allows them to think about themselves as holy.

◇ Answers from the churches

Chapters 2 and 3 discussed what Christians mean by the Trinity. God is not, as Aristotle proposed, a single monad wholly outside this universe. Rather, for Christians, God is triune, three persons, the Father, the Son, and the Spirit. This chapter will focus on the Holy Spirit and on the role of the Holy Spirit both in and outside of the organized life of the church. Over the centuries, some Christians, but not all, have granted to the Holy Spirit an immense role for the individual, while all Christians have acknowledged the power of the Holy Spirit to create and inhabit the church.

What is the Holy Spirit?

To study Christian doctrine, one always begins with the original languages of the Bible and the translations of their core vocabulary into the vernacular. The English noun "Spirit," as well as the archaic English usage "Ghost," translates the Hebrew word *ruah*, which can also be correctly translated as wind or breath. Thus in Genesis 1, when the Hebrew says that a *ruah* from God swept over the face of the primordial waters, this *ruah*—a feminine noun—can be rendered as the spirit of God, wind from God, or breath of God. Traditionally, Christian readers of Genesis, believing that God is ever triune, interpreted this *ruah* as referring to the Spirit of God, who was active in the creation of the world and in the continuing creation of all of life. The usual Greek word in the New Testament for spirit is *pneuma*, which also can mean wind, breath, or life force. Thus in the Gospel of John, when the death of Jesus is described as his "handing over his *pneuma*," this could be interpreted either as his letting go his breath or his giving over his spirit. The Gospel of John also uses a quite different term to designate the ongoing power of God: Jesus says that the *parakletos* will come to uphold and sustain the community. In the Greek of the first century, a *parakletos* could be a defense attorney or a friend, someone who stood up for you and supported you. The church has understood this *parakletos* to be the Holy Spirit.

The two most common ways that English-speaking Christians name the third person of the Trinity are Holy Spirit and Holy Ghost. Although God is not the sort of being that breathes, Christians have also used Breath as a metaphor for the Spirit. Because John's word *parakletos* is especially difficult to translate, some Bibles simply transliterate it into the word "Paraclete." Others use the English words "Comforter" or "Advocate." (Remember that capitalizing words such as "Spirit" or "Advocate" reflects the decision of the English-language translators, since neither Hebrew nor Greek uses the English system of upper- and lowercase.) The Nicene Creed calls the Spirit "the Lord, the giver of life." Some African translations use a noun that connotes feminine power, and some Asian Christians use the term *shakti*, a term that in Hinduism designates divine female energy. The Eastern Orthodox churches and the Western churches disagree about whether the Spirit comes directly from the Father or comes through the Son (recall the discussion in chapter 2 of the *filioque*), and this theological difference is one of the ways that distinguish how churches think about, and thus talk about, the Holy Spirit.

> This same Spirit, which in the creation of the world moved upon the face of the waters, operates on the human character to produce a new heart and a new life.— Hannah More, 1811[3]

Christians have read many passages and poems in the Bible as referring metaphorically to the Holy Spirit. In the Hebrew Scriptures, God is described as present in the form of a cloud. To Moses, God appeared as the fire in a burning bush. Throughout ancient Israel, scented oil poured onto someone's head served as a sign that God had descended into that person, granting power and authority. Thus Christians have used clouds, fire, and oil as **symbols** of the presence and power of God's Spirit. In the story of Noah's flood, it is a dove that signals the end of the catastrophe and the renewal of life (Gen. 8:11), and the Gospels include the vision of a dove as a

symbol = a concrete word, image, or object that represents an abstract truth or value

sign of the presence of God's Spirit in the narratives about the adult baptism of Jesus (Mark 1:10). Thus a white dove has become the most common Christian symbol for the Holy Spirit. Christians cite these biblical references in the claim that, like the wind powerful although unseen, the Spirit of God existed from before time, yet is seen uniquely in the life and work of Jesus Christ. In many churches, another significant symbol is fire, since in the biblical narrative of

In the Acts of the Apostles, the Holy Spirit descended upon the faithful under the image of fire. So was it when Gideon was about to defeat the Midianites; he commanded his three hundred men to take pitchers, and to carry burning torches in the pitchers, and a trumpet in their right hands. Our bodies are pitchers, formed from the clay of the earth, which will burn with the fire of spiritual grace. As the Spirit is the light of the divine countenance, so also is the Spirit the fire that burns before the face of God.— Ambrose, c. 380[4]

Pentecost = the festival fifty days after Easter celebrating the descent of the Holy Spirit into the community

inspiration = a powerful indwelling of the Holy Spirit

ecclesiology = the study of the church

the descent of the Holy Spirit in the Jerusalem community, it appeared as if "tongues of fire" were seen on each person's head (Acts 2:3).

Christians believe that although Jesus of Nazareth is no longer physically on earth, the same Spirit that was in Jesus is now alive in believers. Paul's letters include lengthy descriptions of the Spirit of God in the community, and his metaphor of "the fruit of the Spirit" is popular in the churches: it is as if the Spirit of God is the life force within the tree that is the church, so that "love, joy, peace, patience, kindness, generosity, faithfulness, gentleness, and self-control" are produced in the community by this Spirit (Gal. 5:22-23). In the Gospel of Luke, the Spirit of God brought about the miraculous conception of Jesus, and in Luke's second volume, the Acts of the Apostles, the same Spirit descends on **Pentecost** into the post-resurrection Christian community. In the Gospel of John, when Jesus died, he "gave up his spirit," and the subsequent narratives describing Jesus' resurrection include his giving his Spirit to the community of disciples. Christians say that a believer receives the Spirit of God, and by the **inspiration** of the Holy Spirit the believer lives a renewed existence. Some churches employ the biblical language that the very body of a believer is "a temple of the Holy Ghost." Some churches use the term "sanctification": the Spirit makes one holy, set apart for the things of God and towards the moral life. Yet, like the wind, this Spirit is elusive, mysterious: so in the sixteenth century the theologian John Calvin could write about "the secret efficacy of the Spirit, to which it is owing that we enjoy Christ and all his blessings."[5] For many churches, the annual festival of Pentecost is a significant celebration, with the color red displayed throughout the building and banners depicting the flame of the Spirit carried in procession.

What is the connection between the Spirit and the church?

The dominant Christian tradition has regarded the Spirit as active in the communal activities of the church. Theologians who work on **ecclesiology** agree that it is because of the action of the Holy Spirit that there exists a church at all. Through the Spirit, accessed especially within the church, God is available here and now, even though Jesus Christ is no longer visibly on earth. Christians believe that because sinful humans cannot by themselves live a God-pleasing life, they need the Spirit of God to do so, and if people want to connect with the Spirit of God, church is the place where they can get it. Most churches claim that the Holy Spirit has guided the community of believers over the centuries, leading the development of theology and blessing church endeavors. This attitude may make church authorities hesitant to admit historical errors or contemporary inadequacies, since they hope to ground their tradition in the inspiration of the Holy Spirit.

The connection between the Holy Spirit and the church is evident in the Nicene Creed, in which the third paragraph deals together with the Holy Spirit and the church. What the fifth-century authors of the creed meant by saying the church is "one" is that from God's point of view, there is one church, one vehicle for salvation, one way in Christ. "Holy" meant, not sinless, but set apart, filled with the Spirit of God, and dedicated to the things of God. The word "catholic" written with a lowercase *c* means universal: the church exists throughout the world and includes everyone. By "apostolic," the theologians meant that the church was directly connected with the first century of the apostles, and even as doctrine developed over the centuries, it faithfully represented the teachings of the earliest preachers. All of these qualities of the church are seen as products of the inspiration of the Spirit of God, who gives to the members of the churches a common spirit of fellowship, often called by its Greek word **koinonia**. The Apostles' Creed refers to this communal sharing of salvation as "the communion of saints," because all the baptized, whether dead or alive, are united together in the Spirit.

Christian theology has described the various ways that the Holy Spirit is present in the church. The Bible, also called the word of God, is the collection of books that are recognized as inspired by God to proclaim in an authoritative way the justice and mercy of God. Although churches disagree about precisely what this inspiration is and how it was achieved, all churches

As I turned and was about to take a seat by the fire, I received a mighty baptism of the Holy Ghost. The Holy Ghost descended upon me in a manner that seemed to go through me, body and soul. I could feel the impression, like a wave of electricity, going through me. Indeed it seemed to come in waves like waves of liquid love. It seemed like the very breath of God. I can recall distinctly that it seemed to fan me, like immense wings.—Charles Finney, 1870[6]

koinonia = Christian communal fellowship

Almighty, eternal and merciful God, thus inwardly cleansed, interiorly enlightened, and inflamed by the fire of the Holy Spirit, may we be able to follow in the footsteps of your beloved Son, our Lord Jesus Christ.— prayer attributed to Francis of Assisi, 1226[7]

Fig. 4.3. In 1870, the American printmakers Nathaniel Currier and James Merritt Ives represented the heavenly tree of life with the dove of the Holy Spirit in its branches.

honor the Scriptures as in some way evidencing a divine power from God. In some worship services, the book of the Bible is itself honored as a symbol of the divine authority it carries; it may be carried high in procession, touched, or kissed.

The churches' most important rituals, called variously **sacraments**, **mysteries**, or **ordinances**, are understood as conveying to participants the Spirit of God. Some churches believe that the initiatory ritual of baptism carries the Holy Spirit into the candidate. In other churches, the water is understood as a sign that the Holy Spirit has already entered the candidate.

sacrament/mystery/ordinance = the preeminent ceremonies of Christian worship, through which participants receive blessing from God

The Nicene Creed, 1988 English-language translation:
We believe in the Holy Spirit, the Lord, the giver of life,
who proceeds from the Father [and the Son],
who with the Father and the Son is worshiped and glorified,
who has spoken through the prophets.
We believe in one holy catholic and apostolic church.
We acknowledge one baptism for the forgiveness of sins.
We look for the resurrection of the dead,
and the life of the world to come.

Some churches keep water in their baptismal **font** or in a small dish at the doorway of the building, and worshipers dip their fingers into this water and sign themselves with a cross to recall the Spirit's entry into their lives at baptism.

font = the bowl or tub containing the water for baptism

For some Christians, the baptismal water is sufficient to bring the Holy Spirit into the believer, while for others, a formal prayer calling for the Holy Spirit is necessary. For still others, a later, personal, usually emotional acceptance of this Spirit is the most significant religious event. For these Christians, this individual affirmation of the faith, rather than an earlier church ritual, is called being **born again**, and this emotional event is so central to the faith of these Christians that some claim that people who have not had it are not genuine Christians.

born again = an experience, valued by some Protestants, of an emotional experience of one's life commitment to Christ

For most Christians, the second most important sacrament is participation in a symbolic meal of bread and wine. This ritual is called by various titles and is described in a wide variety of distinctive ways (see chapter 6). Yet Christians agree that Communion is a means by which communicants are unified with God and one another by taking into the community the Spirit of Christ. Especially the Eastern Orthodox churches teach that it is the **epiclesis**, a prayer invoking the presence of the Holy Spirit, that transforms the food into a vehicle for God by bringing Christ into the bread and wine, and in Orthodox worship, this prayer for the coming of the Holy Spirit into the holy things is offered with great ritual solemnity.

epiclesis = a prayer invoking the Holy Spirit

Some churches include five other sacraments on their list: confirmation, reconciliation or penance, ordination, marriage, and anointing of the sick. Those churches that do not refer to these rituals as sacraments still do conduct them, and all Christians recognize these worship activities either as powerful actions of the Holy Spirit or as signs that the Holy Spirit has acted. Depending on whether a church designates these rituals as sacraments or mysteries or only as ceremonies, the specific description differs. But it is possible to give a general definition of each of the five.

In **confirmation**, after baptism, perhaps many years later, believers receive or acknowledge the Holy Spirit to confirm and strengthen their faith. In **ordination**, the community or a representative of the entire church organization prays for the Spirit to enter into a person who then becomes an ordained **minister**. The idea is that the ritual conveys or symbolizes the divine power that stands behind the church's ministers. In the ritual of **reconciliation**, believers confess their sins and receive the assurance of God's forgiveness from the minister; the idea is that the minister's power has come from the Holy Spirit.

At the service that **blesses** a Christian **marriage**, the community or the minister asks the Spirit of God to support the two persons, who vow before God to be united to one another for the remainder of their lives. Since churches see the ceremony of marriage as involving the good will of the Holy Spirit, the question of whether to call the union of homosexuals a marriage is extremely controversial within and across various denominational lines.

With the **anointing of the sick**, a prayer for the Spirit asks for healing or comfort on someone who is sick or dying, and in some churches, this prayer is made a solemn ritual with the use of scented oil. Some churches, however, use the term **the anointing** to refer to any emotional outpouring of the Spirit, and some ministers speak of having been anointed at the outset of their sermons. Many churches that do not use the terminology of "the anointing" still offer up a prayer that the Holy Spirit will speak through the preacher's words. Some churches maintain many other occasions in which the Spirit is invoked: a new building used for worship may be dedicated; a layperson assigned to a task in the community may be consecrated; a new home, a farm's newly planted fields, a family car—the list is long—might be blessed. In each case, the community prays

---

confirmation = a rite at which baptized persons receive or acknowledge the presence of the Holy Spirit

ordination = a rite of designating authoritative leaders in the Christian community by conferring the Holy Spirit upon the candidate

minister = a general term denoting an official leader of a Christian community, who "ministers to," or serves the community

reconciliation = rite of confession of sins and forgiveness from God spoken by the minister

to bless = to ask for God's good will

marriage = a lifelong union of two persons blessed by God in the rite of a wedding that the Holy Spirit will inhabit, bless, and use for good purposes that over which the prayer is said.

Christians believe that when the community worships, the Holy Spirit is operative in places beyond the reading of the word and the participation in the sacraments. Some churches value "speaking in tongues," the experience of **glossolalia** during which the believer enters an altered state of consciousness that expresses the power of God's Spirit in their body. Here individuals become so transported by the power of the Spirit in the preacher's rhetoric and the intense music that they babble their praise and perhaps dance in the aisles. Worshipers testify to the joy and peace they experience during these ecstatic episodes. Although some churches frown on such manifestations of the Holy Spirit, during the twentieth century the world witnessed a large increase of **charismatic** churches that promote such ecstasy as a sign of the indwelling of the Holy Spirit in the worshiping community.

Many churches maintain that the Holy Spirit is present in the music of the worshiping assembly, and over the centuries and throughout the world a wide variety of musical styles has served to carry and express the Spirit. In many churches, a choir or a soloist leads the singing or presents musical pieces that are too complicated for the entire assembly to render. In other churches, the entire assembly participates in enthusiastic singing. For those churches that prize singing during worship, **hymns** so beloved that they are memorized can be the most significant vehicle for individual religious expression both in and outside of worship. If the words of the song are stipulated by the tradition or the church body as a necessary part of the worship, the term **liturgical music** may be used. Some churches maintain their ancient patterns of **chant**, in which the minister, a soloist, the choir, or the entire assembly intones words to a simple musical line. With chant, the text is easy to hear and understand, since the words are more important than the musical pitches.

Concerning the inclusion of musical instruments, there is a wide variation in Christian practice. Some churches reject any musical instrument except the human voice. For centuries Western churches valued the use of an organ, because it could achieve high volume, and now many

anointing of the sick = a rite with prayer and anointing for the healing and comfort of the sick

anointing = a powerful reception of the Holy Spirit by an individual

glossolalia = an ecstatic babble used in praise of God; also called speaking in tongues or being slain in the Spirit

charismatic = filled with and expressive of the Holy Spirit

hymn = a Christian ritual song, often characterized by rhymed and rhythmic stanzas of theological words

liturgical music = music integral to the specific worship occasion

chant = a method of speaking words to a pattern of musical pitches

Fig. 4.4. The Eastern Orthodox icon called The Descent of the Holy Spirit shows the power of the Spirit radiating from heaven onto the assembled disciples. The figure at the bottom is a symbol of the cosmos.

churches worldwide have a band with keyboard, drums, and other sound or rhythm instruments to accompany the singing or to perform on its own. But no matter which instruments are expressive of a specific Christian culture or tradition, the idea is that the Holy Spirit fills the music and as it were travels in the sound into the hearts of the worshipers. Yet it is important to note that in each of these examples of divine inspiration during worship, church leaders are expected to judge whether the excitement is genuinely a sign of the Holy Spirit or merely the enthusiasm of a group of people. Using the biblical idea of "testing the spirits," the community endeavors to determine whether God or some other power is enlivening the community (1 John 4:1).

> Every time I feel the Spirit moving in my heart,
>
> I will pray.
>
> Yes, every time I feel the Spirit moving in my heart,
>
> I will pray.—African American spiritual song

Some Christian music was not composed for worship settings: George Frederick Handel's *Messiah* was composed to be a concert piece. Much Christian music is now composed for and performed in settings outside of worship, where it might function as prayerful devotion or as entertainment. Especially Christian rock is popular around the world in secular settings. Since it is usual for Christians to assert that the Holy Spirit blows like the wind, beyond human control, it may very well be that the Spirit can be conveyed and received through music heard in a concert venue. It is a common Christian assertion that the Holy Spirit blows like the wind, wherever it wills, and does not remain in church; filling the whole world, the Spirit is appropriately experienced also at concert venues.

Churches have different attitudes about the presence of the Holy Spirit in visual art. Some Christians reject any depictions of biblical characters or symbols on the walls of the church. These Christians number Exod. 20:4-5a as the Second Commandment, and they heed its prohibition against any **idol**. They assert that any depictions of holy things will be necessarily so inadequate as to be harmful for the worshipers' access to God. If such art were truly magnificent, it would, like an idol, become more or less adored. In the sixteenth century, Protestants who judged the medieval wall paintings in their churches offensive covered them over with whitewash. Currently, with little of this offense remaining, throughout Europe there are projects to remove the whitewash and restore these medieval wall paintings in many church buildings.

idol = a symbol of holiness that is itself worshiped as divine

However, other Christians, when listing the Ten Commandments, omit the sentence that forbids the crafting of "an idol," instead numbering verse 7 as the Second Commandment. These Christians think that art need not become

piety = a style of religious practice and feeling

liturgical art = art integral to a church's worship

icon = stylized depiction of Christ, biblical characters, or saints venerated in Eastern Orthodox worship

an idol, but can be filled with the Holy Spirit, and so it can enrich worship with the life of God. Certain artistic styles may become extremely important in the **piety** of a group such that worship without the accompaniment of such **liturgical art** is impoverished, if not impossible. The primary example of obligatory liturgical art is the **icon** so beloved by Eastern Orthodox Christians. The icon-maker is not considered an individual artist using personal talent, but rather a servant of the liturgical tradition, rendering the icon as a spiritual vehicle through which worshipers gain entry into the presence of God. When entering their church buildings, Orthodox Christians characteristically kiss some of the icons, in reverence for the presence of the Holy Spirit that they signify. Orthodox theologians defend their devotion for icons by connecting the created icon to the incarnate Christ: they argue that God does indeed use the things of this earth to carry the Holy Spirit to the faithful.

Where else is the Spirit experienced?

Although many theologians have stressed that the Holy Spirit is found in the things of the church, most churches speak of some ways that the Spirit is evidenced in the world. The Spirit of God is free, and like the wind, it blows where it will, beyond the control of even the church. So, since Jesus is described in the Gospels as a faith healer, some Christians have recognized the healing of the faithful as a sign of the power of the Holy Spirit. Such healing may take place in a worship setting, but not always, and especially Roman Catholics revere certain geographical places as so filled with the Holy Spirit as to assist in the healing in the sick. The healing may be either a return to physical health or a sense of wholeness experienced by a person who is filled with God.

Sometimes this healing is seen as so extraordinary that the word "miracle" is used. The Gospels record Jesus' miracles, some of which are extraordinary healings, others of which show Jesus' power over the forces of nature. For many Christians, these biblical narratives are factual reports of genuine events in which Jesus reversed the direction of nature, and for some Christians, such miracles continue in the present through the power of the Holy Spirit. While some such events do not take place within a worship setting, it is common for church leaders to investigate the claim, so as to decide, once again assisted by prayer to the Holy Spirit, whether a genuine miracle occurred.

Some Christians value reports of bizarre occurrences, for example of statues bleeding, as miraculous visitations of the Spirit, while other Christians dismiss these events as having little connection with God. In a culture in which science is highly valued, there is considerable disagreement among the churches concerning the role of the Holy Spirit in any unexplainable occurrences.

Yet another example of the presence of the Holy Spirit is the phenomenon of visions. While awake or asleep, the mystic experiences something that others cannot and reports it to the wider community as a communication from the Spirit. Some Christian pieties prize such extraordinary glimpses beyond the here-and-now and judge that at least some visions are sent by the Holy Spirit. Churches of other pieties are skeptical that such personal experiences have any value for the believing community and so give visions little attention. Some Christians in the churches in Africa are particularly receptive to visions, and with the center of Christianity moving from the northern to the southern hemisphere, it may be that visions will have an increasing role to play as vehicles of the Holy Spirit.

> While unemployed, [the film director Donald W.] Thompson received an offer to make family films in Hollywood, an offer that included a six-figure income and a percentage of the company. Why, his wife asked one day, wasn't he taking the job? "It seems like everything I would want," he replied, "and I don't know why we're not taking it, but I don't think the Holy Spirit is in it."[8]

In the twelfth century, a mystic named Joachim of Fiore popularized the idea that human history was divided up into three periods of Trinitarian activity. The first, concurrent with the Old Testament, was the age of the Father. Then in the life of Jesus came the age of the Son. Beginning in about 1260, the age of the Holy Spirit would be inaugurated. Joachim advocated many substantive changes in the church of his day that would demonstrate the power of the Holy Spirit through all things. Although Joachim's ideas did not gain approval by the leaders of his day, the idea that the Holy Spirit is alive in the world and bringing about a new world order has been important to some Christians, especially during the nineteenth and twentieth centuries. For example, some Christians who claim that women and men ought to be treated equally see that idea as having been born not in the church, but in society. Here the Holy Spirit is credited with working, not only within, but also outside the structures and beliefs of the churches. In another quite different example of the idea of the age of the Spirit, some churches teach that there will come on earth a literal **millennium**, a thousand-year period during which Christ will rule the world, and for some churches, readying for this millennium is a primary task laid upon believers.

millennium = a thousand-year period that figures in different ways in scenarios about the end of the world

Once upon a time we captured God and we put God in a box and we put beautiful velvet curtains around the box. We placed candles and flowers around the box and we said to the poor and the disposed, "Come! Come and see what we have! Come and see God!" And they knelt before the God in the box. One day, very long ago, the Spirit in the box turned the key from inside and she pushed it open. She looked around in the church and saw that they was nobody there! They had all gone. Not a soul in the place. She said to herself, "I'm getting out!" The Spirit shot out of the box. She escaped and she has been sighted a few times since then. She was last seen with a bag lady in McDonald's.—Edwina Gateley[9]

Yet another understanding of the role of the Holy Spirit is becoming more popular in many churches as a response to the earth's ecological concerns. Citing the Genesis account of the creation of the world, these Christians understand that the Holy Spirit was and continues to be operative in the creation of all things. Thanks to the Holy Spirit, springtime arrives and infants are born. In line with this conviction, disregard for nature is a sinful rejection of the Holy Spirit, who intends the entire earth, not merely the church, to be alive to the things of God. Thus churches describing themselves as "green" see ecological ethics as incumbent on those inspired by the Holy Spirit.

Ralph Waldo Emerson, the famous nineteenth-century American philosopher, had begun his career as a minister in the Massachusetts Congregation Church. However, it was not long before he could no longer believe that the sacraments of his church conferred the Holy Spirit, and, being a man of integrity, he resigned the ministry. In a famous address he delivered to the senior class at Harvard Divinity School in 1838, he suggested that persons who wanted to find God should take a walk in the woods. Countless persons raised in some connection with Christianity have followed Emerson out of the church. However, Emerson's choice makes clear the points of this chapter: Christianity affirms that while God is mysteriously present in nature, the Holy Spirit is more clearly evident in the church, and perhaps only through the church can the divine Spirit be accessed and salvation achieved.

Suggestions

1. Review the chapter's vocabulary: the anointing, anointing of the sick, bless, born again, chant, charismatic, confirmation, ecclesiology, epiclesis, font, glossolalia, hymn, icon, idol, inspiration, *koinonia*, liturgical art, liturgical music, marriage, millennium, minister, mysteries, ordinance, ordination, Pentecost, piety, reconciliation, sacrament, social fact, symbol, totemism.

2. Discuss Durkheim's proposal that religion is society worshiping itself by analyzing a situation in which a society has many competing religions.

3. Present arguments for and against English-speaking Christians referring to the Holy Spirit as "she."

4. Choose several Christian rock songs that deal with the Spirit, and contrast their lyrics with that of the ninth-century hymn *Veni Creator Spiritus*.

5. Write a personal essay in which you describe an experience in a church that was for you either disturbingly negative or surprisingly positive.

6. Analyze the theology of Romans 8. In about 57 CE, Paul wrote to the Christians in Rome this earliest description of what Christians believe about the Holy Spirit.

7. Read and discuss the 1991 short story "A New Life" by Mary Ward Brown.[10] A conservative Christian group called the Vineyard attempts to befriend a grieving widow.

8. For a major project, read and write a report on Marilynne Robinson's 2003 Pulitzer Prize–winning novel *Gilead*,[11] in which she describes the many Christians in an Iowan town in 1957, their communal worship, church activities, and personal piety. The protagonist, a Congregational minister, had a life-changing event in church on Pentecost Sunday.

9. View and discuss the 1997 film *The Apostle*, which accurately depicts the worship and communal attitudes in a Holiness church. These Christians understand that their life and worship reflect "Holy Ghost power."

For Further Reading

Dulles, Avery. *Models of the Church*. Expanded edition. New York: Image Doubleday, 2002.

Heron, Alasdair I. C. *The Holy Spirit*. Philadelphia: Westminster, 1983.

Kim, Kirsteen. *The Holy Spirit in the World: A Global Conversation*. Maryknoll, NY: Orbis, 2007.

Pritchard, Rebecca Button. *Sensing the Spirit: The Holy Spirit in Feminist Perspective*. St. Louis: Chalice, 1999.

Why does Christianity have so many denominations and spiritualities?

5

Fig. 5.1. Some Christians display a crucifix with the body of Christ bloody from his wounds.

◇ An answer from a scholar

Ninian Smart (1927–2001), a Scottish scholar who taught at universities in the United Kingdom and the United States and wrote several influential books on the phenomenology of religion, was instrumental in establishing the field of secular religious studies. Before the 1960s, most study of religion was conducted from within a single religious tradition, which then provided the categories for analysis and comparison. Smart's knowledge of non-Western languages and world religions led him to advocate a value-free approach for secular universities, characterized by both information and empathy. He used the term "worldview" to indicate the way that religion, culture, and ideology interact, and he maintained that understanding diverse religious worldviews was essential for humankind's future. He studied both classic world religions and **New Religious Movements**, such as Sun Myung Moon's Unification Church. He described himself as "a Westerner, a Scot, a male, an Episcopalian, albeit with Buddhist leanings,"[1] explaining that no single worldview could contain all truth. Smart is famous for the quip, "She who knows but one religion knows none."[2]

New Religious Movements (NRMs) = recently formed religions that are not connected with the classic world religions

Analyzing the phenomenon of worldviews, Smart proposed that there are seven dimensions to religion. These seven patterns of belief and practice exist in varying degrees in all the world's religions, although one worldview may give ritual the highest significance, and another worldview makes ethics most important. To complicate analysis, each religion varies over time and place, and these seven patterns help the scholar think objectively about religion's complexities.

The insider has certain feelings and beliefs and they are an important part of the data we as religionists are set to explore. But an insider can be terribly wrong about her tradition, ignorant about or insensitive to the variety of her religious heritage. I once heard a Baptist minister give a lecture on Christianity which was, phenomenologically speaking, absurd. What he identified as true Christianity would not be accepted by great swathes of Catholicism, Orthodoxy, Episcopalianism, Methodism and so on. The most important point here is that traditions are plural. The Episcopal church in Fiji may vary greatly from its counterpart in Scotland.—Ninian Smart[3]

Describing this order as random, Smart delineated seven dimensions of the sacred. (1) The ritual or practical dimension includes worship, prayer, pilgrimage, and other formalized communal activities that have sacred meaning and connect the visible with the invisible. (2) The doctrinal or philosophical dimension is a worldview's organized system of beliefs that intellectually explain seeming contradictions. (3) The mythic or narrative dimension includes traditional stories that undergird present identity by presenting the script for rituals, explaining origins, imagining the future, and connecting the divine and the human. (4) The experiential or emotional dimension has been especially evident in world history, when a religious emotion has altered individual or communal life. (5) The ethical or legal dimension includes imperatives to moral behavior and describes optimal virtues, which may or may not involve any divine authority. (6) The organizational or social dimension is necessary for

Fig. 5.2. How many of Smart's seven dimensions stand behind this photo of a worshipping community?

the maintenance of the worldview and for the effectiveness of the leadership. (7) The material or artistic dimension includes the concrete things—buildings, art, musical instruments, symbolic objects—important in expressing and maintaining the religious worldview.

Smart's proposal, that every religious worldview spanning centuries and cultures will evidence these seven dimensions, helps explain the diversity of Christian branches, denominations, and **spiritualities**. Each Christian community will incorporate all seven dimensions, but will perhaps focus on one. (1) The ritual dimension is especially important in Roman Catholicism, with its emphasis on worship. (2) The doctrinal dimension is important to the Protestant churches that arose during the sixteenth-century European **Reformation**. (3) The narrative dimension, emphasizing biblical stories and the biographies of its leaders, is especially significant for African and African American denominations. (4) The emotional dimension is essential in **Pentecostal** churches, which promote experiences of ecstasy. (5) The ethical dimension is especially significant for the contemporary movement called **evangelical**, in which personal, family, and social codes of behavior receive great attention. (6) The social dimension is primary in the countless independent churches, which stress local identity-markers. (7) The artistic dimension is paramount in the Orthodox churches, with their reverence for icons and traditional ethnic style of music. Smart's categories thus provide one answer to the inquiry about Christianity diversity: every religion will contain each of these seven features, and in Christianity, this diversity is expressed through its denominations.

◈ Answers from the churches

One complication in considering the many Christian denominations and spiritualities is a confusion in labeling. Imagine trying to place a certain First Church in a diagram of Christianity. Historically, First Church is Baptist, a denomination that originated in the late sixteenth-century Reformation. However, during the nineteenth century, this **congregation** aligned itself with others that were entirely African American

---

spirituality = concern for the moral life and an appreciation of wholeness which may or may not be connected with organized religion

Reformation = a movement in sixteenth-century Europe hoping to reform the Roman Catholic Church that resulted in the rise of new denominations

Pentecostal churches = those churches that emphasize Pentecost and the gifts of the Holy Spirit, ecstasy, and healing

evangelical churches = those churches that emphasize the authority of the Bible, personal commitment to Jesus, witnessing to Jesus, and conservative social reform

congregation = usual Protestant designation for a local church in membership. Thus, ethnically, First Church is called **Black Church**, and now its African heritage is more important to its identity than its Baptist origins. In the mid-twentieth century, First Church bonded with other evangelical churches, actively promoting conservative social agendas. Because a conservative biblical interpretation marks all the preaching and education at this church, other Christians call it a fundamentalist church. Finally, in the late twentieth century, First Church built an immense, 7000-seat theater that is filled each Sunday for worship, and it now calls itself a **megachurch**. So it is not clear whether First Church is to be labeled Baptist, Black, evangelical, fundamentalist, or megachurch.

Black Church = those Protestant churches with a majority African American membership and worship that features enthusiastic preaching and singing

megachurch = a church, usually independent Protestant, serving thousands of worshipers

Christianity is comprised of institutions, local, national, international. To remain alive, every institution needs to perpetuate itself. Some churches accomplish this by encouraging large families or urging their members to evangelize. Successful institutions also provide their members with a sense of belonging. For churches, this belonging may be achieved through a beloved theology, a distinctive spirituality, a style of music, or a bonding through social action. Any successful group needs to promote a clear sense of purpose. A church may have as its focus to keep people from sin, to comfort all who suffer, to nurture a lively local community, to remake society at large. A successful group needs to preserve order and authorize its leaders but also to systemize change. Even when churches relish their historic connections, every branch, denomination, spirituality, and local church undergoes continual change. Some churches welcome change as a sign of the continual working of the Holy Spirit, and others resist change, judging that God has blessed especially their historic patterns.

Fig. 5.3.

Fig. 5.4.

Which churches claim to be the oldest?

The Eastern Orthodox churches

Already in the third century, the area east and northeast of the Mediterranean Sea was home to many Christians. Its central city Byzantium, later named Constantinople and now Istanbul, was the eastern capital of the Roman Empire. Here, in present-day Syria, was found the remains of the earliest church; here, in Egypt, monasticism began; here, in what is now Turkey, the fourth- and fifth-century councils that determined Christian creeds were held. Most Christians now residing in this area are members of Eastern Orthodox churches, which are organized by language and geography into national churches. Thus both in those countries and wherever there are immigrant groups there may be Orthodox churches that are Albanian, Antiochian, Armenian, Bulgarian, Carpatho-Russian, Coptic, Ethiopian, Greek, Romanian, Russian, Serbian, Syrian, and Ukrainian, and their ethnic identity may be paramount in their **parish** life. In keeping with their label, Orthodox Christians value their heritage as maintaining the right teaching and worship.

> parish = the usual Orthodox and Roman Catholic designation for a local church

Two thousand years have seen considerable development within Orthodox churches. Yet usually Orthodoxy prefers what is oldest. At the head of each national Orthodox church is a **patriarch**, who is equal to the other national patriarchs. This polity is understood as the most ancient and thus, in their judgment, the best. As in the early church, priests can marry. Orthodox thinkers continue to honor Platonism, the philosophy that was important

> patriarch = usually, the Orthodox bishop of a national church

in early Christian theology. Plato wrote that everything we see and experience on earth is merely an inadequate copy of an unchanging "ideal," a kind of eternal pattern beyond this earth to which we aspire. Orthodoxy, by upholding Christian Platonism, always reaches beyond this earth to the everlasting truths of God.

Orthodox Sunday worship, usually conducted in their historic language and lasting several hours, is filled with poetic texts that aim to draw the community up to God. Orthodox Christians refer to their sacred ceremonies as mysteries. The

The matins service of the Armenian Orthodox Church includes a week's cycle of hymns that celebrate God's acts of creation as recorded in Genesis. The Sunday hymn recalls the four primal elements—fire, earth, air, and water—that God has ordered into a harmony. . . . God is like a cantor who chants his Creation into existence and rejoices everlastingly over its beautiful harmony. His song continues, and its melody moves and inspires humankind to restore beauty and harmony to a Creation that is fallen and misshapen.—Vigen Guroian[4]

Fig. 5.5. In Orthodoxy, some candles are three-in-one, as symbols of the Trinity.

primary symbols in Orthodox churches are icons, which are meant to connect the human with the divine. Following an early Christian understanding, the Orthodox churches place primary emphasis on Easter and Christ's resurrection. They revere the mystery of a three-in-one Trinity, and the goal of divinization is to make humans more fully what the Trinity intends. The most revered Orthodox theologians are monks, some in monasteries and others wanderers, known for their mystical writings and poetic prayers. Since the Orthodox resist innovations in theology, they use the version of the Nicene Creed without the *filioque*, a later Western addition. Because the Orthodox churches have always been tied to their nation-state, Orthodoxy has tended to be politically and ethically conservative, valuing their past and resisting disruptive change. In the past, most citizens of these countries were baptized into their national Orthodox church, and so church membership strengthened ethnic identity.

The Roman Catholic Church

Orthodoxy is not alone in claiming an original priority within Christianity. The Roman Catholic Church claims first-century origins, since both Paul and Peter were martyred in Rome, the first capital of the Roman Empire. Several offshoots of Roman Catholicism exist, such as the Polish National Catholic Church and the Old Catholics; and several **Uniate** church bodies, for example the Ukrainian Catholic Church, maintain allegiance to Rome but in other ways resemble Orthodoxy. But the vast majority of Catholics are members of a single international organization centered in an area of Rome called Vatican City, and many Roman Catholics honor the **Vatican** by making pilgrimages to it.

Having inherited from the Roman Empire the model of a single authority figure, Roman Catholicism has established the **pope** as head of its worldwide organization. In 1870, the Roman Catholic **magisterium** affirmed **papal infallibility**, meaning that when formally articulating central matters of the faith, the pope cannot err. Throughout history, the pope has exercised varying degrees of control over the other clergy, baptized Roman Catholics, and secular heads of state.

Western theologians, believing that the Holy Spirit continues to inspire the church in the development of doctrine, replaced the older Christian interest in Plato with one grounded in Aristotle. Aristotle, Plato's student, rejected the mystical Platonic ideals and valued instead the objective study

Uniate churches = a grouping of churches that retain Orthodox characteristics but acknowledge the primacy of the pope

Vatican = the headquarters of the Roman Catholic Church; its hierarchy

pope = usually, the bishop of Rome and international bishop of the Roman Catholic Church

magisterium = the teaching authority of Roman Catholic bishops

Fig. 5.6. In Saint Peter's church in Rome, the elaborate canopy marks the place where it is believed that St. Peter was buried.

of this earth. Embodying Aristotelian precision, Western theologians used reason to compose doctrinal treatises that explained matters of faith and practice, and all Roman Catholics are expected to accept the authorized theology.

An example of the development of Roman doctrine is the thought about the afterlife. Early church doctrines about heaven and hell were supplemented with teachings about **purgatory** and **limbo**, but in the twentieth century, limbo was removed from the list. Another innovation in the Roman Catholic theological tradition has been the twentieth-century movement called **liberation theology**, which proposes that communal care for the poor, rather than individual entry into heaven, ought to be Christians' main concern. Yet especially in sexual ethics, Roman Catholic teachings remain traditional. Woman's role as mother is highly valued, and any sexual intimacies that are not open to conception are prohibited. A valuing of all human life, the primary role

papal infallibility = Roman Catholic doctrine of 1870 designating when the pope speaks without error

purgatory = an experience of suffering after death to ready a sinner for heaven

limbo = a neutral state after death for those for whom neither heaven nor hell is appropriate, such as unbaptized infants and righteous pagans liberation theology = twentieth-century teaching, identified especially with Latin American Roman Catholicism, about God's preferential option for the poor

religious order = a single-sex religious organization requiring lifelong vows for communal life and work

In this present situation when people are starving to death because there is an overabundance of food, our Catholic young people still come from schools and colleges and talk about looking for security, a weekly wage. They ignore the counsels of the gospels as though they had never heard of them. . . . The only security comes in the following of the precepts and counsels of the gospels.—Dorothy Day, 1935[5]

excommunication = removing from a baptized person the right to receive the other sacraments

for women, and God's purpose for sexual intercourse provide background to the Roman Catholic bishops' absolute prohibition of abortion.

In Roman Catholicism, the doctrine of original sin became central, and the focus that the ancient church gave to the resurrection was transferred to Christ's crucifixion. Western theologians proposed theories of atonement to explain how humans are saved. The primary symbol for Roman Catholics is a crucifix, in which the figure of Jesus is on the cross dying for humanity's sins. A distinctive feature of Roman Catholicism is a high reverence for the Virgin Mary, Jesus' mother. Without her submission to the will of God there would have been no salvation through Christ, and Roman Catholics grant Mary a continuing role in bringing about salvation by pleading to God for humankind and by modeling obedience.

In Roman Catholicism, God's grace is made available primarily through seven sacraments, most of which are presided over by priests, and the necessity of the priesthood has raised serious questions in those places where now there are not enough priests. Catholicism encourages the faithful to participate in weekly worship, daily devotional prayer, even pilgrimages to sacred sites. Catholic institutions of education, health, and social service have been maintained largely by the **religious orders**. Benedictines, Dominicans, Franciscans, and Jesuits are among the major orders, whose members, while receiving no personal salary, vow to participate in the ministry of their order to the benefit of Roman Catholics and the society at large. The religious orders model the Roman Catholic emphasis on doing good and sacrificing for others.

From the third century on, controversies arose between the churches of the East speaking Greek and those of the West speaking Latin. The differences in Christian and cultural viewpoints culminated in 1054, when the patriarch of Constantinople and the pope of Rome **excommunicated** each other. Thus the single church became two branches, each of which shaped its faith in light of its language, philosophy, aesthetic, and institutional structures.

The Restorationists

It is appropriate here to describe the several **Restorationist** churches. In the nineteenth century, some American Protestants were distressed at the growing number and complexity of Christian denominations, and several new denominations attempted to restore a simple, pristine first-century church, as if to re-create what the church had been at its inception.

Restorationist = denominations that sought to restore first-century Christian teaching and practice

One group, the Christian Church Disciples of Christ, sought a biblical pattern of church organization, doctrine, and worship, which stresses the unity of all Christian churches, rather than their diversity. Following the New Testament, they celebrate communion weekly. The Seventh-Day Adventists assert that Christians should obey the original Jewish command by worshiping on the seventh day, that is, Saturday, and they focus on the second coming of Christ to the earth. Although such denominations are not centuries old, they are similar to the Orthodox churches and to Roman Catholicism by grounding themselves in the earliest Christian usage.

> The colony of Pennsylvania possesses great liberties above all other English colonies, inasmuch as all religious sects are tolerated there. We find there Lutherans, Reformed, Catholics, Quakers, Mennonites or Anabaptists, Herrnhutters or Moravian Brethren, Pietists, Seventh Day Baptists, Dunkers, Presbyterians, Newborn, Freemasons, Separatists, Freethinkers, Jews, Mohammedans, Pagans, Negroes and Indians. But there are many hundred unbaptized souls there that do not even wish to be baptized. In one house and one family, 4, 5, and even 6 sects may be found.—Gottlieb Mittelberger, a visitor to colonial Pennsylvania who gladly returned to Europe in 1754[6]

Which churches arose during the Protestant Reformation?

During the fifteenth century, the political, cultural, and economic patterns that had held European society together since the fall of the Roman Empire were shifting. Individual nations, their monarchs, and local languages were gaining power, and thus a smaller role was allotted to a church centered in Italy. The cultural Renaissance attempted to replace narrow beliefs and ignorant practices with a learned worldview inspired by the study of the philosophy, literature, and the arts of classical Greece and Rome. Scholars noted that the authorized

mainline denominations = those Christian churches with several centuries of history whose members participate in the dominant culture

Protestant = churches that arose in protest of the Roman Catholic Church

Roman Catholic Latin translation of the Bible included problematic mistranslations. The adventures of explorers altered the received understanding about the earth and human life. The feudal system of lords and peasant farmers was giving way to urbanization, where cities promised more individual freedom. More individuals envisioned and sought, not merely survival, but a better life. The invention in 1450 of the printing press made literacy a high value, and literacy often challenges authority. These societal changes brought about three waves of European Christians reacting against some of the beliefs and practices of the church of Rome, the first and second waves constituting what are sometimes called the **mainline Protestant** denominations.

The first-wave Lutheran and the Anglican churches

The first wave of the Protestant movement originally intended only to reform the Western church. Yet as positions hardened, separate church institutions developed. Those churches that followed the teachings of Martin Luther (1483–1546) resulted in Lutheran churches, many of which continue the legacy of Luther's career as a university professor of Bible by stressing biblical study and correct theology. The first-wave Reformation in England proceeded politically, with monarchs executing Christians they deemed either too Protestant or too Catholic, with a final compromise in a centrist Anglican Church that emphasized harmonious tolerance, rather than theological precision. Because of the extent of the British Empire, Anglican churches, usually in the United States called Episcopalians, became a worldwide Christian denomination.

liturgy = the format of text and action used by a Christian assembly in its worship

The first-wave churches retained much that had developed in the Western church over 1500 years: adherence to the ancient creeds, a formal authorized Sunday **liturgy**, high reverence for sacraments, an ordained priesthood, traditional religious art and music, social services for the sick and the poor. Yet the Reformers believed that over the centuries many errors had been introduced into Christianity, and backtracking was necessary to erase them. The primary resource was to be the Bible, studied in its original languages of Hebrew and Greek. The Reformers made vernacular translations of the Bible and of the Latin liturgy. Citing the Bible as their sole authority, they placed their focus on only two sacraments, baptism and Holy Communion. By emphasizing God's grace freely granted to every sinner, less emphasis was placed on the clergy and

Fig. 5.7. Martin Luther is usually shown wearing his university teaching robe and holding an open Bible.

on the church's prescribed ceremonies. Reacting against the serious sexual and financial scandals involving Roman Catholic clergy and the Vatican, the Reformers rejected both clerical celibacy and an authoritative pope, giving the **laity** greater roles in church life. This history influences the spirituality of most Lutheran and Anglican churches to this day. Some first-wave churches are theologically conservative, maintaining their original emphases, and other first-wave churches are theologically liberal, imagining that the church's reformation requires continual change. In many cities, worshipers can choose among Lutheran and Episcopal congregations that are either conservative or liberal in their worship style, theological preferences, and social agendas.

laity = Christians who are not ordained to ministry

The second-wave Presbyterian and the Reformed churches

Some Reformers believed that the first wave had not gone far enough. The second wave was led by John Calvin (1509–1564), and Calvinists strongly influenced the theology and the legal practices of the seventeenth-century American colonies. Many contemporary denominations have their roots in this second-wave movement, including the several Presbyterian and Reformed church bodies and the United Church of Christ, a twentieth-century merger of smaller church bodies. Some of these churches continue a strong connection with their historic mother church, and others, proud of how they have changed with the social situation, have little that is Calvinist remaining in their spirituality.

In considering the seriousness of sin, Calvin wrote of **total depravity**. Humans cannot on their own please God, and Calvin understood the church as an arm of God to maintain discipline and guide believers to godly living. Because Calvin thought there should be only one church in each geographical area, he established a **theocracy** in Geneva, Switzerland, and he mandated that the government should pass laws that support a single chosen denomination. For example, if keeping Sunday as a Jewish-style Sabbath day of rest is religiously necessary for Christians, then a Calvinist government will make any commerce illegal on Sunday. Currently even some

total depravity = the Calvinist doctrine that by nature all humans are sinful and incapable of pleasing God

theocracy = a government run by religious authorities

Fig. 5.8. What is important, and what is not, in this second-wave church?

Christians who are not descendant from Calvin advocate his position that the government should support one religion.

elder = lay leader

Because Calvinists resisted any religious hierarchy, Calvinist congregations have lay leaders called **elders**, and a council of clergy has responsibilities over a geographical area. Most Calvinists reject the liturgy that had developed in Europe over 1500 years, replacing it with a service marked by lengthy Bible reading and instructional sermons that educate the people in Bible and Christian living. Calvin judged that religious art on the walls of churches led people's imagination away from the Bible, and so many second-wave churches have plain interiors. Calvin had been trained in the law, and Calvinist churches have inherited a spirituality that honors God as the Lawgiver and adheres to established church procedures.

The third-wave Baptist and Plain churches

The third-wave was convinced that neither the first nor the second wave had gone far enough. The third wave is sometimes called the Radical Reformation, because its leaders sought truly radical changes in church and society. During the crises of the third wave, Europe witnessed riots in which laypeople trashed the local Roman Catholic buildings in order to destroy religious items that they viewed as contrary to God's word, and some third-wave Christians refused to obey laws that they believed infringed on their religious beliefs. These denominations are called **Free churches**, because they see themselves as free from any exterior authority in either church or government. Sometimes these freedoms are balanced with an unquestioned authority granted to the local minister. Most of these churches maintain a strong countercultural identity, calling their members away from the sin-filled secular society to live a righteous life, following Jesus.

Free churches = those churches that advocate freedom from government control and outside church authority

The Free churches that originated during this period of history include the several Baptist affiliations, from the more liberal American Baptists to the more conservative Southern Baptists and Free Will Baptists. Each Baptist congregation is independent of all others, although their members meet in conventions to vote on cooperative positions and actions. Some third-wave churches, such as the Church of the Brethren, are called **Peace churches** because they advocate pacifism and refuse to serve in the armed forces. The perpetual social pressure to raise one's standard of living is rejected especially by the **Plain churches**, such as the Hutterites, the Mennonites, and the

Peace churches = those churches that teach pacifism as the only way to follow Jesus

Plain churches = those churches that advocate a countercultural economic simplicity in lifestyle

Amish, which advocate simple attire and minimal possessions. Some groups, such as the Amish, reject higher education as placing a nonscriptural value on things that do not matter to the Christian life. Most of these churches maintain no religious hierarchy and no shared system for training clergy. For Baptists, the term "bishop" means the head minister of a large congregation. With no authorized pattern of worship, each congregation can worship as it pleases.

The theological position of third-wave churches that was originally the most socially disruptive was believer's baptism. Since the New Testament does not speak of the baptism of infants, and since not even parents should be allowed to determine the religious situation of their children, the third-wave churches abolished infant baptism and replaced it with believer's baptism. This meant that the original third-wave Protestants, then called Anabaptists because they rebaptized their members, claimed that persons who had been baptized as infants were not genuine Christians. Many European Christians refused to tolerate this opinion, and governments collaborated with church authorities to persecute and even execute third-wave Protestants. For third-wave Protestants, the Bible is sovereign, and by the late nineteenth century, many of these Christians had become fundamentalists, teaching biblical inerrancy. The church's sacraments are viewed as nonessential signs of one's interior faith. Baptism is only a sign of one's commitment, and communion is celebrated perhaps twice a year.

Since American culture so strongly values individual autonomy, it is not surprising that Baptists have become one of the most populous denominations in the United States. Yet some of the third-wave groups balance this emphasis on individualism with a strong communal ethic. Amish Christians dress in what are essentially uniforms, since their communal identity, not any individual choice, determines their identity, and they teach the acronym JOY, which means "Jesus first, others second, yourself last." In some places in the world there remain Hutterite and Bruderhof communities that resemble monasteries in which families share a common religious devotion, and simplicity of house, furnishings, and dress is maintained.

Which churches are recent additions?

The Holiness churches

The Anglican priest John Wesley (1703–1791) stressed that Christians should strive to live a holy life. As proof that they had received the Holy Spirit, Christians needed actively to reject the sinful society and the sin-filled self, and the

Fig. 5.9. Many independent churches adapt commercial sites for their worship space.

church should offer methods of prayer and discipline to assist believers for this challenge. Phoebe Palmer (1807–1874) followed Wesley's teachings by preaching about perfection and the experience of being sanctified by the Holy Spirit. Thus arose the Holiness churches, which include the many Methodist churches, named for Wesley's "methods," and many Holiness church bodies. Some Holiness churches have titles that recall the New Testament, such as the several Apostolic denominations and the Church of the Nazarene, to indicate their desire to replicate the transformed and countercultural lifestyle of early Christians.

Urbanization meant that neighbors with different languages, ethnicities, religious and social practices, and modern ways offered choices that did not accord with strict Christian holiness. Thus churches in the Holiness movement sponsor worship and communal activities that attempt to strengthen believers against the many temptations of contemporary society. Methodist and Holiness churches are known for their intense prayer practices, with Methodists most famous for their enthusiastic hymn-singing, which is seen

Fig. 5.10. The Salvation Army is a Holiness church famous for its charity to the poor.

as a significant support to the faith of the individual. Methodists have urged members to reform the wider society to minimize sinful practices: it was Methodist women who in their opposition to alcohol picketed saloons in Ohio, thus having a significant impact on the emerging prohibition movement. Many Holiness Christians avoid movies, dancing, revealing attire, and anything that might incite occasions for sin. Many of them meet in simple storefronts. Holiness churches were among the first to ordain women to the ministry, since they so strongly honor the Holy Spirit as a living reality in their midst, and Holiness churches are among the most racially integrated. Many Holiness churches sponsor religious **revivals**, often in camp settings, which many participants find transformative in their lives.

Theologically, Methodists stress God's **prevenient grace**. But after persons accept God's grace, the Holy Spirit works on them to sanctify them. This sanctification will spill out from the heart of the believer into the wider society, and especially in care for the poor and sick. Methodist theologians stressed human reason as a tool in interpreting the Scriptures. However, the Holiness churches have been less interested in theological systems and more focused on holding enthusiastic worship events through which the Holy Spirit transforms believers, and they emphasized personal spiritual well-being over the repair of the society.

revival = a lengthy worship event, sometimes held outdoors, characterized by inspirational song and enthusiastic preaching, with the goal of reviving the religious commitment of Christians

prevenient grace = God's mercy that comes before humans seek it

Black Church

A grouping of churches usually termed Black Church is said to have begun in 1787 in Philadelphia, when at a Methodist church service an African American member was forcibly moved away from the area reserved for whites up to the crowded balcony, which was reserved for Africans, slave and free. Richard Allen (1760–1835) led a walkout of that congregation's black members and established the African Methodist Episcopal Church, known now as A.M.E. Soon another group arose called A.M.E. Zion. Over the next two centuries, these and other breakaway groups, many of them Baptists, allowed African immigrants to worship in their own unique style and to function outside of white authority. For many of these congregations, their identity as Black Church is more important than their history as Methodists, Baptists, or other denominational groupings.

Participation in Black Church has been immensely important for the spirituality of many African Americans, and a majority of African Americans who have become leaders in the wider society received their training in the Black Church. The dominant spirituality proclaims that Jesus has freed them from sin and from the oppression of white society, and in worship they celebrate this freedom with enthusiasm. Some scholars believe the worship style and theological emphases of Black Church keep alive African religious patterns by means of song, dance, drumming, ecstasy, and incantatory preaching. Black Church retains language of spirit possession, both of the Holy Spirit and of the devil, and members are encouraged to read the Bible daily for inspiration and comfort. Black Church preachers see the story of the Exodus, God's freeing of the chosen people from slavery to Egypt, as their own story. Thus the Bible functions as their existential autobiography, and their lengthy sermons are usually filled with references to Bible stories.

The Pentecostal churches

Some Protestants who emphasize the Holy Spirit hold that a baptized person can experience spiritual gifts, which may include the power of healing and the ecstatic experience of the indwelling of God. In 1906, a several-month-long revival that was held at 312 Azusa Street, Los Angeles, signaled the beginning of the twentieth-century movement of Pentecostal churches. Pentecostal denominations include the Assemblies of God, the Church of God in Christ, the Foursquare Gospel Church, Calvary Chapel, and Vineyard, as well as countless independent church groups. The Pentecostal movement is currently the growing arm of Christianity in the developing world, and increasingly Pentecostalism is listed as a fourth branch of Christianity, along the standard three of Orthodoxy, Roman Catholicism, and Protestantism. A recent phenomenon in the United States is that immigrants from Latin America who had been Roman Catholics in their homeland now align themselves with a local Pentecostal church.

Centered in the story in Acts 2 of the first Christian Pentecost, this movement stresses the "the baptism of the Holy Ghost" as a personal ecstatic experience of speaking in tongues. What is usually called the **second blessing** goes beyond the first baptism by pouring additional power of the Holy Spirit into the believer. Pentecostal churches baptize believers "in the name of Jesus," rather than in the name of the triune God. Jesus is Savior, Baptizer in the Spirit, Healer, and soon-coming King. Many Pentecostals are fundamentalist interpreters of the Bible, and their valuing of ecstasy makes theology less important than it is for mainline churches. Pentecostals' critical stance toward church hierarchy and systems of clergy

second blessing = a post-conversion, post-baptismal infusion of the Holy Spirit

---

Frank Bartleman describing the Azusa Street Revival: It was a spontaneous manifestation and rapture no earthly tongue can describe. . . . Some have condemned this "new song," without words. But was not sound given before language? And is there not intelligence without language also? . . . No subjects or sermons were announced ahead of time, and no special speakers for such an hour. No one knew what might be coming, what God would do. All was spontaneous, ordered of the Spirit. Those were Holy Ghost meetings, led of the Lord. . . . A dozen might be on their feet at one time, trembling under the mighty power of God.[7]

preparedness means that they can easily establish themselves in mission situations. Their informal worship of song, Scripture, and prayer, filled with laughing, crying, singing, clapping, and embracing, tends to nurture a conservative theology, social values, and lifestyle.

Evangelical churches

Of all groupings of denominations and spiritualities, the evangelical is among the most commonly discussed in contemporary media. The term "evangelical" does not name a denomination but rather denotes an increasingly popular style of Protestantism. Many people find the label evangelical more appealing than a church's historic denomination, and some evangelical churches describe themselves as **nondenominational**.

With little interest in the complex history of Christian doctrines, evangelical churches keep to what they see as several Christian basics. All persons are to accept Jesus Christ as their personal Savior, thus avoiding hell and gaining everlasting life in heaven. Most evangelicals describe themselves as born again, and they treasure their memory of the moment they accepted Jesus as their Savior. Salvation grants believers

nondenominational = free from connection to the structures, beliefs, or practices of named denominations

a personal relationship with God, and thus private prayer as conversation with Jesus is stressed. In thanksgiving for this salvation, believers are to live a recognizably Christian life and to spread the good news to others. Preaching usually includes a call to accept Jesus as one's Savior, since even worshipers need to be called again to faith.

Evangelical churches tend to stress personal ethics and traditional sexual mores more than social or communal sin. Many evangelical churches are marked by a pessimistic attitude toward current culture, and yet their worship styles counter the negativity with positive experiences that encourage believers to feel good about their faith. The intense network among the evangelical churches has meant that their interest in any particular social issue can function as a significant conservative political force.

Independent churches

The twentieth century witnessed the expansion of independent churches, which in some areas of the world have become the most significant arm of Christianity. An inspirational preacher or a small team simply begins to hold public worship, and a congregation might arise. No regional, national, or international consortium supports such a church, and many people find this independence an attractive feature. The church's name and title will have been decided on by the evangelist or by the original group of worshipers.

What is most important in these churches is the given resident community, and many call themselves a Community Church. That particular minister, those musicians, that education program, those midweek activities are what matter to the members. Some of these churches emphasize their openness to persons who have been unchurched, and they describe such participants as **seekers**. Some independent churches fill immense stadiums for Sunday worship, and they may prefer to use the descriptor "megachurch." Many people like the impersonal tone of a massive meeting, finding it similar to their experiences at sports events. Megachurches intend that truly committed members will participate in the midweek events that pursue education, service, or friendship. One of the most renowned of these megachurches is Willow Creek Community Church in Barrington, Illinois, founded in 1975, at which each weekend some 24,000 people worship. However, an independent church might be instead a storefront with several dozen worshipers for whom the intimacy available in a small group nurtures their faith. Among independent churches are the snake-handlers of the American Appalachian region. They focus on a single verse, Mark 16:18, which most Christian theologians consider to have been a late addition to the Gospel manuscript, which speaks of safely handling snakes and drinking poison, which they do during worship.

seeker = an unchurched person seeking religion

China has two officially sanctioned and thus legal Christian churches, one Catholic and one Protestant, but some Chinese Christians instead attend small independent underground churches, which are periodically subject to harassment by the government. But especially in Africa there is an immense movement of what are called the African Instituted Churches—also called African Indigenous Churches or African Independent Churches (AICs). AICs may be single congregations or a mother church with its offshoots, and they cultivate a wholly African flavor. A usual characteristic of the African independent churches is a focus on liberation from an evil and oppressive world culture by means of some indigenous leaders, narratives, tribal symbols, or traditional rituals. This **inculturation** gives the African churches a distance both from the Europe they perceive as home to a decadent Christianity and from the missionary movements of the nineteenth century.

inculturation = adapting a received pattern to correspond with another culture

In the African Instituted Churches, Jesus is honored as Liberator, Ancestor par excellence, Deliverer, Savior. These

Fig. 5.11. An interior of a megachurch, fully equipped with state-of-the-art technology for sight and sound.

churches prize their local prophetic leaders, accept the validity of visions, remain connected with the spirits of the dead, and revive tribal rituals and symbols, incorporating them into basic Christianity or amending historic beliefs and practices so as to include them. Most of these churches absolutely reject homosexuality, and some accept polygamy, two historically African attitudes about sexuality.

Are these groups Christian churches?

While some African churches are regarded as fascinating examples of inculturated Christianity, some have evolved to be far distant from the doctrine and
practice that generally defines Christianity. Thus arises the inquiry as to which
religious groups are called Christian. There is currently a long list of religious
groups that originated in Christianity which may or may not be currently considered Christian, depending on who is compiling the list.

In the African churches founded by Isaiah Shembe (1870–1935) and by Simon
Kimbangu (1899–1951), the role of Jesus Christ has been lessened to the extent
that the founder is honored. In the Bible, Zion is another name for the city of
Jerusalem and becomes a metaphor for the city of God's people
and God's home on earth. For some of the **Zionist** Africans,
their own national or tribal identity functions as the sacred city
for God's holy people, and the narrative of their founder takes
center stage.

Zionist = a title used by some
churches that regard themselves as the beginning of God's
work to save the world

Arising among the European third-wave Protestants,
the Society of Friends, usually called Quakers because they
"quaked" only before God's word, rather than before the king,
believe that all people are equal and are "friends" of everyone in the world.
Some contemporary Quakers honor the Bible and affirm Christian doctrine,
and others no longer do. The Unitarian-Universalists are a twentieth-century
merger that brought together the Unitarian belief that God is one, not triune,
and thus Jesus is not divine, and the Universalist assertion that all peoples,
regardless of their beliefs, will be saved. Historically, these several groups
included many prominent social reformers. In the present, some of their members consider themselves Christian, while many do not.

sect = a small exclusive religious
community demanding of its
members a total allegiance that
often requires a separation from
the wider society

One group that began as a **sect** but evolved into a major
religious institution is the Church of Jesus Christ of Latter-Day
Saints. Usually called Mormons, they had revived the polygamy
of the Old Testament and so were forced outside what was then
United States territory. For them, Joseph Smith's 1820s *Book
of Mormon* has greater authority than does the Bible, and several of their key doctrines and practices, especially the secrecy
that surrounds some of their rituals, are so distinctive that most
lists of Christian denominations omit them. Also arising in the nineteenth century, the Jehovah's Witnesses were Restorationists who attempted to restore
the original pure community of believers before any first-century theological
developments. For Jehovah's Witnesses, God is not triune, and Jesus is not God,
but believers are to continue Jesus' proclamation of God's kingdom. As part of

their countercultural witness, they avoid symbols and rituals of allegiance to their secular government, such as the pledge to the American flag. Some New Religious Movements such as Reverend Sun Myung Moon's 1954 Unification Church use the term "church," albeit with beliefs and practices that differ significantly from mainstream Christianity.

Some groups, by isolating themselves from the wider society and from other Christians and by professing idiosyncratic beliefs, are termed **cults**. The tragic suicide of nearly every member of Jim Jones's People's Temple brought an end to a community that originally worked for interracial justice and alleviation of poverty. Branch Davidians reside in heavily armed and secretive communes readying themselves to survive the apocalyptic battle at the end of time. Yet historians have shown that some groups which began as sects or cults later evolved into regular Christian denominations.

cult = a usually small group of religion adherents whose primary devotion is to its current leader; see chapter 8 for other usage

Some religious groups are **syncretistic**. Voodoo and Santería are the most well known of those faiths that arose among the slave populations in the Caribbean. Some of the worldviews and practices of their native West African religions are maintained under labels borrowed from the Christianity of their slaveholders. Another syncretistic group, the Native American Church has replaced the bread and wine of communion with communal experiences under the influence of peyote, its ensuing visions understood to have come from the divine for the good of all.

syncretism = the meshing together of two ostensibly contradictory ideas or systems

Several reasons why there are hundreds of Christian denominations and spiritualities are evident. The primary Christian principle that God became incarnate in Jesus Christ has opened the religion to a continuing incarnation in peoples, languages, and systems. The two branches of Orthodoxy and Roman Catholicism show that Christians in different cultures, languages, and aesthetics will think, speak, and celebrate their faith in different ways. The Reformation demonstrated that technological advances and evolving systems of government may alter the religion of believers. Recent denominational additions show that individual freedoms can supplant traditional authority. Not surprisingly, those at opposite ends of the economic ladder will practice their religion and educate their clergy in different ways. Because some people prefer to associate with others who are like them, racial and ethnic groups will flourish. Because religious faith can be a life-altering worldview, small intense communities of the faith will thrive. The human interest in combining symbol systems will make for inculturated Christianity. And because many countries value religious liberty and cultural diversity, all these options may be available in the same city at the same time. Thus the student of Christianity must beware of any sentence that begins with the words "Christians believe that . . ." or "The Christian spirituality is. . . ." Christianity is far too complex for most such statements to be true.

Suggestions

1. Review the chapter's vocabulary: Black Church, congregation, cult, elders, evangelical, excommunicated, Free churches, inculturation, laity, liberation theology, limbo, liturgy, magisterium, mainline, megachurch, New Religious Movements, nondenominational, papal infallibility, parish, patriarch, Peace churches, Pentecostal, Plain churches, pope, prevenient grace, Protestant, purgatory, Reformation, religious orders, Restorationist, revival, second blessing, sect, seeker, spirituality, syncretist, theocracy, total depravity, Uniate, Vatican, Zionist.

2. Access and discuss a listing of the numbers of current members of the Christian branches and denominations. How ought such numbers be determined?

3. Present arguments for and against Christian acceptance of Voodoo.

4. Research the Mar Thoma Church of India.

5. Write a personal essay in which you analyze and react to a news report about a recent church event.

6. In the Bible, John 17 is often called Jesus' High Priestly Prayer, in which he prays that the church will be one. Discuss John 17 in light of this chapter.

7. Read and discuss "Parker's Back," a short story by Flannery O'Connor posthumously published in 1965.[8] A Methodist man whose name means "servant of Yahweh" and "My God is he" gets an Orthodox icon of Christ tattooed on his back, thinking his wife will like it.

8. For a major project, read and write a report on James Agee's short novel *The Morning Watch*,[9] which narrates the thoughts of a pious adolescent boy as he participates in a prayer vigil during Holy Week. Identify and describe his denomination and spirituality, using the categories outlined in this chapter.

9. View and discuss the 2006 film *The Island (Ostrov)*. The Eastern Orthodox tradition honors the holy hermit called a *starets*, a monk who serves as a spiritual counselor and healer. Some of these hermits are known for their bizarre behavior. In this film, the twentieth-century Anatoly suffers obsessive guilt, and much of his speech is either the Jesus prayer or

excerpts from the Orthodox liturgy. The film depicts a denomination and spirituality unknown to many Westerners.

For Further Reading

Bednarowski, Mary Farrell, ed. *Twentieth-Century Global Christianity.* Vol. 7 in *A People's History of Christianity*. Minneapolis: Fortress Press, 2008.

Berry, Carmen Renee. *The Unauthorized Guide to Choosing a Church*. Grand Rapids: Brazos, 2003.

McLaren, Brian D. *A Generous Orthodoxy: Why I am a missional, evangelical, post/protestant, liberal/conservative, mystical/poetic, biblical, charismatic/calvinist, anabaptist/anglican, methodist, catholic, green, incarnational, depressed-yet-hopeful, emergent unfinished Christian*. Grand Rapids: Zondervan, 2004.

Shea, Suzanne Stremper. *Sundays in America: A Yearlong Road Trip in Search of Christian Faith*. Boston: Beacon, 2008.

Tyson, John R., ed. *Invitation to Christian Spirituality: An Ecumenical Anthology*. New York: Oxford University Press, 1999.

How do Christians worship? | 6

Fig. 6.1. On this 1561 Danish altar painting, a crucifix is central to baptism, Communion, and a sermon, with ministers dressed in different garb.

◇ An answer from a scholar

Catherine Bell (1953–2008) is renowned for her substantial contributions to the field of ritual studies. Describing ritual as a cultural practice, she wrote often about "ritualizing," as well as about "ritual," because her interest was in the process and the effects of such human activities. Rituals are flexible, continually undergoing alterations, both in what is done and in what is meant. Ritualizing is always situated within a specific context. Thus Bell argued that the meanings of any ritualizing are appropriate to that unique group, and any generalized theories that suggest a universal explanation to a certain behavior pattern are bound to be wrong. Bell wrote that ritualizing is undertaken to make and protect the cultural patterns that are necessary to healthy human community. Rituals impose order within a group, perhaps account for that order, and shape the attitudes of the participants to accept that order. Rituals always support the authority of some persons and map out the interrelationships between the participants.

The degree to which activities are ritualized—for instance, how much communality, how much appeal to deities and other familiar rites, how much formality or attention to rules, and how much emphasis on performance or appeal to traditional precedents—is the degree to which the participants suggest that the authoritative values and forces shaping the occasion lie beyond the immediate control or inventiveness of those involved.—Catherine Bell[1]

Ritualizing has immense power to shape the sensibilities of the participants. Yet Bell stresses that how such ritualizing functions for each participant may differ substantially from what the group leaders imagine is the purpose of the activity. Traditional ritual patterns might be reproduced, but they may be reinterpreted to fit current values and meaning. For example, in some cultures a bride was veiled because her husband was not allowed to see her prior to the wedding, while contemporary Western brides wear veils because the veils are judged beautiful wedding garb. The outsider cannot know precisely the meaning of the veil for any individual bride: perhaps the bride is donning a veil to please her mother, in which case the power relationship is between mother and adult daughter.

In Western societies, it is usually expected that participants affirm the values expressed in the ritualizing, as if the physical activity is secondary to the primary role of personal belief. Many Christian churches hold that for genuine religious participation, individual commitment is required. Therefore, a person born and raised in a Christian environment who does not believe in the central ideas of Christianity is likely to feel that he or she has little reason to continue involvement in its ritual and communal life.

Ritualizing can be a highly effective method of maintaining the traditional values of the dominant culture. However, ritualizing can also alter past values or inculcate alternative beliefs. Bell gives the example of African Americans celebrating Kwanzaa, a ritual that means to counter the dominant Anglo value system and to build communities based on an alternative vision. Yet no observer or even participant can say how much the individuals are internalizing or are ignoring what goes on in a ritual, or what parts of the ritual are the most or least effective. Bell avoids universal judgments, doubts any rational improvement of human community, and stresses local value and individual subjectivity.

Using Bell, one can say that Christian worship constitutes and celebrates the relationships within the church. The worshipers are confirming the power dynamics that the rituals delineate, that is, God's power over the world, the leaders' authority within the community, and the participants' relationships within the group. The more value a Christian ritual has, the more that ritual is seen as established by God or by uncontested Christian authorities. To change worship patterns is to alter power relationships within the Christian community. Bell warns against declaring what a Christian ritual means over time and place, since ritualizing is continually changing and is perpetually understood differently. Bell stresses that some ritualizing is necessary for group cohesion, and thus Christian communities will be expected to dedicate considerable effort into planning and executing their worship.

> Washington and his wife were regular attendants [at Episcopal churches] while residing in Philadelphia. The President was not a communicant, notwithstanding all the pretty stories to the contrary, and after the close of the sermon on sacramental Sundays, had fallen into the habit of retiring from the church while his wife remained and communed.—Rev. E. D. Neill[2]

◇ Answers from the churches

All churches teach that communal worship is not only expected of all the baptized, but is in some way necessary for the full life of a Christian. This chapter will outline the major similarities and some of the differences in what Christians do at worship.

What are some differences in worship styles?

Christian churches teach that people who believe in God, that is, people who at least try to trust in God as the center and meaning of life, will want to worship that God, sing praises to God, and honor God with their time and attention. This is no different from the pattern among friends and lovers, who want to praise and honor one another. Anthropologists describe the worship of many ancient peoples as an attempt to pacify an angry deity, as if sacrifices of dead animals will appease a god or goddess who has been offended by immoral behavior or inadequate ritual. This idea is present in some Christian worship. For these Christians, God is rightfully angry over human sinfulness, and the hour of worship deletes the negatives that have accrued over the last week. In these churches, a necessary part of the service is the **confession of sin**, for facing God always entails acknowledging human failings. Other Christians stress God as perpetually forgiving and Christ as having achieved the only sacrifice that is necessary. These Christians may conduct worship as a wholly pleasant experience. Yet both types of churches encourage believers to worship regularly.

Some Christians answer that the primary event of worship is God making the move to come into the worshiping community, but others stress that the community is going towards God. Some claim that the main purpose of worship is to strengthen one's intimate connection with Jesus, and others teach that the goal of worship is the transformation of society. For some, getting to heaven is the primary goal of believers, while for others, the afterlife is less an issue than is a renewed life while here on earth. Yet both sides of these emphases will likely be at least minimally present in all Christian worship.

Some Christians proudly maintain their centuries-old inherited ritual pattern. Others are adapting inherited worship to include more local or ethnic symbols, while still others are proud of inventing new symbols and rituals with which to worship. Churches advertising **ancient-future worship** combine the archaic with the postmodern. Churches of the same branch or denomination may differ in the details of how they worship, since despite the expectations of church officials, congregations may develop their own ways to use symbols and enact rituals.

Some churches claim that since symbols embody meaning, and since significant symbols pull participants into embracing that meaning, the more symbols in the room and in the

confession of sin: a prayer admitting personal and communal failings and a plea for God's forgiveness

Worship is the weekly opportunity to practice not being God.—Peter W. Marty[3]

Our funky little church is filled with people who are working for peace and freedom, who are out there on the streets and inside praying, and they are home writing letters, and they are at the shelters with giant platters of food. —Anne Lamott[4]

ancient-future worship = a worship style blending historic symbols and rituals with those of contemporary world cultures

ritual, the better off worshipers are. These churches believe that religious rituals carry sacred intent, and so they fill their worship with elaborate personal and communal rituals. Such churches may for example encourage everyone to kneel or to sign their bodies with a cross at various times during the service. The **altar** may resemble an elaborate golden throne, or in most Orthodox churches, be hidden behind an **iconostasis**. The **nave** and **chancel** of their **sanctuary** may be filled with art. Clergy will dress in historic **vestments**, such as **albs** with **chasubles**, or perhaps in traditional festive ethnic garb, and participants wear their Sunday best. Among these churches it would be understood that worshipers will learn the meaning of the symbols and rituals over many years of participation.

Other churches fear that symbols and rituals clutter up time, space, and mind so much that the main point of worship—the connection between God and the community—gets obscured; thus the fewer symbols, the better. Thus at these churches there may be no art on the walls, there will be few ritual movements, the room may resemble a lecture hall, the ministers may wear a **Geneva gown** or may join the community to dress in street clothes. There may be no permanent altar, with a simple dining room table brought in for Sundays with Communion. Many churches are somewhere in the middle of these extremes. It is likely that Christian churches are convinced that their type of worship is best, since for those Christians, that style of symbol and ritual has indeed connected them with God and one another.

Another example of how Christian worship differs has to do with who is authorized to lead worship and what those ordained persons are called. Some churches maintain a hierarchy of clergy, rising up through the ranks of **deacon**, **priest**, **monsignor**, **metropolitan** or bishop, archbishop, **cardinal**, and finally patriarch or pope. It is customary to address these priests as Father. Each rank of clergy will have appropriate roles to play in worship. Some churches have only two levels, ministers and bishops. In yet other churches, all the ordained persons are equal, and may be called minister, **reverend**, **pastor**, **mother**, or **preacher**. For more examples of

altar = the table on which the bread and wine are set for Communion; also, the area in which the piece of furniture is set

iconostasis = a room divider that separates the altar area from the rest of the room on which icons are hung

nave = the area in which the participants stand or sit

chancel = the area that houses the altar, usually in the front of the church

sanctuary = the entire worship space, or the area designated as most sacred

vestment = the ceremonial dress of leaders of worship

alb = a white robe that means to recall baptism

chasuble = a poncho, usually in a specific color for the time of year, worn by presiding clergy

Geneva gown = black academic robe that symbolizes the education of the clergy, first worn by ministers in the churches of Geneva

Titles used in various churches for their authorized leaders: deacon, elder, priest, father, minister, reverend, pastor, preacher, mother, monsignor, metropolitan, bishop, archbishop, patriarch, pope.

ordo = the classic four-part Sunday worship pattern of Gathering, Word, Meal, and Sending

Eucharist = a classic title for the meal of bread and wine, recalling the Greek eucharistia, which means thanksgiving

Divine Liturgy = Orthodox name for Eucharist, stressing the movement from the human toward the divine

diversity, Presbyterians have ordained lay leaders called elders, and some churches use the term "deacon" to designate non-ordained persons who tend to details of the worship and the building.

What usually takes place when Christians gather on Sunday?

Over the millennia, humans have met in community and shared food together, using symbols and rituals that connect them with one another, with their specific and prized historic past, and with the cycles of the cosmos. For about two thousand years, Sunday has been the usual meeting day on which the Christian community meets to achieve these purposes. Because Christians intend to center their lives around God, the connections between the participants are grounded in God's connection with the entire community. Despite a recent cultural move to think of Sunday as the end of a weekend, for Christians Sunday is regarded as the first day of the week, the day to imagine that God began creation, but primarily the day that according to the Gospels, Jesus rose from the dead. It is customary for churches to urge all baptized persons to gather each week to worship God, to celebrate the risen Christ, and to connect with one another. Actual attendance by Christians varies greatly, depending on many social conditions, and statistics about both membership and attendance are unreliable. Some members are referred to as Easter Christians, since they come to worship only on Easter.

All Christian Sunday worship from about the year 100 to 1525 and perhaps half of Christian worship since 1525 follows a four-part **ordo**: Gathering, Word, Meal, and Sending. The community gathers together, reads selections from the Bible and considers their meaning for the assembly, shares a meal of bread and wine, and is sent away to live a renewed life. It is likely that this ordo was developed by combining two first-century patterns: Jewish worshipers meeting on Sabbath, our Saturday, to read from and consider the Torah, and small Christian assemblies gathering in homes on Sunday for a weekly meal. Depending on the denomination, the Sunday

Fig. 6.2. This Roman Catholic Church in New Mexico exemplifies a middle position, with some few significant symbols.

event may be called **Eucharist**, the **Divine Liturgy**, **Mass**, the liturgy, worship, **Holy Communion**, the **Lord's Supper**, service, meeting, or even just plain "church."

The opening ritual of the Gathering often includes music, perhaps congregational singing, that unites the group and focuses attention on the event. In some places, worshipers may move freely to the music. Especially in Africa, there are parishes in which troupes of dancers wearing distinctive dress accompany the music by filling the aisles with their practiced movements.

The Word section usually includes the reading of two or three passages from the Bible, followed by a homily or sermon that expounds on the meaning of those passages for contemporary believers. Some churches use an authorized lectionary, while in other churches the preacher is expected to choose which passages to proclaim and discuss. The preaching may last from five minutes to an hour. The people may receive the message in meditative silence or may join with the preacher by jumping and shouting with ecstatic joy. There

Mass = common Roman Catholic title for Eucharist, from the closing Latin phrase ita, missa est, "go, you are dismissed"

Holy Communion = common Protestant title for Eucharist, stressing the community's unity with Christ and one another

Lord's Supper = common Protestant title for Eucharist, stressing the origin of the meal in Jesus' last supper

may be a short address directed at small children. It is common for the Word part of the service to be most important in Protestant churches, with the **pulpit** a significant piece of furniture and the sermon judged to be what best conveys the mercy of God and inspires the assembly.

In the classic ordo, food is served as part of worship. Originally a full meal, now the food is the bread and wine identified with the story of Jesus' last meal with his disciples before his death. Some churches hold the meal weekly, others daily, and others quarterly or semi-annually, and it is usually the specific historical development of each church that determines how often the meal is served. Some churches use leavened or flat bread, purchased locally or baked by members of the assembly, while others use prepackaged **hosts**. For the wine, some churches offer a common **chalice** for everyone to drink from, others use tiny individual glasses, and in the Orthodox churches, the priest uses a spoon to commune the people. Since Thomas Welch invented the process of making grape juice in 1869, some churches have been offering grape juice as well as, or instead of, wine. Many Roman Catholics continue the practice begun in the late Middle Ages that the laity receives only the bread. In some churches, even toddlers commune, while in other churches members must have completed a course of instruction first. In some churches all visitors are welcome to commune, and in others the table is open only to members.

Depending on the church, Communion can be interpreted in many different ways. It might be described primarily as thanksgiving, as a time to meditate on the sufferings of Christ, as providing mystical union with the Trinity, as a

> pulpit = an elevated podium, usually with a waist-high enclosure, at which the preacher stands

> host/wafer = small round circle of unleavened bread used for communion

> chalice = a goblet used for communion, sometimes elaborately adorned

Fig. 6.3.

continuing sacrifice for sin, as a time for private devotion, as an expression of God's forgiveness, or as a communal bonding experience. It is common for the Meal part of the service to be most important for Orthodox and Roman Catholic churches, focusing on the role of priest to **consecrate** the bread and wine and judging that receiving the sacramental food is what best conveys the mercy of God and inspires the assembly.

to consecrate = to set apart for religious use by prayer; to make holy

The Sending part of the service is short but important, since it includes a blessing on the community to live during the forthcoming week a renewed life, forgiven by God, following the words of Christ, connected with other members, and attending to the needy. The participants have received grace from God, and now they go out to share that peace with the world.

Worship services usually connect the present community with its specific historical past. Thus it happens that a five-hundred-year-old debate about the bread and wine is still apparent throughout the world's churches. Following the pattern of Jews and Christians whenever they eat, early Christians spoke a substantial prayer of thanksgiving to God before they shared the bread and wine of the Sunday meal. This prayer is termed variously the **Great Thanksgiving**, the **Eucharistic prayer**, the **anaphora**, and the **canon** of the Mass. As part of this prayer, the presider repeats the story of Jesus' meal with his disciples before his death, in which, appearing in four variants in the New Testament, Jesus says something like, "Take, eat, this is my body. This is my blood of the covenant." These words of Jesus, or the actions of the Holy Spirit during the prayer, are viewed by most churches as central to Communion, consecrating the ordinary food into the sacramental meal that brings God's blessing into the assembly.

Great Thanksgiving / Eucharistic prayer = prayer praising God for creation and salvation, recalling Jesus' last supper, and invoking the Holy Spirit on the meal and community

anaphora = Orthodox designation for the prayer over the bread and wine

canon of the Mass = Roman Catholic designation for their most traditional Eucharistic prayer

For the first thousand years, preachers and theologians spoke in general terms about the bread and wine as the body and blood of Christ. Orthodox churches maintain the ancient practice by speaking only mystically about the bread and wine as the body and blood of Christ. By the thirteenth century, Western theologians explained the transformation of the food into sacrament by using philosophical categories from Aristotle. In brief: first, everything is made of something, which were called the accidents; and secondly, everything *is* something, which is called its substance. So for example, flour, sugar, shortening, baking powder, frosting,

Fig. 6.4. This church illustrates one common way that communion is served to the congregation.

transubstantiation = the Roman Catholic doctrine that the substance of the Eucharistic elements of bread and wine become the body and blood of Christ

and candles are the accidents; the substance—what it is—is a birthday cake. Medieval Westerners taught that the accidents of bread and wine remain the same, but the substance is transformed by the word of Christ: thus the technical term **transubstantiation**.

In the sixteenth century, Protestant reformers rejected this use of the Aristotelian categories, and third-wave Protestants taught instead that the change from bread and wine to the body and blood of Christ occurs in the heart of the believer. Depending on one's views on this issue, the assembly will deal differently with the role of the presider, the text of the prayer, the rite of communion, and any left-over bread and wine. In especially the sixteenth and seventeenth centuries, both Protestants and Roman Catholics were martyred over which explanation they used. Today some theologians are proposing explanations that accord with contemporary physics and psychology and that begin to heal old divisions.

A second order of worship developed in Protestant churches and accounts for perhaps half of contemporary Sunday worship. This alternative order was a response to several different historical situations. In some places, many worshipers attended worship but did not commune, and some churches then

Over all that we take to eat, we bless the Creator of all things through God's Son Jesus Christ and through the Holy Spirit. And on the day named after the sun, all, whether they live in the city or the countryside, are gathered together in unity. Then the records of the apostles or the writings of the prophets are read for as long as there is time. When the reader has concluded, the presider in a discourse admonishes and invites us into the pattern of these good things. Then we all stand together and offer prayer. When we have concluded the prayer, bread is set out to eat, together with wine and water. The presider likewise offers up prayer and thanksgiving as much as he can, and the people sing out their assent saying the Amen. There is a distribution of the things over which thanks have been said, and each person participates, and these things are sent by the deacons to those who are not present.—Justin, c. 150 CE[5]

eliminated the communion meal. In geographical areas with few or no Christians to assemble for communion, preachers wanted rather to evangelize by preaching. Thus during the nineteenth century there developed in North American revivals a three-part pattern now called the **frontier ordo**: warm-up, message, and conversion. To gather into one group the many people who were not regular members of a single community, the warm-up, sometimes referred to as **Praise and Worship**, featured enthusiastic song, perhaps several hours long.

frontier ordo: the nineteenth-century three-part worship pattern of warm-up, message, and conversion

After the music comes the message, which usually includes a short Bible reading and a lengthy sermon. Often the preacher invites the worshipers to accept Jesus Christ as their Savior. The event concludes with a ritual of conversion, in which people are invited to come forward to dedicate, or rededicate, their life to Christ and to church involvement. The frontier ordo is the one most common in contemporary megachurches, in televised worship, and among those churches that hope to appeal to seekers.

Praise and Worship = lengthy time of opening singing, to ready worshipers to receive the word

Many Christians include as part of Sunday worship the sacrament or ordinance of baptism. As with the sacrament of bread and wine, there is a range of theological opinion about the water of baptism and what the ritual achieves. Some churches consider baptism as necessary for salvation: without being baptized, a person cannot go to heaven. Many Christians teach that baptism is like

Fig. 6.5. The popular hymn "Amazing Grace," written in 1779 by ex-slaver John Newton, speaks poetically about one's conversion.

the Red Sea or the Jordan River, which believers cross over to arrive at the Promised Land, and they describe baptism as washing away one's sins and, like the womb waters that embrace an infant, symbolizing one's new life in Christ.

Since at least the third century, it has been customary to baptize even infants, who also need salvation. However, the third-wave Reformers construed baptism as a sign of individual commitment, and thus some churches baptize only believers who publicly confess their faith. Thus the emphasis may be on the

Fig. 6.6. Some churches maintain the original practice of baptizing in streams or lakes.

action of God or on the choice of the candidate. The ritual of baptism may require any amount of water, from three drops of water on the head to a plunge in a river. Baptism can be administered by any lay Christian in an emergency, for example for a dying newborn, or it can be part of a full congregational festival, at which numbers of people are baptized together.

What about special festivals and observances?

Christian worship also connects worshipers with the cycles of the universe. The most important Sunday of the Christian year is Easter, the foremost celebration of the resurrection of Jesus Christ from the dead. This celebration is scheduled to accord with the cycles of the cosmos, as if the sun, moon, and earth itself are moving in celebration of Christ. Easter's placement in spring-time has a long prehistory. Many ancient peoples in the northern hemisphere observed the spring equinox, which falls near March 21, as a significant celebration, since it marked the outset of spring and suggested a perfect balance in the universe. During the first millennium BCE, Jews fixed Pesach—their celebration of Passover, a historic memory of God's salvation—on the first full moon after the spring equinox. During the 30s CE, it was at the time of Jewish Passover that Jesus was executed. Thus when in the second century Christians

Holy Week liturgies, one after the other, have begun to accumulate in me. Each service of the Triduum strips away a layer of defensive, outer cells. The whole church is organized in a cycle of seasons, liturgies, holy days, and Gospel readings that may be connected to how life unfolds. We need to revisit our experience over and over again; each time, each visit, another layer is peeled away, another piece or aspect is revealed. Our cells carry memories that rise on anniversaries, demand another look. Holy Week is a distillation of this repetition.—Nora Gallagher[6]

decided to mark a specific Sunday as the primary celebration of Christ's resurrection, they chose the first Sunday after the first full moon after the spring equinox, and they called this day the Christian Pascha. Because most Orthodox Christians use an ancient calendar in their calculations, the Eastern and the Western celebrations of Easter are sometimes on different Sundays.

By the third century, the celebration of Christian Pasch was a three-day event. This Triduum began on Thursday evening, with a service recalling Jesus' last meal with his disciples and his washing the disciples' feet. Friday was a service focusing on the positive effects of Jesus' suffering and death. Saturday night was the first great celebration of the Resurrection, which included a fire-and-candle ceremony, many biblical readings, a majority of the year's baptisms, and the first Eucharist of Easter. Although this three-day ritual fell out of use, some churches are now reviving it. Some areas hold rituals throughout Holy Week, beginning with Palm Sunday's palm procession, recalling Jesus' entry into Jerusalem and into the worshiping community now.

Because Easter was the preferred occasion for all baptisms, the forty-day season of Lent developed as a time to prepare the candidates for baptism. In the Middle Ages, when most persons were baptized as three-day-old infants, Lent evolved into a time for all Christians to repent of their sins and prepare to receive Christ at Easter, especially by remembering their baptism. It has become clear to historians that many Christians during these centuries communed only once a year, at Easter. Many churches maintain what are called the disciplines of Lent: fasting, prayer, and giving money and time for the needs of others. Many churches begin Lent with Ash Wednesday, on which worshipers' foreheads are marked with a cross of ashes, to symbolize their sin and mortality, as they await the forgiveness and eternal life of Easter. Many churches think of Easter as lasting fifty days, with Ascension on the fortieth day, and culminating in the festival of Pentecost.

There is no memory of when Jesus was born, and the earliest Christians conducted no observance of his birth. However, when in the fourth century the Roman Empire legalized and then popularized Christianity, Christians decided to keep an annual celebration of Christmas. They chose the winter

---

The liturgical year as commonly practiced in Western churches:

Advent = four Sundays before Christmas

Christmas = December 25, the celebration of Jesus' birth

Epiphany = January 6, the celebration of the visit of the Magi to the infant Jesus

A variable number of Sundays

Ash Wednesday = beginning of Lent, a focus on sin and death

Lent = forty days of preparation for Easter, focusing on amendment of life

Holy Week = the last week of Lent, observing Jesus' last week of life

Palm Sunday = the Sunday in Holy Week, observing Jesus' entry into Jerusalem

Triduum/Three Days = commemoration of the death and resurrection of Christ

Maundy Thursday / Holy Thursday = commemorating Jesus' last supper

Good Friday = commemorating Jesus' death by crucifixion

Easter Vigil = the first celebration of Jesus' resurrection

Easter = the annual celebration of Jesus' resurrection

Ascension = fortieth day of Easter, commemorating Jesus' ascension into heaven

Pentecost = fiftieth day of Easter, celebrating the presence of the Holy Spirit

Remainder of standard Sundays of the year

Fig. 6.7. In many Hispanic cultures, an elaborate passion procession called Semana Santa takes place on the city streets during Holy Week.

solstice as a symbolically important time, since on that day the light of the new year is born, and since the society already celebrated that date with elaborate festivities, especially the pagan celebration of the Unconquered Sun. It came to be that some baptisms were held at the close of the twelve-day Christmas celebration on Epiphany, and so the four weeks of Advent developed as a time to prepare the candidates for baptism.

Although seventeenth-century Puritans—for example, the pilgrims of Massachusetts—forbade the celebration of Christmas as nothing more than excessive partying, most contemporary Christians keep a calendar that revolves around Easter and Christmas, both of which are flanked by seasons before and following. Some churches have developed a far more detailed calendar, with continuous observances that mark either an event in the life of Jesus, the death day of a saint or beloved leader, or a contemporary concern. The Orthodox churches arrange the festivals of Christ in a pattern different from that of

Western churches. Some churches judge that an elaborate liturgical calendar is not spiritually useful, but only obscures the focus on salvation.

What worship goes on throughout the week?

Some Christians worship throughout the week. One pattern is to attend a short daily Mass. Members of vowed religious communities meet daily for prayer services, at least for morning and for evening prayer. The most rigorous monastics assemble seven times daily, even gathering in the middle of the night for communal prayer. This set of services, called the **Divine Office**, imagines each day as a full life, going from day's birth to the death of sleep, illumined by the events in the life of Christ. A central feature of these daily prayers is the praying of the Psalms. Many Christians worship privately throughout the week. Some read from the Bible and pray about its meaning; others use some prayer technique, such as a **rosary**, to assist their devotion. Some Christians prefer the repetition of what is called the Jesus prayer: "Lord Jesus Christ, Son of God, have mercy on me, a sinner." Throughout history, for an intensified experience of worship, Christians have gone on retreats or **pilgrimages** to sites identified with the life of Jesus or the saints. All Christians are taught to say a prayer of thanks before meals. When any such worship is conducted by a lone person, the idea is that millions of other Christians are praying in a similar way at the same time around the world.

Divine Office = a daily pattern of psalms and prayers for communal or personal worship

rosary = a string of beads used in counting prayers

pilgrimage = a religious journey to a sacred site

But like people in all the world's religions, Christians also meet to mark the life stages of their community members. The traditional **rites of passage** occur at birth, puberty, marriage, and death, personal events that are understood as affecting the whole community. Communities need to know who has been born, who is sexually mature, who is authorized to have sex with whom, and who has died. For Christians, these rites of passage, which some churches consider sacraments, observe these situations by tying them to the words of Christ and asking for God's blessings on everyone.

rites of passage = communal observances of an individual's change of status

To celebrate birth, some churches keep a naming ceremony, while others think of infant baptism as the first rite of passage. Some Christians keep a ceremony for young teenagers, to mark their entry into adulthood, such as confirmation or a quinceañera, a party for a sixteen-year-old young woman.

A controversial issue in world Christianity is whether clitoridectomies can be blessed by Christians or must be forbidden as abusive. Most Christians bless weddings with services of prayer. Some churches are now holding worship services to bless the union of same-sex couples, and some churches call this a Christian marriage. However, other churches consider homosexual activity as sinful and so cannot bless it. A communal service at the time of burial is the rite of passage that earliest in Christian history was regularized. The community gathered to bury its dead and to pray God to give to the dead eternal life. Other rites of passage are practiced in some churches. Following the example of the healer Jesus, many Christians conduct rituals of healing. Some churches in Africa regularly conduct **exorcisms** as part of worship. Depending on the church, there may be worship gatherings to pray at the time of adoption, divorce, retirement, and natural or national disaster.

exorcism = a ritual to free a person from the power of evil

What about architecture, art, and music?

For millennia, humans have chosen specific places as sites for their religious gatherings. The term *axis mundi* is applicable when the worship space is seen as the symbolic center of the earth, as if there everything is perfect, since there is where the deities arrive. Some early Christians spoke about Jerusalem as the center of the world, since there Christ was crucified and risen. But beginning in the fourth century, sliver fragments of what was revered as Christ's true cross were sent throughout Christian lands. This practice demonstrates the more usual idea: Christians do not have a single specific *axis mundi*, because wherever a group of Christians gather for worship, there is sacred space. This belief is seen in the word "church," which comes from the Greek *ekklesia* and originally meant an assembly of people, not a building. Christians have used a great variety of buildings for their communal worship. Currently on a Sunday, some are meeting secretly in homes; others gather in their local consecrated building; some are renting a storefront; others have traveled to a renowned church building; some are gathered under a tree in the outdoors.

In many contemporary church buildings the entire history of Christianity is evident. From Judaism came the **ambo,** the reading desk that holds the Bible. From the first century came the table around which the community gathers for bread and wine. In the second century, Christians popularized what we call a book, as being easier to use in worship than a scroll. From the third century came the baptismal font; before that, many baptisms took place in a river

ambo = the lectern from which the Scriptures are read.

or lake. From about the third century came religious art, depictions that Christians borrowed from pagan temples and adapted for Christian use. From about the eighth century came side altars that honored dead saints. From the early Middle Ages came any gold or precious jewels, as wealthy churches copied the opulent adornments of throne rooms. About that time a low railing set off the altar area, keeping the lay people—and wandering animals—away from the holy space. From the thirteenth century came the **Gothic** arch, a technological advance that allowed for high ceilings and many windows. From the later Middle Ages came the elevated pulpit. From the fourteenth century some places installed **pews**: prior to that, worshipers stood around or sat on the floor. In the nineteenth century hymnals, which had been privately owned, came to be provided. Perhaps during the last century items used for worship were donated in memory of deceased members. Those churches that display a national flag are copying European national churches, a practice that became popular in the United States during wartime as a sign of patriotism. When in the twentieth century copy machines became common, worship folders came to be printed out each week. Some churches have recently installed projectors and screens. Finally, the prayers may reflect the morning's news. As many churches can testify, the past lives on into the present.

Gothic = the pointed arch, and the architecture it made possible

pew = a backed bench for seating in church

About art in the church, Christians continue to disagree. The earliest Christians followed the dominant Jewish practice, which followed the commandment never to draw or sculpt the divine (Exod. 20:4). But by the third century, Christians were borrowing images from Greek and Roman art. For example, images of the Greek shepherd god Hermes were used to depict Jesus and images of Jupiter used for God. Orthodox churches developed icons, a unique style of religious painting that is revered as sacramental in its ability to draw the worshiper into the presence of God. Western churches copied secular art, with painting, stained glass, and statues becoming less symbolic and more realistic. By the late sixteenth century, the third wave of Reformers rejected such Renaissance art and returned to the opinion of primitive Christians, judging church art to be idolatrous. Currently, Christians around the world are adorning their churches with art of their culture, with Jesus depicted as ethnically similar to the congregation. Some churches now are projecting religious art that is especially applicable for that Sunday onto walls or screens. Many churches use colors to designate the season of the year, for example white and gold for festivals, red to recall the Holy Spirit, purple for Lent, and green for the standard Sundays of the year.

Since the earliest Christian centuries, theologians have discussed which music to allow in worship: music that was identified with secular theater and dance might detract worshipers. Currently all Christians welcome music into worship, albeit with judgment about which type of music is appropriate. Some churches maintain the ancient Near Eastern style of chant, in which the words that are sung are more important than the musical line. Some churches continue to sing ancient hymns, such as those written by John of Damascus (c. 675–c. 750). Reformation churches popularized congregational hymns that contain the preferred theology and at their best are both inspiring and enjoyable to sing. One beloved style of congregational song is the African American **spiritual**, which arose in the early nineteenth-century American South when the slaves sang words about biblical freedom as they worked in the cotton fields. Global music is now popular in many churches and means to connect each singing congregation with those on the other side of the world. Churches have different practices concerning the use of instruments, some preferring the organ, others employing any and all instruments, and still others rejecting any instruments except the human voice.

> spiritual (n) = an emotional biblical song

> Movements of a musical setting of the Mass:
>
> Kyrie—Lord, have mercy
>
> Gloria—Glory to God in the highest
>
> Credo—I believe in God, the Father almighty
>
> Sanctus—Holy, holy, holy
>
> Agnus Dei—Lamb of God

In summary, in worship Christians praise God, petition for their needs, ritualize their beliefs, strengthen their community, and inspire themselves for service. For some worshipers, but not for all, worship, at least some of the time, achieves these goals. To consider the effectiveness of these rituals in meeting their goals, it may be an interesting experience to visit churches for their Sunday worship. Visitors do well to show respect for the event by dressing as if for an important appointment. In some churches, members will be wearing their "Sunday best" as a sign that they are meeting with God, and attire that is too casual may be offensive. Some churches have greeters at the door who will offer hospitality and assistance. Usually it is acceptable for visitors to stand or sit throughout the ritual in respectful silence. A visitor need not feel obligated to participate in any way. However, in some churches, visitors will be asked to introduce themselves to the entire assembly and may even be invited to commune. Depending on the church, the Sunday service may last anywhere from a clipped forty minutes to a meandering three hours. Attending several worship services is the best way to see what this chapter has been about.

Suggestions

1. Review the chapter's vocabulary: Advent, alb, altar, ambo, anaphora, ancient-future worship, Ascension, Ash Wednesday, canon of the Mass, cardinal, chalice, chancel, chasuble, Christmas, confession of sin, consecrate, deacon, Divine Liturgy, Divine Office, Easter, Easter Vigil, Epiphany, Eucharist, Eucharistic prayer, exorcism, frontier ordo, Geneva gown, Good Friday, Gothic, Great Thanksgiving, Holy Communion, Holy Week, host, iconostasis, Lent, Lord's Supper, Mass, Maundy/Holy Thursday, mother, nave, ordo, Palm Sunday, pastor, Pentecost, pew, pilgrimage, Praise and Worship, preacher, priest, pulpit, reverend, rites of passage, rosary, sanctuary, spirituals, transubstantiation, Triduum/Three Days, vestments, wafer.

2. Apply Catherine Bell's theories to the worship practices of the Church of Jesus with Signs Following, the Appalachian snake-handlers.

3. Present arguments for and against worship services lasting precisely one hour.

4. In a one-year period, Suzanne Strempek Shea attended Sunday worship at fifty different churches. Her book *Sundays in America*[7] records her adventures. Read some or all of her reports. Choose the one about which you have most questions, and discuss.

5. Write a personal essay in which you contrast two Christian worship services that you have attended.

6. In the New Testament, Paul comments on how the Christians in Corinth were worshiping. Read and discuss 1 Cor. 11:2-34.

7. Read and discuss the 1935 short story by William Saroyan titled "Resurrection of a Life." A dying man's recollection of his life and of the slaughter of soldiers in World War I is interspersed with quotations from the hymns he sang in worship.

8. For a major project, read and write a report on Margaret Craven's 1973 novel *I Heard the Owl Call My Name*. In a Kwakiutl village on the west coast of British Columbia, an Anglican priest ministers to a tribe that faithfully participates in Christian worship while also maintaining their traditional rituals.

9. View and discuss the 1989 film *Romero*, the story of the ministry and 1980 assassination of Archbishop Oscar Romero in San Salvador. The film includes clips of Roman Catholic worship. How does worship function in this movie?

For Further Reading

Foley, Edward. *From Age to Age: How Christians Have Celebrated the Eucharist.* Revised and expanded edition. Collegeville, MN: Liturgical Press, 2009.

Spinks, Bryan D. *The Worship Mall: Contemporary Responses to Contemporary Culture.* Harrisburg, PA: Church Publishing, 2011.

White, James F. *Documents of Christian Worship: Descriptive and Interpretive Sources.* Louisville: Westminster/John Knox, 1992.

Zelensky, Elizabeth, and Lela Gilbert. *Windows to Heaven: Introducing Icons to Protestants and Catholics.* Grand Rapids: Brazos, 2005.

How did the church develop? | 7

Fig. 7.1. This crucifix is the earliest extant depiction of Christ on a cross. From about 425, it is the side of a small box carved in ivory.

◇ An answer from a scholar

Clifford Geertz (1926–2006) was a sociologist whose focus on cultural anthropology was important in the twentieth-century study of religion. In his 1973 book *The Interpretation of Cultures*, he defined culture as "an historically transmitted pattern of meanings embodied in symbols, a system of inherited conceptions expressed in symbolic forms by means of which men communicate, perpetuate, and develop their knowledge about and attitudes toward life."[1] Culture is the traditional matrix of the symbols that supports human communities by motivating people for living and by ordering social life. Geertz maintained that little is understood about how these symbol systems can be so determinative of human behavior, and he called on cultural anthropologists to study these symbols and rituals that so shape human life. Geertz wrote that a primary locus for such symbols and rituals is religion.

In his essay "Religion as a Cultural System," Geertz explained that these symbol systems, for example religion, are not invented by each individual, but are passed down and developed through the generations. The symbol system that is religion provides both a model of life, that is, a description of what is, and a model for life, that is, an image of what life ought to be. By highlighting the gap between how things should be and how they actually are, religion transmits through the generations a developing code of ethics. People adhere to religion because an aura of factuality surrounds it. This powerful aura, which is experienced through the community's rituals, receives much of its validity because of its age and its past successes. Thus religion's past and present development prepare the community for its future.

The symbol system of religion produces "powerful, pervasive, and long-lasting moods and motivations"[2] without which the human would be incomplete, unable to function well and fully within the society. Three areas in which

> The degree to which religious systems themselves are developed seems to vary extremely widely, and not merely on a simple evolutionary basis. In one society, the level of elaboration of symbolic formulations of ultimate actuality may reach extraordinary degrees of complexity and systematic articulation; in another, no less developed socially, such formulations may remain primitive in the true sense, hardly more than congeries of fragmental by-beliefs and isolated images, of sacred reflexes and spiritual pictographs.—Clifford Geertz[3]

Fig. 7.2. Catherine Ferguson (1779–1854), born a slave, had her freedom purchased by a friend, and, although illiterate, established the first Sunday School in New York City.

religion offers considerable help for human society are the intellectual, the emotional, and the moral. As people quest for meaning, experience suffering, and analyze evil, their historic religious system gives some answers about the meanings of life; it helps individuals extend their ability to endure; and it deepens and widens their moral insight.

Using Geertz, one can say that Christianity is a complex symbol system that has developed over time. It is taught from one generation to another, and it alters from decade to decade. No adequate understanding of any religion can omit attention to its historical development. Much of the authority that Christianity has over its adherents comes from their belief that the religion has assisted previous generations. Christianity helps believers to conceptualize and understand human life: thus there exists a long and learned tradition of Christian philosophers and theologians. Second, Christianity gives believers a schema for their suffering: thus stories of how and why Christians suffered and the meaning of their suffering are valued. Third, Christianity extends the moral insight of its participants; thus we can expect that over the centuries and in various cultural situations, Christianity presents codes of moral behavior.

Since these systems develop over time, and since Christianity is a world religion in which there are "extraordinary degrees of complexity," studying Christian history is a massive task. Lengthy historical studies present one way to see the complex development of Christianity, in which successive historical periods and multiple world cultures have each played their role.

◈ Answers from the churches

In constructing a history of the church, that is, a chronological account of past events that are known to the compiler, many historians began with data from the biblical book of the Acts of the Apostles. Luke was assumed to be a trustworthy recorder of primitive Christianity, even inspired by God. Yet written perhaps in the late 80s, Acts may be shaped more by Luke's narrative skill than by any prior written accounts or accurate memories, and many biblical scholars now cite the difficulties in reading Acts factually. For example, although Luke narrates an encounter between Ananias and Paul, who had been struck blind (Acts 9:10-19), Paul himself had written thirty years prior (Gal. 1:11-24) that he consulted no one after his meeting the risen Christ, nor does he mention any episode of blindness. Thus historians must judge whose account is more factual, Luke's or Paul's. Ought records of outsiders be trusted? In about 112 CE, a Roman governor named Pliny the Younger warned the Emperor Trajan about the growing movement of Christians, and he defended their executions, since he judged their beliefs to be dangerous superstition. Yet many scholars have valued Pliny's description of the early church and find his benign description of Christians at odds with his defense of the policy of execution.

Some historians judge that what is currently meant by "religion"—a worldview with stories, beliefs, rites, and morals, that extends by volunteer participation not determined by ethnicity or geography—was first seen in Christianity. Christians may want to trace their background to help understand their current situation. Christianity has often shaped the non-Christian world. For example, it was Dennis the Short, a sixth-century monk living in Eastern Europe, who invented the chronological scheme of BC and AD (now BCE and CE), dividing up history Before Christ and *Anno Domini*. Although his

> The Christians were accustomed to meet on a fixed day before dawn and sing responsively a hymn to Christ as to a god, and to bind themselves by oath, not to some crime, but not to commit fraud, theft, or adultery, not falsify their trust.... It was their custom to depart and to assemble again to partake of food—but ordinary and innocent food.—
> Pliny the Younger, 112[4]

calculations were four to six years off, his centering of all human history in the birth of Jesus is used by even non-Christians around the globe. Thus to learn world history, the study of Christian history is essential.

Each chapter of this textbook includes some references to Christian history. This chapter presents (1) seven individuals who most influenced the later church; (2) seven events occurring within Christianity that most determined future development; (3) and seven circumstances from outside the church that greatly altered Christianity. Each is paired with later similar developments. The chapter concludes with examples from the arts and literature that helped to shape Christianity. A linear chronology of Christian history is available in an appendix.

Which individuals had the most influence in shaping Christianity?

Paul, apostle, New Testament author (d. 60s)

Paul, originally a devout Jew who had opposed the emerging Christian movement, had an encounter with the risen Christ that inspired him to become a fervent apostle for the new faith. During the 50s, Paul traveled throughout the areas north and northeast of the Mediterranean Sea preaching the gospel, establishing churches, and writing letters to these churches, teaching theology and giving advice about controversies. Written two to four decades before the Gospels, this correspondence is the earliest Christian writing extant, and Paul's understanding of Christ's death and resurrection remains seminal for Christian consideration. His letters discuss a wide range of topics, from the meaning of Christ's death and resurrection to Christian interpretation of the Hebrew Scriptures, from care for the poor to sexual ethics.

Jesus had conducted his ministry in Aramaic, a language similar to Hebrew. But Paul wrote in Greek, the dominant language of the Roman Empire. Paul's **Hellenizing** of the Jewish Jesus means that from the very beginnings of Christianity, the gospel was articulated in a new language for a different culture. For example, when Paul interprets a Jewish story from Genesis about Abraham and his family, he uses a Hellenistic literary technique, the allegory (Gal. 4:21–5:1). Thus Paul discussed the Jewish tradition using Greek modes of thought and Greek vocabulary.

At least seven books in the Bible are letters of Paul. The New Testament includes six more letters that claim Pauline authorship but may have been

> Hellenism = the continuing effect of the Greek language and culture in the Roman Empire

The undisputed letters of Paul: 1 Thessalonians, 1 and 2 Corinthians, Galatians, Romans, Philippians, and Philemon. Biblical letters either by Paul or by his disciples: Colossians, Ephesians, 2 Thessalonians, Titus, 1 and 2 Timothy.

ascetic = a person practicing extreme self-denial

Fathers of the church = the most influential theologians of the second to sixth centuries, sometimes numbered as twenty, who formulated Christian doctrine

written by his disciples, who would have understood their work as continuing the apostleship of Paul. All thirteen letters are continually studied by theologians, read by individuals, and proclaimed in worship as Scripture, and countless missionaries have continued Paul's ministry of evangelizing the world. Paul's role in the beginnings and continuation of Christianity is so great that some historians view him, rather than Jesus, as the originator of the religion.

Jerome, Bible translator (about 345–420)

Although Jerome was an **ascetic**, a scholar, a priest, a monk, and an assistant to a pope, he was primarily important as a biblical translator. Jerome found errors in the existing Latin translations of the Greek New Testament, and he spent twenty-three years crafting the Vulgate, his own Latin translation of the Hebrew and Greek of the Bible. The Vulgate became the authoritative biblical text in the West for a millennium and remained so for Roman Catholicism until the twentieth century. Thus Jerome had untold influence in Christian thinking. Jerome also wrote extensive commentaries on the meaning of Scripture that were consulted for centuries. Honored as one

Fig. 7.3. Bibles are provided to hotel rooms by the Gideon International Society, which claims to have given away 1.7 billion copies of Scripture since it began in Montana in 1908.

of the **Fathers of the church**, Jerome has been called the Father of Biblical Studies, and illustrations always picture him working on a page of Scripture.

Christianity does not require its adherents to learn an ancient sacred language. Following Jerome, translators have now rendered the Bible into more than 10,000 languages. Many of the world's languages were first reduced to writing by Christian missionaries, who had to invent alphabets in order to accomplish a translation. The translation that has achieved eminence similar to that of Jerome's is the King James Version, an English translation completed in 1611, still used by some churches today, even though its Shakespearean English is difficult for many people to understand.

Augustine of Hippo, bishop and author (354–430)

Born in the North African region of the Roman Empire, Augustine was a teacher of rhetoric, until at age thirty-three, after an arduous intellectual and religious journey, he became a Christian. By 398 he was bishop of Hippo in what is now Algeria. For decades he wrote extensively about the Christian faith, using contemporary philosophical categories as intellectual foundation for doctrine, condemning current heresies, and proposing ethical positions about controversial matters. He dealt with many topics central to Christian thought, and his works are still consulted by theologians today.

The most monumental of Augustine's positions that is accepted as doctrine by most churches is his category "original sin." Because all humans since Adam and Eve are born with sin, everyone needs Christ, and even infants need to be baptized. God's grace heals the human will, so it can then love God and the neighbor. Augustine taught that the sacraments are given their power by God, not by the moral life of the priest, and most churches have adopted this position. That Augustine chose not to marry his common-law wife of eighteen years bolstered the growing Western preference for clerical celibacy, which was finally mandated in the West in 1123. Augustine's teaching that God's intention for sexual intercourse is conception and thus any contraception is sinful remains central to Roman Catholic sexual ethics. Augustine considered that Christians can engage in warfare only if the war is judged to be just, and his just-war theory remains important as churches consider the morality of modern warfare.

There was a pear tree close to our own vineyard, heavily laden with fruit, which was not tempting either for its color or for its flavor. Late one night—having prolonged our games in the streets until then, as our bad habit was—a group of young scoundrels, and I among them, went to shake and rob this tree. We carried off a huge load of pears, not to eat ourselves, but to dump out to the hogs. Doing this pleased us all the more because it was forbidden. I loved my error—not that for which I erred but the error itself.—Augustine, *Confessions*[5]

The *Confessions*, in which Augustine analyzes his intellectual, moral, and theological growth, is usually considered the world's first autobiography. Many Christians copied his pattern, writing spiritual autobiographies or accounts of their conversion and subsequent life as believers. One famous spiritual autobiography is *The Story of the Soul*, by a nineteenth-century French nun, Thérèse of Lisieux (1873–1897). Thérèse's commentary on the "little way" of her short restricted life and her painful dying was an inspiration to many readers who also had lived uneventful lives marked by suffering.

Benedict of Nursia, monk (480–547)

abbot/abbess = the elected superior (i.e., father/mother) of a vowed monastic community

cloister = an enclosure, sometimes a wall, that symbolizes the separation of monastics from the wider society

religious, as a noun = a vowed member of a religious community

habit = the uniform, usually a robe, of a vowed religious

charism = the focus of a religious order's work and spirituality

Especially after Christianity had become an approved, and then a popular, religion in the Roman Empire, monasticism developed from some hermits in the Egyptian desert into large communities of men and of women who sought to live an especially rigorous Christian life. The monk who most influenced the development of Western monasticism was Benedict of Nursia. While the **abbot** of a monastery in Italy, he composed *Rule for Monks*, a set of principles for the management of a community of monks or nuns. With wisdom about human nature and a spirit of moderation, Benedict designed a daily schedule of prayer, study, work, and rest that meant to ensure lives of health, contentment, and productivity.

For fifteen hundred years, monasteries and convents have trained theologians, prepared clergy, hand-copied Bible manuscripts, sewed church vestments, created religious art, trained liturgical choirs, run schools, fed the poor, operated hospitals, maintained orphanages, traveled as missionaries, provided social services, hosted spiritual retreats, and prayed for those who have less time and energy for prayer. Some work inside their **cloister**, and other **religious** work daily in the outside world. These men and women take solemn vows, among which may be poverty (having no or very few personal possessions), chastity (living sexually continent lives), obedience (obeying the community's elected superior), or stability (remaining in one religious community). Some wear historic **habits**, and others do not.

Although social attitudes and secular opportunities have contributed to the decline of Western religious orders, some orders continue the work of their historic **charism**. A monastery with considerable contemporary influence is the Taizé community in France. Begun in 1940 by Roger Schutz, a Protestant minister, this ecumenical community has approximately 100 Protestant and Roman Catholic brothers, and it is visited annually by some 100,000 young people. The unique Taizé music has been exported throughout the world, and many churches sponsor midweek worship that is modeled after that of Taizé, with Latin chants, darkened rooms, dozens of votive candles, Orthodox icons, and meditative silences.

Francis, friend of the poor (1182–1226)

Feudalism, the economic system of medieval Europe, attempted economic stability by keeping the rich rich, and the poor poor. With modern capitalism emerging in Europe, many Christians adopted the pattern of getting richer than their parents. However, a child of a successful merchant in Assisi, Italy, Francis was convinced that Jesus had been poor and that Christ was calling him to live with the poor. He donned a ragged robe of sackcloth, survived by begging, and traveled around preaching in the fields and streets. His parents and many church leaders rejected this embrace of poverty, but he influenced many people towards a life of humility.

His identification with peace comes both from the prayer "Make me an instrument of your peace," and from the story of his visit to the Muslim sultan. Francis is associated with the love of nature, since for Francis "the poor" included the little creatures of earth. By the time of Francis's death, dozens of men had joined his community, and Clare of Assisi, inspired by Francis, had begun a women's community. Francis is famous for the **stigmata** found on his body when he died. It is as if by such close identification with Christ, he came to share Christ's wounds.

stigmata = wounds in the palms, feet, and side, replicating the wounds of Christ on the cross

sister/brother, also friar = possible titles for vowed religious

The spirit of Francis lives on in the Franciscan religious orders of both men and women, and dozens of persons have claimed to have the stigmata. His focus on the poor energizes the work of those theologians who teach that throughout the Scriptures, God is always to be on the side of the poor, and thus to be close to God, a Christian should be close to the poor. One famous **sister**, Mother Teresa of Calcutta (1910–1997), founded a new religious order called the Missionaries of Charity to care for the poor of India. Daily the sisters walk the streets of Calcutta gathering up the dying, to attend to them in death. Under the nuns' care, some lived, and so she established an orphanage. In 1979, she received the Nobel Peace Prize for her work.

Fig. 7.4. Father Peter Damien (1840–1889), the "leper priest," overcame objections from the government and his religious superiors to minister in a leper colony on Molokai, Hawaii. He contracted leprosy and died on the island.

Thomas Aquinas, theologian (1225–1274)

Thomas, from Aquino, Italy, entered the religious order of the Dominicans because he was attracted to its charism of learned study and preaching. Since he believed that all learning pointed to and emanated from God, his goal was to synchronize into one encyclopedic system the Bible, the Fathers of the church, and Aristotle, who in the thirteenth century was considered the greatest Western philosopher. Aquinas is acknowledged as the greatest theologian of the Middle Ages, and the Thomist proposals on some key theological issues became established doctrine in the Western church.

revelation = God's conveying of the truth of salvation

Thomas's combining of Christian **revelation** and human reason is called **scholasticism**, which maintained that religious truth is not irrational. When searching for truth, theologians must use their intellect: since God's unique gift to humans is rationality, rationality could not then lead people away from the Creator. In his *Summa Theologiae*, Aquinas's method demonstrated immense learning and acute reasoning,

scholasticism = a Christian movement from the ninth through the seventeenth centuries that applied Greek philosophy to religious thought and he is famous for proposing rational proofs for the existence of God. Some of his proposals reflect Scripture, for example when arguing against the claim that women were mistakes of nature, for revelation teaches that God does not make mistakes. Other times he leaned toward Greek philosophy, for example when agreeing with Aristotle that men had more rationality than women. Scholasticism was a primary force behind the establishment of Western universities.

Among the later theologians who constructed a single theological system was John Calvin (1509–1564). The primary theologian of the second wave of the Reformation, Calvin worked for years perfecting his tome *The Institutes of the Christian Religion*, which is famous for its thousands of Bible citations and its intellectual precision. Calvin taught that humans are totally depraved: no part of the human being is exempt from sin. Calvin's submission to the sovereignty of almighty God led to his most controversial proposal, that God has predestined some persons to salvation and others to damnation. His desire that the true religion ought to encompass everyone in the community led to his establishment of a Swiss theocracy, which later the Puritan immigration introduced in North America.

Martin Luther, reformer (1483–1546)

Sixteenth-century Europe witnessed growing nationalism, scholarly skepticism, increased literacy, and criticism of some aspects of Roman Catholicism. Into this situation came Martin Luther, a German monk and professor of Scripture, who after years of scrupulous efforts to gain God's good favor, became convinced by his biblical study that because of the death of Christ, God's forgiveness is a free gift. To make this gracious God more available to believers, he translated the Bible into vernacular German. Luther ignored the pope's excommunication of him, asserted that the church hierarchy had often erred, criticized contemporary church practices, wrote voluminously about the Christian life, and urged every believer to read the Bible. Inspired by him, a reformation of the Western church resulted in the rise of Protestantism, as entire geographical areas of Europe designed ways to remain Christian without adherence to the pope in Rome or to an Orthodox patriarch. Luther's 1517 *95 Theses* delineated his objections to the medieval church's approach to purgatory, and the Protestant churches that later evolved rejected the doctrine of purgatory altogether.

Subsequent centuries have seen other reformers. Two hundred years after Luther, Margaret Fell (1614–1702) challenged the authority of male dominance in the churches. One of the founders of the Religious Society of Friends,

Fell is called the Mother of Quakerism. While imprisoned in England in 1666 for her activities, she wrote the essay *Womens Speaking Justified*. Beginning with the first creation story in Genesis, Fell used the Bible to argue that there ought to be equality between women and men in the church. Her work inspired many Christians of later centuries to reform their churches' practices of male dominance and to lobby for women's ordination.

What happened within the church that shaped Christianity in new ways?

Decisions of bishops' councils

During the first three centuries of Christianity, bishops gained increasing authority to interpret the Scriptures, clarify doctrine, condemn heresies, direct the clergy, and model worship. However, bishops disagreed with each other, and beginning in the fourth century, bishops met in councils to debate and then to vote on fundamental aspects of the Christian beliefs. Some councils were marked by fierce quarrels among obstinate theologians, and sometimes the Roman Emperor supported one side of the fight. The first such council was held in 325 at Nicea, in present-day Turkey, after which the Nicene Creed is named. Another important council was held in 451 at Chalcedon, also in present-day Turkey. At the Council of Chalcedon, bishops voted to affirm the two natures of Christ: Christ Jesus was fully divine and fully human, in two distinct but united natures. Most churches continue to affirm the statements of Chalcedon.

Later councils continued to define doctrine and mandate practice. In 1962, the pope convened the world's Roman Catholic bishops for the Second Vatican Council, which made decisions that affected most aspects of Roman Catholicism. Ecumenical conversation with Protestants and Orthodox was encouraged, and non-Christian religions were recognized as conveying some divine truth. The spirituality of the lay life was affirmed. Catholics were urged to read the Bible, and the Latin liturgy was to be translated into the vernacular. However, some Romans Catholics opposed these reforms and in subsequent decades worked to reverse them.

Reports of pilgrims

Probably in 381–384, a woman named Egeria made a pilgrimage from what is now Spain to the Holy Land and to Christian sites in Egypt and Syria. Her journal includes detailed descriptions of the liturgy of the churches in Jerusalem and of the special services held during festivals, especially Holy Week.

By traveling to sacred sites and telling others about her religious experiences, Egeria illustrates a Christian practice that became important in later centuries. By choice or as imposed punishment, Christians walked across continents to pay reverence to the places associated with Jesus or to do penance for their sins near **relics** of the **saints** in **shrines** or churches. Written before 1400, Geoffrey Chaucer's poetic collection of stories *The Canterbury Tales* describes a pilgrimage to the city revered as the site of Thomas Becket's martyrdom in 1170, and Chaucer includes both religiously sincere pilgrims and tourists simply seeking adventure.

Still today, pilgrimages give Christians the opportunity for sustained spiritual reflection. A pilgrimage site revered by especially Roman Catholics is Lourdes, France, where in 1858, a fourteen-year-old girl named Bernadette Soubirous (1844–1879) claimed to have had several visions of the Virgin Mary. A spring at the site became associated with divine healing, and today five million people annually make the pilgrimage to Lourdes, some of whom are hoping for physical or spiritual healing.

Travels of missionaries

From Paul to the present, some Christians have traveled to distant places to preach about Christ in hopes of converting non-Christians to the faith. Missionaries see their commitment as obedience to Jesus' commissioning his disciples to "Go therefore and make disciples of all nations" (Matt. 28:19). One renowned missionary is Patrick (389–461), who evangelized the people of Ireland. Patrick is famous for describing the Trinity as like the shamrock, for composing the hymn called *St. Patrick's Breastplate* that evidences Ireland's past paganism, and, by legend, for expelling all the snakes from Ireland.

The continuing missionary endeavor has carried Christianity throughout the populated world. Not only clergy became missionaries; laypeople who could not receive authorization to preach and teach in their own churches were funded to do so in foreign places. One such lay missionary was the Irish Presbyterian Amy Carmichael (1876–1951), who for over fifty years conducted missionary work in India. Although she

relic = a piece of the body, clothing, or personal possession of a dead eminent Christian

saint = a person revered for extraordinary holiness; here, an eminent dead Christian who inspires devotion and can intercede for the believer before God

shrine = a site revered for its identification with a sacred event or saint

The bishop grips the ends of the sacred wood [of the True Cross] with his hands, while the deacons, who are standing about, keep watch over it. There is a reason why it is guarded in this manner: it is the practice here for all the people to come forth one by one to bow down before the table, kiss the holy wood, and then move on. It is said that someone took a bite and stole a piece of the holy cross. Therefore, it is now guarded by the deacons lest there be anyone who would dare come and do that again.—Egeria, c. 380[6]

Fig. 7.5. Albert Schweitzer (1875–1965) was renowned both for his theological writings, such as *In Quest of the Historical Jesus*, and for his thirty-five years living in the Cameroon as a medical missionary.

dressed in a sari and lived with the people, she was a fierce opponent of the Hindu caste system, especially of the practice of requiring some girls to be temple prostitutes. Carmichael established a school, a hospital, and an orphanage. Her writings, such as her 1903 *Things as They Are*, were filled with photographic illustrations of life in India and convinced many Christians to support her mission work.

Ecstasy of individuals

One way that individuals express their religious devotion is to succumb to ecstatic episodes, which then may greatly affect the onlookers and challenge the more pedestrian church authorities. Beginning in the eleventh century, a number of women had ecstatic experiences that took the form of visions of Christ, Mary, or other saints. Church authorities investigated the validity of these visions, since there is a difference between someone claiming to see Mary and Mary actually appearing to someone. Most visionaries were cloistered in convents, and thus had limited influence during their lifetime. But Catherine (1347–1380), who lived in Siena, Italy, spoke openly about the church controversies of her day, criticizing the pope and inadequate clergy. She was revered in part because of the power of her episodes of ecstasy, through which God was thought to direct her thoughts and behavior.

Far more common than visions is glossolalia. The countless Christians who have the experience of speaking in tongues attest that the episodes give them an abiding sense of the presence of God, and in Pentecostal churches, they are honored by other worshipers for what is seen as divine visitations. Charles Harrison Mason Sr. (1866–1961), the son of freed slaves, was the founder of the African American Pentecostal denomination called the Church of God in Christ, which currently has over six million members. Mason popularized the phrase "Yes, Lord," that worshipers shout out during Pentecostal worship.

Enthusiasm of revivals

Although in European countries with state churches most residents were baptized in infancy and active involvement in church activities was not expected, in the volunteer and competitive market of American Protestantism, ministers wanted to "save souls" and to arouse slackers back to active membership. Beginning in the eighteenth century, enthusiastic Protestant preachers presided over lengthy and often entertaining events, marked by emotional preaching and inspiring music. One of the most famous revival preachers was George Whitefield (1714–1770), a British evangelist who traveled in colonial America. Most clergy barred him from their pulpits, but audiences of thousands gathered outdoors to be swept up by his extremely effective preaching style.

In the twentieth century, the most famous evangelist was Billy Graham (b. 1918), who led what were termed Crusades to arouse enthusiasm for Christian commitment. The prominence he achieved by preaching to great crowds gathered in

I happened to attend one of [Whitefield's] sermons, in the course of which I perceived he intended to finish with a collection, and I silently resolved he should get nothing from me. I had in my pocket a handful of copper money, three or four silver dollars, and five pistols in gold. As he proceeded I began to soften, and concluded to give the coppers. Another stroke of his oratory made me asham'd of that, and determin'd to give the silver; and he finish'd so admirably, that I empty'd my pocket wholly into the collector's dish, gold and all.—Benjamin Franklin's autobiography, 1739[7]

sports stadiums led to his becoming an unofficial chaplain to twelve Presidents of the United States. These emotional revivals, with audiences of thousands and music provided by professional performers, increasingly suggested that Sunday worship replicate these experiences.

Challenges from inculturation

In the sixteenth century, Matteo Ricci (1552–1610), a member of the intellectually rigorous Jesuit order, attempted a new approach to mission work. Moving to China, he perfected his grasp of the language, dressed and lived as did the Chinese, and studied the Chinese classics, with the hope that by thus honoring the Chinese, he could convert them to Christianity. He translated part of the Scriptures into Mandarin Chinese, but when he sought to translate the Latin liturgy into Mandarin, he was refused permission by the Roman Catholic authorities. His innovative techniques towards inculturation did not fit with the more traditional understanding that whatever is alien to Christianity must be discarded and totally replaced by a European understanding of salvation.

By the twentieth century, many Christians moved closer to Ricci, adapting their received tradition so that it could be more readily accepted by others. In so doing, they altered their church's message in small or great ways. One example is the African theologian John S. Mbiti (b. 1931). Mbiti writes that traditional African religions, far from being filled with evil, paved the way for the Christianization of the continent because of many parallels between the two. For example, traditional tribal healers are now a substantial part of the African Christian experience, since their miracle cures are seen as continuing the healing ministry of Jesus Christ.

Proliferation of denominations

The dominant Christian idea for centuries was that there is one church. When in 1054 the Great Schism led to separate churches in East and West, each presented itself as the one true church, and during the Reformation, many Protestants maintained the policy that each geographical area should have only one denomination that was determined by the ruler. However, the third-wave Radical Reformers, under the leadership of Menno Simons (1496–1561), an ex-Catholic priest, refused membership in one of the established churches, met in homes, rejected infant baptism, attempted a countercultural communal life, and practiced pacifism. These Dutch Protestants did not imagine that they would become the sole Christian church in the area, but rather presented their faith as an option available to other Christians, who had to be rebaptized to become members.

Thus geographical areas became home to several competing denominations, and the idea of church option was born. With option comes individual choice. With choice comes comparison and competition. By some counts, there are currently 41,000 different Christian denominations, and many Christians do not object to this proliferation.[9] Some social scientists suggest that the existence of option, whether or not it is a sin against Christian unity, greatly increases church commitment, since believers feel empowered in membership by the fact of their personal choice.

A translation of pictograms of the Lord's Prayer drawn by Franciscan friars for sixteenth-century Nahua Christians in colonial Mexico: Oh, our Father! In heaven, God the Father is found. Noble people worship the Name. . . . The faithful kneel to receive the sacred tortilla, which the Father gives to Christians each day. May the faithful have tortillas on their tables. . . . May the Father defend and protect the fearful and afflicted faithful with the sword and the Cross as they beg Him for protection from the cowardly Evil One who flees. May there be flowers![8]

What happened outside the church that influenced Christianity the most?

The government outlaws Christianity.

By mid-first century, periodically some Christians were imprisoned, tortured, or executed, because the Roman Emperors judged their beliefs to be politically unsettling. Although scholars agree that the vast numbers of martyrs sometime cited are an exaggeration, the fact is that from about 35 to 313, when Emperor Constantine gave official sanction to Christianity, many believers were martyred. But in the words of Tertullian in 197, "The blood of the martyrs is the seed of the church": such martyrdoms tended to inspire believers to more fervent faith. Two martyrs who captured Christian imagination for centuries were the North African women Perpetua (c. 180–203) and her slave Felicity. Perpetua wrote a journal describing her trial and imprisonment, and an onlooker completed the account by chronicling her death in the arena. Perpetua's and Felicity's names are included in the list of saints in the historic Eucharistic prayer of Roman Catholics.

Martyrdoms took place through the centuries and around the world. In 1877 Christianity was successfully introduced to the royal court in Uganda, but a decade later King Mwanga II was incensed by those whose primary allegiance was not to him, but to Christ. He burned to death thirty-two young Christian men, but the persecution led to more numerous Christian believers in Uganda. Currently 85 percent of Ugandans are Christian.

Hilarianus the governor said to me, "Have pity on your father's grey head; have pity on your infant son. Offer the sacrifice for the welfare of the emperors." "I will not," I retorted. "Are you a Christian?" said Hilarianus. And I said, "Yes, I am." Then Hilarianus passed sentence on all of us: we were condemned to the beasts, and we returned to prison in high spirits.— Perpetua, 203[10]

The government imposes Christianity.

However, some monarchs mandated their preferred style of Christianity. The first nation-state that imposed Christianity was Armenia in 315. Later, the Empress Theodora (c. 810–862), while reigning in Constantinople, used her authority to support the use of icons in worship. The continued veneration of icons in Orthodoxy is credited to her, and a procession with icons that she led in 843 is celebrated each year in Orthodox churches on the first Sunday of Lent.

Fig. 7.6. Jacques Callot's 1627 etching of the martyrdom of twenty-three Franciscan monks who were crucified in Japan in 1597

Fig. 7.7. An icon of Vladimir (c. 958–1015), ruler of Kiev. Choosing Orthodox Christianity over Judaism and Islam, he ordered the baptism of all Russians in 988.

Queen Isabella of Castile, in present-day Spain (1451–1504), a devout Roman Catholic, wanted her dominions to be solely Roman Catholic. In 1480 she authorized the interrogation of suspect Christians, to eliminate anything that seemed to the Inquisitors heretical, and in 1492 she ordered the conversion or expulsion of Jews and Muslims from her lands.

Other religions influence Christianity.

Already in the first century, the dominant religion of the Roman Empire influenced early Christianity in several ways. Greco-Roman art depicted the deities as Judaism never did, and within several centuries also Christians were drawing and sculpting Jesus on the model of pagan gods. As Christians encountered the lively practice of religions in which a goddess was dominant, church officials responded by converting the goddess devotion into the increasing veneration of Mary. In 431 at the Council of Ephesus, a city renowned for its worship of the mother goddess Artemis, Mary was affirmed not only as the mother of Jesus, but as Theotokos, the mother of God.

Christians continued to absorb beliefs and practices of what had been the dominant religion. Contemporary Asian Christianity is marked by echoes of Confucianism, especially in its ethics of filial piety and the authority of male elders. Many manifestations of African Christianity incorporate rituals from traditional paganism in which, for example, the community's dead remain powerful forces among the living, both for good and for evil.

Other religions threaten.

Although originally Christianity successfully replaced prior religions, in the second millennium Islam presented itself as an unstoppable religious power. Christians responded to actual threats and imagined fears with violence. The Crusades (1095–1291) were failed military attempts to push back Muslim populations and to wrest the Holy Lands back into Christian hands. No longer could Christianity present itself as a sign of peace, since popes and prominent theologians supported these military Crusades. Two Crusades were especially notorious: in 1204, the Western Christians sacked the Eastern Christian city of Constantinople; and the Children's Crusade of 1212, for which a young boy gathered thousands of children to walk to the Holy Land and convert the Muslims, ended with most of the children starved to death or sold into slavery.

From approximately 1480 to 1750, the Western churches engaged in what is called the **witch**craft craze. Considerable scholarship has attempted to understand the reasons behind the imprisonment, torture, lynching, or legal execution of tens of thousands of persons, mostly women, many of whom were healers or midwives. Authorities believed that persons received power either through channels or illicitly from the devil. Such devil worshipers, called witches, were blamed for causing tragic events, hunted down, and killed. The witchcraft episode in 1692 in Salem, Massachusetts, was exacerbated by the testimony of adolescent girls, whose claims of for example old women as apparitions torturing them at night in their bedrooms were believed by church authorities.

witch = here, a person whose power is assumed to have come from the devil

Plagues kill millions.

Typically, religions suggest reasons why there are disasters and disease, but especially when the Bubonic Plague hit Europe in 1348, the magnitude of the disaster went beyond usual explanations. It is estimated that about 50 percent of the European population died of plague, and this tragedy greatly affected the churches. The ranks of the clergy were depleted, and the survivors became obsessed with death. Since the plague was widely understood as divine punishment, God was viewed as a vindictive judge, and penitential rituals such as **flagellation** and extreme fasting increased. In subsequent decades, some church art included brutal scenes of death and destruction, for example a depiction of Herod's slaughter of the innocent babies (Matt. 2:16-18).

flagellation = punishing oneself with a whip

In the twentieth century, the pandemic of HIV/AIDS coincided with a societal consideration of gay rights, and many Christians mistakenly blamed AIDS on male homosexual behavior. For several decades, some Christians denounced AIDS as divine punishment, although other Christians asserted that, like the Black Plague, AIDS claimed victims of all kinds. In the early twenty-first century, the debate about divine punishment continues among Christians.

The Enlightenment criticizes revelation.

Until the eighteenth century, most theologians believed that God had revealed divine truth through the Scriptures and that God guides the church in its development of doctrine. This trust in revelation was challenged by the Enlightenment, a new intellectual attitude by which scientific examination sought to increase knowledge through the discovery of fact. Many Enlightenment thinkers rejected the Christian faith or reduced it to a rational ethical system, and in reaction some churches rejected scientific methods of discovery. However, Jean Astruc (1684–1766), a renowned physician and author of scientific writings about midwifery and sexually transmitted diseases, was a Roman Catholic who used his scholarly skills to study Genesis. His 1793 book *Conjectures* was the first systematic theory to delineate four sources for the Book of Genesis: this accounted, for example, for stories that appear several times and for textual inconsistencies. Astruc's theory became the basis of what is now called the **documentary hypothesis** of the **Pentateuch**. Although fundamentalist Christians reject his proposals, many Christian churches accept the work of Astruc, who has been called the Father of Biblical Criticism.

Pentateuch = the first five books of the Hebrew Scriptures

documentary hypothesis = a theory delineating the four source documents that were edited and assembled to become the Pentateuch

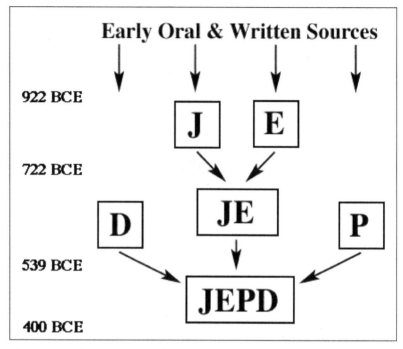

Fig. 7.8. In this diagram of the widely held documentary hypothesis, J, E, P, and D denote four different sources for what became the Pentateuch.

Applying intellectual analysis to things theological has continued. Although since the third century some theologians have wondered how a merciful God could punish anyone eternally, the dominant Christian tradition has maintained that some persons will suffer eternally in hell. However, applying the modern thought championed by the Enlightenment, Rob Bell (b. 1970), a conservative evangelical pastor of a large church, has challenged traditional teachings about everlasting punishment. His slogan "Love Wins" summarizes his understanding of the gospel as God's universal gift to all.

The spirit of the age asserts itself.

The dominant beliefs and practices of a culture influence the faith of some Christians. The modern worldview of the twentieth century spoke optimistically about scientific advancement, rejected archaic myth, and proposed that, with enough education, everyone in the world would agree about some universal truths, such as the value of individual rights. This spirit of modernity inspired Christians in several areas. The ecumenical movement encouraged all denominations to downplay their historic differences and to collaborate in common work and mission to the world. An organization that nurtures ecumenism is the World Council of Churches, established in 1948. Another consequence of modernity was the liturgical movement, in which clergy and scholars of many denominations worked together and learned from each other ways to improve their worship practices.

The contemporary idea called postmodernism has rejected the modernist hope for universals, saying that there is no undergirding truth. All reality is local. There is little reason to be optimistic about human improvement. One example of postmodernism beginning to affect the churches is a diminished interest in world missionary work. A new respect for all world religions and skepticism about Christianity as the only truth translate into less urgency toward the Christianization of all peoples.

Fig. 7.9. The church in Garden Grove, California, called the Crystal Cathedral, was dedicated in 1980 and seats 2700. It is built with 10,000 rectangular panes of glass.

How did the arts and literature contribute to the development of Christianity?

Buildings: Often considered the most magnificent Gothic church in the world, the cathedral of Notre Dame in Chartres, France, was constructed during the twelfth and thirteenth centuries and still today is visited by thousands each year. Such grand edifices with their spectacular interiors were the most impressive buildings most persons could encounter and thus attested to the power of God and the church.

Art: The frescos on the ceiling and walls of the Sistine Chapel in the Vatican in Rome were painted by Michelangelo Buonarroti (1475–1564). Their depiction of the Creation of Adam and the Last Judgment are embedded in the religious imagination of countless Christians.

Literature: The thirteenth-century epic poem called *The Divine Comedy* by Dante Alighieri (1265–1321) became so seminal in the Western Christian

Fig. 7.10. *Family Grace*, a 1938 painting by Norman Rockwell, illustrates Christianity being passed down from the older to the younger generations.

Fig. 7.11. "Blessed Assurance" is one of the 8500 hymns written by the blind American Evangelical believer Fanny Crosby (1820–1915).

imagination that much of what was believed about hell, purgatory, and heaven came not from the Bible or church teaching, but from Dante's imagination.

Spiritual classics: *The Imitation of Christ* by Thomas à Kempis (c. 1380–1471) is a devotional book beloved by centuries of both clergy and laity. Its accessible prose means to inculcate in believers the mind of Christ.

Children's stories: Now being made into popular films, the Narnian chronicles are beloved children's books by the British Anglican C. S. Lewis (1898–1963). The first in the series, *The Lion, the Witch and the Wardrobe*, is an allegory of the Christian doctrine of the atonement.

Fiction: The sixteen novels in the Left Behind series by Tim LaHaye (b. 1926) and Jerry Jenkins (b. 1949) depict one Christian idea about the end times, when all believers in Christ have been drawn in rapture to heaven. What is left is hell-on-earth. Over 60 million copies of the books have been sold.

Music: Composed as a concert oratorio, *The Messiah* by George Frederick Handel (1685–1759) was written in just twenty-four days to words provided by Charles Jennens (1700–1773), a fervent Christian who hoped that the texts he had selected from the King James Version of the Bible and Britain's *Book of Common Prayer* would inspire faith in the hearers.

Song: "Hark! The Herald Angels Sing"—the opening line was originally "Hark, how all the welkin rings"—is perhaps the most well known of the 6000 hymns composed by Charles Wesley (1707–1788) for congregational worship. Because people tend to remember the words to songs they have memorized, it is claimed that to understand someone's piety, listen to the hymns that person sings.

Film: It is too soon to judge whether feature films that portray the life of Jesus or the saints will significantly influence Christian spirituality. Christian leaders and viewers both lauded and condemned the 2005 movie *The Passion of the Christ*, which interleaves Gospels with the visions of Anne Catherine Emmerich (1774–1824) and the Stations of the Cross.

There never was a time when Christianity stood still, without moving somehow forward in time, while simultaneously shifting to the right or to the left. Because of the persons and events that this chapter has highlighted, the religion was not the same as it had been previously, and all had consequences that could not have been anticipated. About each, one can ask: What if this person had not lived? What if this decision went the other way? What if those events had never occurred or had changed the religion in some other way? Some Christians take comfort in their faith that the development of Christianity has been led by God, while other Christians judge that a wrong turn was taken and that the church ought to go back before it can move forward again.

Suggestions

1. Review the chapter's vocabulary: abbot/abbess, ascetic, charism, cloister, documentary hypothesis, Fathers of the church, flagellation, habit, Hellenism, Pentateuch, relic, religious (n.), revelation, saint, scholasticism, shrine, sister/brother, stigmata, witch.
2. Apply the insights of Clifford Geertz to the Protestant denomination called Calvary Chapel.
3. Present arguments for and against the practice of Christian missionaries who evangelize people who are not Christian.
4. Discuss a current Christian news item or controversy, and in your analysis, list everything in this chapter that must be considered as necessary background.
5. Choose an individual highlighted in this chapter, and write a personal essay in which you explain your interest.
6. Read Romans 16, and list everything you learn from Paul's comments about the church in Rome in about 55.
7. Read and discuss Nathaniel Hawthorne's 1836 classic short story "The Minister's Black Veil." In this story, Hawthorne casts his own light on the Puritan ideas of sin and retribution.
8. For a major project, read the allegory that was read by more Christians than any other: John Bunyan's 1678 *The Pilgrim's Progress*. Why for nearly perhaps three centuries would this have been such an influential piece of writing for Christians?
9. The 2001 Polish movie *Quo Vadis Domine?* blends historical data about first-century Christians with the famous legend in which Peter, running away from Rome to escape martyrdom, meets Christ on the road, and then turns back to face his own death. View the film, and separate out history, legend, and the filmmaker's imagination.

For Further Reading

Anderson, William P., ed. *A Journey through Christian Theology, with Texts from the First to the Twenty-first Century*. Illus. Richard L. Diesslin. 2nd ed. Minneapolis: Fortress Press, 2010.

Backhouse, Stephen. *The Compact Guide to Christian History*. London: Lion Hudson, 2011.

Ellingsen, Mark. *Reclaiming Our Roots: An Inclusive Introduction to Church History*. 2 vols. Valley Forge, PA: Trinity Press International, 1999, 2000.

Stark, Rodney. *The Rise of Christianity*. San Francisco: Harper, 1996.

What are saints? | 8

Fig. 8.1. In the San Damiano crucifix that Francis of Assisi saw in 1206, which inspired his life among the poor, Christ is surrounded by the Virgin Mary, John the Evangelist, Mary Magdalene, Mary Clopas, and other unidentifiable saints.

◈ An answer from a scholar

William James (1842–1910) was an eminent multidisciplined scholar who taught at Harvard University for three decades and wrote extensively in the emerging field of psychology. He worked to chronicle and credit individual experience, and having himself suffered various psychological and physical distresses, he sought to identify and analyze those experiences that help to bring about happiness. Philosophically an American pragmatist, he judged that experiences are true if they prove to be useful in producing a happiness that positively affects the self and others. Thus individual experiences should to be analyzed, in hopes of determining their usefulness for themselves and others.

In contrast with many of his scientific colleagues, James judged that a sense of the spiritual was a natural and healthy psychological function. In his famed lectures published in 1902 as *The Varieties of Religious Experience*, he defined religion as the feelings and experiences of individuals in their solitude as they stood in relation to what they considered the divine. Religious feeling, he said, is "an absolute addition to the subject's range of life."[2] Religious institutions and their doctrines, he said, were only the social descendants of what was primary, which is individual experience.

Several of James's lectures dealt with saintliness. Individuals with saintly character, he said, have extraordinary energy and hopefulness. As "great-souled persons," their lives of virtue led them to become "a genuinely creative social force."[3] James outlined four characteristics of a saintly character: (1) a conviction of the existence of an ideal power, which for Christians is God; (2) a sense of friendly continuity between the self and that ideal power, and a willing self-surrender to that power; (3) because of a diminution of focus on the

The more commonplace happinesses which we get are "reliefs," occasioned by our momentary escapes from evils either experienced or threatened. But in its most characteristic embodiments, religious happiness is not mere feeling of escape. It cares no longer to escape. It consents to the evil outwardly as a form of sacrifice—inwardly it knows it to be permanently overcome. There are saints who have literally fed on the negative principle, on humiliation and privation, and the thought of suffering and death,—their souls growing in happiness just in proportion as their outward state grew more intolerable. No other emotion than religious emotion can bring a man to this peculiar pass.—William James[1]

Fig. 8.2. The lower right of this 2011 Hungarian postage stamp honoring Martin of Tours shows him giving half of his cloak to a beggar.

self, immense elation and freedom; and (4) growing loving and harmonious affections. From these flow practical consequences: sacrifice and asceticism, strength of soul, purity and charity. These individuals have replaced a focus on the ego with attention to God and the other. James examined the lives of many saintly persons, among whom were persons named saints in the Roman Catholic Church as well as Christians honored by Protestant churches and secular society, and in his lectures demonstrated the usefulness of such individuals. Thus James could validate the truth of their experiences, even when they engaged in what might be viewed as extreme or eccentric behavior.

Using William James, one can say that central to any world religion are its most saintly individuals, since it is in individual experience that religion arises. These saintly characters, even when their actions appear bizarre or psychologically fanatical, are actually open to the divine in a way that the average person is not. This widening of the self by the divine has accrued untold good for the human community and lays out a path to follow for others in the religious society. It is wholesome, then, for Christian communities to recognize and emulate these saintly individuals, and when studying the Christian religion, it is imperative to pay attention to the saints and to the communal response to them.

◇ Answers from the churches

The word "saint" has multiple meanings. Popularly, the word often functions as a synonym for perfection, with no specific connection to religion, and thus sometimes is used satirically. Christian usage includes a range of meaning, saints being all baptized persons, or those noted for their dedication to Christ, or those extraordinary deceased Christians who are able to effect miracles. This chapter presents an overview of the diversity with which Christians over time and across denominations honor their saintly persons.

What was the earliest Christian understanding of sainthood?

The earliest extant Christian writings are the letters of Paul to various communities of believers, and repeatedly in his letters, Paul refers to everyone in these assemblies as "holy ones" (e.g., Phil. 1:1). By "holy" Paul meant the Hebrew idea of "holiness," being set apart by God for godly living. The Greek for "holy ones," *hagios*, is usually translated in English as "saints." An account of a saint's life is called a hagiography, although that term usually implies that the account is idealized. For Paul, saints are all those who believe in Christ, bear Christ's Spirit, and live the new life inspired by the cross and resurrection. Several times Paul urges his readers to "contribute to the needs of the saints" (e.g., 2 Cor. 9:12), that is, to give money for the care of poor Christians. Thus to be a Christian was to be a saint.

> A saint is a person so grasped by a religious vision that it becomes central to his or her life in a way that radically changes the person and leads others to glimpse the value of that vision.— Lawrence Cunningham[4]

It was not long before Christians narrowed the meaning of the term. A saint was one who was in some way extraordinarily close to Christ, and throughout the history of Christianity one can see how in every time period, churches identified persons in different lifestyles and with various virtues as those living especially close to Christ, who then were held up as models for everyone else. Examining the lives of those whom the churches have honored as saints is a way of studying church history, since the saints functioned as mirrors of each age and spirituality. Once several branches of Christianity developed, it was sometimes even the case that persons might be honored as saints by one set of Christians because they persecuted another set of Christians.

From the earliest church through the peace of Constantine, nearly all the persons honored as saints were martyrs. The first believer to be martyred was Stephen, whose story is told by Luke in the Book of Acts. Stephen was a **deacon**, one of seven men who served with the apostles in the primitive church by helping with the daily distribution of food to the needy. Stephen was later accused of having slandered Moses in his preaching, and Luke wrote that he was tried before the Jewish religious court and stoned to death (Acts 6–7). Luke uses this story as a parallel to the death

deacon = an assistant to the other clergy, especially in the practical matters of church work

Fig. 8.3. Michelangelo's painting of the Crucifixion of St. Peter depicts the second-century memory that when martyred, Peter chose to be crucified upside down, feeling unworthy to die in the same way Jesus did.

of Jesus, since Luke believed that the work of Jesus continued into the life of the church. Many Christians over the ages have kept December 26 as the day to remember Stephen. This scheduling means to say that the joyful birth of Christ, celebrated since the fourth century on December 25, opens to the reality of death, both Christ's and the martyrs'.

Another early famous saint was Lawrence, yet another deacon, serving in the city of Rome. As a deacon, his task was to provide for the poor, a practice of the early church that received considerable notice, especially since caring for the poor was supposed to be an obligation of the emperor. According to the famous story, when in 258 Lawrence was ordered to hand over the church treasury to the civil authorities, he told the soldiers to meet him three days later, at which time he presented them with a group of Christians who were blind, maimed, and poor, as he said: "These are the treasures of the church."

patron saint = a saint specifically designated as protector of a region, occupation, or activity

The authorities were not amused, but executed him by roasting him on a gridiron. The story goes that Lawrence's last words were, "Turn me over, I'm done on that side." The account of this saint, as often happened throughout history, served to encourage and increase Christian practice in third-century Rome, and some churches now call him the **patron saint** of treasurers. A depiction of a man holding what looks like a barbeque grate is an image of Lawrence, revered for his care for the poor, if not also for his sense of humor, perhaps popular because he presented such a macabre image of saintliness.

At certain periods, devotion to a particular saint became so popular and intense that scholars speak of the **cult** of the saint. It was as if these saints connected the living with the dead, and by being so close to God, bridged heaven and earth. People wanted to be near their tomb, visit a shrine or church dedicated to their honor, gaze at their possessions, or touch their bones or relics. Many people in antiquity did not know the date of their birth, and so it was their death day that became the date to celebrate their "birth" into heaven. Patron saints were assigned to regions, occupations, and activities, and religious persons wore amulets that symbolized the protection the saint gave. Since it was believed that the saints were already in the presence of God, the medieval church taught that the saints could intercede to God for human needs. On the model of the monarch's court, it is as if God was too supreme to hear personal prayers, but beloved and still-powerful saints were

I arise today surrounded by cherubim, obedient to angels, protected by archangels. I hope in resurrection, strong in the prayers of the patriarchs, the predictions of prophets, the words of the Twelve, the innocence of virgins, the deeds of righteous men.—St. Patrick's Breastplate[5]

listening, and they would relay the request to the Almighty, or perhaps work a miracle by themselves. It was usual to ask saints to intercede to God for dead relatives and friends who were suffering in purgatory, that they might soon be released from their punishment and welcomed into heaven.

cult = here, an intense popular devotion to an eminent dead Christian

By the late Middle Ages, many believers prayed to saints more than to God. Literate believers read the devotional writings or biographies of the saints. Founders of many religious orders were honored as saints, ensuring a steady stream of veneration by the members of their community. Devotion to saints became big business, as pilgrims by the hundreds traveled to churches that displayed saints' relics, thus making those churches important economic centers. Uneducated people accepted fanciful tales as factual, and some church authorities questioned the value of the resulting religious practices. Even today Roman Catholics debate the value of such rituals as burying a statue of St. Joseph in one's yard to ensure rapid home sales. Theologians urge the faithful to distinguish between magic, that is, miraculous actions effected by a specific ritual for the good of the petitioner, from miracle, which is a sign in this world of the power of the resurrection of Jesus Christ.

Composed in the fifth century, the Apostles' Creed included the Latin phrase *communion sanctorum*, usually translated into English as "the communion of saints," although the words can also mean a sharing in holy things. The Apostles' Creed is accepted by all churches as an ancient statement of essential Christian beliefs, and in many churches the recitation of the creed is part of the rite of baptism. The creedal words "I believe in . . . the communion of saints" is one way that Christians have affirmed the life of the church itself. The phrase has been variously interpreted, usually to mean either that, despite appearances to the contrary, all baptized Christians around the world are united by God into one fellowship, or that all dead Christians are mystically connected with all the living. As with the popular annual Western festival of All Saints Day on November 1, which arose as churches in northern Europe Christianized the pagan appeasement of the dead at early winter (an event called Samhain), the emphasis may be on the local community, the wider church, or all the dead along with the living.

How do the Christian branches differ concerning saints?

Once the persecution of Christians by the Roman Empire ended, people acclaimed as saints were those who had lived in some extraordinary way for the faith. In the Eastern Orthodox churches, there came to be six categories of saints. The Apostles, named in the New Testament, were the first Christians to preach the gospel. The Prophets of the Old Testament had predicted the coming of Christ, and so although they were not baptized Christians, they too were honored as saints. The Martyrs sacrificed their lives in order to confess Jesus as the Son of God. The Fathers of the Church had elucidated the Christian faith for the benefit of all. The Monastics lived apart from society in order to perfect their faith and thus modeled an extraordinary obedience. Finally, the Just are the clergy and laity who become examples of faith in daily life and practice.

Orthodoxy teaches that all Christians are to imitate the holiness of God, and those we revere as saints are models of this imitation of Christ and become more and more like God. Saints can intercede for the faithful before God. Many Orthodox monks and nuns, living independently rather than in regulated communities, lived somewhat outlandish lives as hermits, were sought out as miracle-workers, and were honored as saints. One of the most famous is Simeon Stylites, a fifth-century Syrian monk who served as pastoral counselor and catechist to many, in spite of the fact that for thirty-seven years he lived on a small platform on top of a pillar that was many feet high. Rather than establish an official system that determines who is designated a saint, the Orthodox churches use the term widely, so that Orthodox children might invoke the prayers of, for example, their dead grandmother, since she is being thought of as one of the Just.

One of the most beloved of saints in Orthodoxy is St. Nicholas. A fourth-century bishop of Myra, a city in Asia Minor, Nicholas was famed for his leadership in the church. However, it is in tales involving his care for children that he is best remembered. Three poverty-stricken girls were to be sold into prostitution by their father, but to rescue them from this fate, Nicholas threw into their window three bags of gold: today a signboard displaying three gold balls marks a pawnbroker's shop. Over the centuries and through several languages, St. Nicholas morphed into the secular Santa Claus, but Orthodox families keep the **feast day** of the saint on December 6 with parties and gift-giving. Several Orthodox saints are revered for their role in establishing church art. Most honored is Romanos the Melodist, a sixth-century poet who composed over a thousand hymns called kontakia that are sung weekly in Orthodox worship.

feast day = the date on which to celebrate the life and death of a saint

Since devotion to the saints remained central to the piety of many laypeople, over time the bishops in the Western church worked to bring order to this piety, by designating a procedure by which the hierarchy determined who

Fig. 8.4. In a new Orthodox church in Finland, one of the many icons depicts the revered fifteenth-century iconographer Andrei Rublev, holding his famous icon of the Trinity.

were deserving of the title "saint," and thus whom the entire church could invoke in prayer. The first formal **canonization** of a saint by a pope occurred in 993. The process toward canonization in the Roman Catholic Church has since 1983 included first an exhaustive examination of the dead person's life, writings, virtuous actions, signs of sanctity, and even the corpse, followed by examination of claims that since death, the dead person has been credited with two miracles. Most of the miracles that are considered are inexplicable healings.

The Roman Catholic Church has a current listing of over 10,000 saints. The apostle Peter is honored with the title of the first bishop of Rome. A sampling of saints are: the Church Fathers Ambrose and Augustine; the pope Gregory

canonization = the Roman Catholic process of officially declaring a person to be a saint

A real miracle is something that is difficult to understand and impossible to explain through ordinary means. It is never luck, never a coincidence. It is, as St. Thomas Aquinas says, "beyond the order commonly observed." It is divine and supernatural, gilded by grace and understood only through faith. . . . If we've never experienced a miracle, we believe it through faith. And if we have experienced a miracle, we don't try to explain it. We just accept it.—Justin Catanoso[6]

the Great; the monarchs Queen Helena and King Louis IX of France; the theologians Anselm and Thomas Aquinas; the mystics Catherine of Siena and Teresa of Avila; the educator Jean-Baptiste de la Salle; the missionary Peter Claver; the authors John of the Cross and Thérèse of Lisieux; and the founders of religious orders, among whom are Benedict, Dominic, Francis, Clare, and Ignatius Loyola. Some saints come with gripping biographies, for example Joan of Arc, the French military enthusiast burned as a witch in 143 and canonized in 1920. Many saints were honored for their lives of extreme self-denial, depriving themselves of food, sleep, warm clothing, or sexual relations, which traditionally was interpreted as devotion to Christ. In 2012 the pope canonized a seventeenth-century Algonquin-Mohawk woman Kateri Tekakwitha as a patron saint of Native Americans. The values implied in some canonizations are debated among Roman Catholics, for example, that of twelve-year-old Maria Goretti, who by resisting rape was knifed to death by her attacker.

The historically significant leaders of the church were not necessarily the most popular saints. Sometimes quite minor saints gained fame, for example Blaise, because he was invoked each February at rituals where Roman Catholics had their throats blessed. It was sometimes the case that the less that was known about a dead saint, the more likely that an elaborate devotional legend could develop, since there were few facts to contradict the story. An example is the popular cult of St. Christopher, whose statue in the twentieth century was affixed to many automobile dashboards as a prayer for safety. The legend told of a man named Christopher who carried an increasingly heavy child across a river, only to discover on the other side that the child was Christ, who himself was shouldering the whole world. The saint symbolized a life in which bearing someone's burdens was actually service to Christ. However, there appears never to have been such a man: the name Christopher means "Christ-bearer," and thus the legend is merely an elaboration on the name. Yet many people accepted the tale and believed that God protected them through the invocation of St. Christopher. A similar situation involves St. Veronica, said to be the woman who wiped the brow of Christ as he carried his cross and was rewarded by his true image on her veil. Despite the role this woman plays in the popular Lenten devotion of the Stations of the Cross, the story is not told in the Bible, but rather illustrates the name: Veronica means True-Image.

At the time of the Reformation, Protestant theologians strongly opposed the centrality in European piety of the cults of the saints. Protestant clergy taught that believers needed no intermediaries when they approached God, and likening the medieval practice to a kind of polytheism, said that only God should to be addressed in prayer. Many laypeople, in their rejection of the authorities in Rome, responded positively to this new worldview, and during some sixteenth-century riots mobs of laypeople trashed local churches, smashing the statues of the saints.

Most Protestant churches continue to speak against the veneration of a special group of saints. However, some Protestant churches now publish a list of the faithful departed, who are to be commemorated as models of faith and who illustrate God's continual shaping of the church. Some Protestants keep death days in remembrance, and some local churches are named after especially biblical saints. Some Protestant church buildings display images of the most significant Reformers, such as Martin Luther. Many Protestants have revived the New Testament meaning of "saint," calling all baptized persons, or all dead baptized persons, saints. The Separatists of England who immigrated to North America as the Pilgrims referred to their small branch of Christians as "the saints." In the African independent churches and in some African American churches in the United States, the founder of the community is granted immense reverence, functioning as a kind of saint. Yet even with this looser use of the term "saint," questions arise—for example, whether Martin Luther King Jr. is to be honored as a martyr and a saint, or only considered a murdered Christian.

A saint who is growing in acclaim across denominations and among persons who are not Christian is Francis. Much of Francis's current fame arose from within the ecological movement. Francis's sense of himself as one of the poor of God's creation opened him to love of nature and communion with animals, which he referred to as his brothers and sisters. This spirituality was uncharacteristic of his time period, in which an increasingly urban society hoped to conquer nature and to utilize animals for economic good. Currently many Christian assemblies sponsor an event near his death day, October 4, at which parishioners bring pet animals to church for a blessing. Whether Francis himself, who advocated extreme poverty, would have approved of spending large sums of money on pets is an example of the countless questions posed to contemporary believers by the intriguing biographies of the saints.

The first stanza of a Protestant children's song:

I sing a song of the saints of God, patient and brave and true,

Who toiled and fought and lived and died for the Lord they loved and knew.

And one was a doctor, and one was queen, and one was shepherdess on the green:

They are all of them saints of our God, and I mean, God helping, to be one too.

—Lesbia Scott, 1929[7]

Fig. 8.5. At St. Gregory of Nyssa Episcopal church in San Francisco, iconographer Mark Dukes painted a 2,300-square-foot mural of eighty-eight dancing saints, including both Christian saints and "friends of God," such as Gandhi.

What about the two Mary's?

The saint who has received the most widespread veneration is Mary, Jesus' mother. Mary is the Greek spelling of the Aramaic name Maryam, perhaps a common name in honor of Moses' sister (Exod. 15:20). Often called the Virgin Mary, because two of the Gospels, Matthew and Luke, tell stories of Jesus' miraculous birth from a virgin woman, Mary's rise over the centuries from a young woman living in Nazareth to Queen of heaven exemplifies the way in which saints mirror their age, and her place in theology illustrates the development of doctrine.

The Orthodox churches laud Mary as Theotokos, Mother of God, a title that expresses the theological belief that Jesus was God: thus Mary, as mother of Jesus, was mother of God. Icons depicting the Theotokos are in all Orthodox churches, and Orthodox Christians revere her role as intercessor for believers.

It was especially in the Western church that Mary became honored not only as the mother of Jesus, but in her own right as the primary believer. By the second century, apocryphal stories that elaborated on the few biblical references to Mary and Jesus' birth became popular. One noncanonical

Fig. 8.6. This sculpture by Elizabeth Frink depicts the Virgin Mary, not as a young virgin or mother, but as an old woman.

gospel included a story about the midwife at the stable. Centuries of Christian theology accepted the prescientific idea that the female was merely a passive recipient of male sperm, and theologians speculated about the details of Jesus' conception and birth. For example, Mary was so exceptional that she did not suffer labor pains. Celibates stressed that she lived and died a perpetual virgin. Preachers contrasted Eve, who had brought sin into the world, with Mary, who brought forth the salvation of the world. In the fifth century, churches honoring Mary were built on sites that had housed temples to the pagan mother goddess. Although Francis of Assisi maintained that Mary was a humble peasant, most of the hierarchy during the Middle Ages described Mary as a queen, and this at a time when several European realms had powerful queens. Many churches and cathedrals were dedicated to Notre Dame, "our lady," a complement to Christ, "our lord." Medieval celibate males wrote of Mary as their bride. During the Black Plague, Mary became the Mother of Sorrows. Yet throughout, Christian women were counseled to be like Mary, that is, obedient mothers of children who were sent by God.

Over the centuries in the Orthodox churches, icons of Mary retained their classical design, in which the altered human form means to draw the worshiper to the God beyond the icon. However, Western church art used realism, and the changing depictions of Mary greatly influenced how the faithful reflected about Mary. The rosary, in which the believer asks for Mary's intercession, became an increasingly popular form of prayer, and statues of Mary showed her with rosary beads attached to her belt. When in the fourteenth century it became popular for women of means to hire a nursemaid, rather than to nurse their own infants, church officials commissioned art for the churches in which Mary was shown nursing the baby Jesus. At the rise of the bourgeois family, church art depicted Mary, Joseph, and the child Jesus together. When in the eighteenth century Mary's role as submissive mother was emphasized, perhaps in reaction to the increasing women's movement, church artists no longer clothed her in regal red, but rather in pastel blue.

The primary prayer of the rosary, repeated fifty-three times: Hail, Mary, full of grace. The Lord is with thee. Blessed are thou among women, and blessed is the fruit of thy womb, Jesus. Holy Mary, Mother of God, pray for us sinners, now and at the hour of our death. Amen.

In the last few centuries, the Roman Catholic Church has validated several apparitions, in which persons of no status describe visions of the Virgin Mary. The vision of Mary with most consequence has been the story of her appearing in 1531 to the native peasant Juan Diego in Guadalupe, Mexico, and the resulting depictions of Jesus' mother as Our Lady of Guadalupe, in which Mary is shown as a cosmic goddess, rival the crucifix as dominant Christian images in Mexican Christianity.

Lourdes, France is renowned for an apparition of Mary to a young girl named Bernadette Soubirous in 1858; Fatima, Portugal for a 1917 apparition to three children; and Medjugorje, in Bosnia-Herzegovina, where six children received apparitions of the Virgin Mary in 1981. These sites are visited annually by thousands of pilgrims, many of whom are seeking healing, thanks to the intercession of the Virgin.

Theologically the Roman Catholic Church has promulgated several Marian doctrines, which only Catholics espouse: in 1854 the doctrine of Mary's **Immaculate Conception**, which is often confused with the virginal conception of Jesus, and in 1950 the doctrine of the **Assumption** of Mary into heaven, which means that she is already experiencing the life of the resurrection. Most Roman Catholics accept Mary's role in salvation as truth revealed over the centuries, and they see the historical development as a sign that God's mercy can take new forms appropriate to each culture.

Immaculate Conception = the Roman Catholic doctrine that Mary, when conceived in her mother Anne's womb, was kept from the stain of original sin, so that she lived a sinless life

For Protestants, Mary became the exemplar of the faithful Christian, for with no merit of her own, she received grace from God, and, a sinner like everyone else, she accepted in faith the word of God. Martin Luther held the Virgin Mary in high regard as the woman who believed what the angel said to her and was willing to bear shame for Christ, but he ridiculed Marian items in the relic trade, such as vials of her breast milk. Most Protestants reject the elevation of Mary that began in the second century, especially teachings about Mary's sin-

Assumption = the raising of Mary's body into heaven already at her death

lessness and her role as intercessor, as well as practices of Marian devotion. Some contemporary Christians give the biblical stories of a virgin birth little religious value, judging them to be late first-century adaptations of the commonplace Greco-Roman myths of the virgin births of deities. On the other

Around eleven the apparition came, and everything became absolutely still. Near us, I could hear the visionaries praying in Croatian. I sensed that Mary was praying with them. . . . Each of us was savoring the tiny miracle we had just experienced. We had actually been there for an apparition— and the Mother of God had blessed us. The signs and wonders were indeed the goal of many. They didn't seem to realize the real phenomenon was the miraculous change in those who came here and those who lived here.—Wayne Weible, on his pilgrimage to Medjugorje[8]

hand, fundamentalist Protestants list the belief in the virgin birth as one of the essential Christian truths necessary for salvation.

The other Mary who has continually captivated Christian imagination is Mary of Magdala, a town next to the Sea of Galilee. That she is named for herself, rather than by a husband or son, suggests that she was single. The New Testament says of her only that Jesus cured her of seven devils (Luke 8:2) and that she was present at the tomb on Easter Day (e.g., Mark 16:1). Early preachers called her the Apostle to the Apostles because, according to the Gospel of John (20:18), she ran from the tomb to announce to the disciples, who were in hiding, that Christ was risen.

Already in the second century, noncanonical gospels elaborated on her story, describing her close association with Jesus and lauding her as a rival with Peter for church authority. In about 600 Pope Gregory, to simplify the teaching of the Bible, combined several scriptural stories about women and taught that Mary Magdalene had been the adulterous woman whom Jesus forgave (John 8:1-11). Because of this conflation of New Testament stories, artistic depictions of Mary Magdalene usually include a small jar of ointment, to connect her with the repentant woman who poured precious oils on Jesus' feet (Luke 7:36-38). Since Augustine had used the sin of sexual lust as his primary example of human sin, Gregory was then able to contrast the holy and sacred Virgin Mary with the prostitute Mary Magdalene. The practice of depicting the two Mary's at the cross was set in Western church art, the noble Virgin Mary veiled and her body swathed in fabric, and the voluptuous Magdalene with long disheveled hair wearing an off-shoulder dress. By the thirteenth century, a detailed legend of her adventures was popular, and the clergy of Vézelay, France claimed to have her relics, to which pilgrims thronged.

Continuing the pattern that each age describes the saints according to the current worldview, contemporary Christian writers have appropriated Mary Magdalene for several new purposes. Some Christians find that debunking the portrayal of her as a prostitute is a way to challenge the church's habit of demeaning women. Reviving her title as Apostle to the Apostles, women striving for equality in the church describe her independence from males and her role as a preacher of the resurrection. To fit with contemporary media that celebrate explicit sexuality, fiction and film exploit the noncanonical description of her as Jesus' lover or wife.

Saint as martyr, theologian, cloistered virgin, visionary, evangelist, social activist, miracle-worker, or extraordinary inspiration: what binds this motley group together is the willingness to live in countercultural ways. The saints' fervent belief in Christ led them to espouse and enact values other than those

Fig. 8.7. This medieval depiction of Mary Magdalene is based on the resurrection account in John 20:11-18.

of the majority culture, and one cannot tell the story of either the Christian religion, or indeed world history, without attending to these saintly persons and to their achievements.

Suggestions

1. Review the chapter's vocabulary: Assumption, canonization, cult, deacon, feast day, Immaculate Conception, patron saint.
2. Contrast William James's theory about the social benefits of selflessness with the contemporary idea that productive persons must attend first to the self.
3. Present arguments for and against the religious value of reverencing as a saint someone who never actually lived.
4. Investigate the life of one of the ascetic women, such as Marie of Oignies (1177–1213), Beatrice of Nazareth (1200–1268), Margaret of Cortona

(1247–1297), Angela of Foligno (1248–1309), or Catherine of Siena (1347–1380), whose extreme fasting would in our day be called anorexia nervosa.

5. Write a personal essay in which you describe a person whose extraordinary faith and behavior has inspired you.

6. Using a concordance, locate and read the passages about saints that are in the Book of Revelation. What did the author of Revelation, a visionary at the beginning of the second century who was facing persecutions, mean by "saint"?

7. Read and discuss the 1991 short story "Little Miracles, Kept Promises" by Sandra Cisneros,[9] which records the many notes invoking the saints that are posted at a Marian shrine. A retablo is a small wooden plaque depicting a saint.

8. For a major project, read and write a report on the 2011 *The Maid* by Kimberly Cutter,[10] a novel based on the life of Joan of Arc (1412–1431). Cutter presents Jehanne d'Arc as an extraordinary young woman who both celebrates and doubts God's choice of her as the Maid of Lorraine, the savior of France.

9. View and discuss the 1996 film *Entertaining Angels*, which tells the story of Dorothy Day (1897–1980), Roman Catholic journalist and activist for the poor. Decide whether you would call her a saint. Of the many films that focus on saints, several are relatively historically accurate and worth seeing: *A Man for All Seasons*, about Thomas More (1478–1535); *Becket*, about Thomas Becket (1118–1170); *Molokai*, about Father Peter Damien, the "leper priest" (1840–1889); *Thérèse*, about Thérèse of Lisieux (1873–1897); *Tsar*, about Metropolitan Philip II of Moscow (1507–1569).

For Further Reading

The Book of Saints: A Day-by-Day Illustrated Encyclopedia. New York: Metro Books, 2011.

Cunningham, Lawrence S. *A Brief History of Saints.* Malden, MA: Blackwell, 2004.

Haskins, Susan. *Mary Magdalen: Myth and Metaphor.* Old Saybrook, CT: Konecky & Konecky, 1993.

Warner, Marina. *Alone of All Her Sex: The Myth and the Cult of the Virgin Mary.* New York: Vintage, 1976.

Woodward, Kenneth L. *Making Saints: How the Catholic Church Determines Who Becomes a Saint, Who Doesn't, and Why.* New York: Simon & Schuster, 1990.

What do Christians say about their relationship to the state?

Fig. 9.1. Haitian artist Jacqes Chery designed the Misereor Hunger Cloth to accompany the Lenten lectionary readings. Surrounding the tree-of-life crucifix are images of both political oppression and religious hope.

◇ An answer from a scholar

The German professor Max Weber (1864–1920), one of the founders of the field of sociology, spent much of his career in independent scholarship. At a time when many social theorists were either dismissing or condemning the role of religion in society, Weber used his encyclopedic knowledge to argue a far more nuanced position. In analyzing the complexities of social behavior, he claimed that a combination of many ideologies forms, maintains, and furthers society. The differing values of these ideologies interact in a complex way, and through the meshing of these diverse values, the people shape the society—however, a society that has already shaped the people.

Weber wrote that religion is one such factor that in both past and present can be a powerful force in shaping social behavior. Religious attitudes sometimes are granted high value in society, and especially when the religious leaders are seen as acting on God's behalf, religion can provide a reversal of values that creates the will and the conditions for proposed change. Weber's most famous example was from sixteenth-century European Protestantism, particularly in its Calvinist form. Calvinism taught its adherents that their religious faith called them to be active, and also financially successful, members of the society, since through this activity they would demonstrate their salvation within the wider world. Although medieval Christianity had taught that avarice was a deadly sin, the new religious ideas in Calvinism were a primary factor in the acceptance of an ethical capitalism. Protestants rejected monasticism and its escape from the world, believing instead that they were to use their religious vision to improve society. Weber presented many other examples of religion sponsoring social change; thus to understand the state, one must study the religions practiced within it.

routinization = the ordering of individual charism into a sustainable institution

Weber discussed the religious figures of magician, priest, and prophet. He described the prophet Jesus as having had extraordinary charismatic authority, and Jesus' religious view was later **routinized** into the Christian religion. The prophet and later the religious institution preach ethics and hope to shape society to adopt these values. The symbols utilized by religious communities have far-reaching power to effect change. Christians, shaped by their time and place, strive to inculcate the political situation with the values of Jesus, albeit that the charismatic prophet and the religious establishment may be in tension with one another as to the practicality of any specific goal.

Using Weber, one can say that the religion Christianity sees itself as having institutionalized the extraordinary values of the charismatic prophet Jesus, and the religion hopes to direct its own energies to further his values. Because of this, some Christians will actively engage in the political process, and Christians, as citizens of a nation, will function in the wider society guided by their religious worldview. Christian symbols and rituals can be examined for their role in forming, conserving, or altering the society. However, Weber stresses that society has already influenced these Christians, and thus they will have sometimes substantial differences in how they see society, what in the society needs addressing, and how best to institute Jesus' values. The many societies populated by Christians differ, and so Christians will differ, as they work to shape society according to their religious view.

◈ Answers from the churches

There is no simple answer to the question, "What do Christians say about their relationship to the **state**." History includes Christians who advocated isolation from the secular world, those who suffered from persecution by the state, those who actively engaged in social reform, and those who forced all citizens to adopt their own brand of Christianity. In analyzing this complex situation, two twentieth-century theologians who happened to be brothers proposed ways to think about humans in relation to their culture, and their work provides a helpful background to the chapter's many "answers from the inside."

One brother was the historical theologian H. Richard Niebuhr, a professor of Christian ethics at Yale University and an ordained minister in what is now the United Church of Christ. Niebuhr stressed the absolute sovereignty of God and the demands God lays on humans in a world in which situations are always in flux. In his most famous work, *Christ and Culture* (1951), Niebuhr outlined five different Christian attitudes that have been significant over the ages. (1) For some believers, Christ is against culture. Contemporary society and government are the enemy, and the church arises to embody a wholly new type of society. (2) Medieval Christians may have accepted a Christ of culture. Their society and its state established a Christianity that purported to be faithful to the gospel, and so for them Christ functioned within culture. (3) For some Christians, Christ is above culture, calling individual humans to

Every permanent political association had a special god who guaranteed the success of the political action of the group. In principle this god accepted offerings and prayers only from the members of his group, or at least he was expected to act in this fashion. The stranger was thus not only a political, but also a religious alien. In general, political and military conquest also entailed the victory of the stronger god over the weaker god of the vanquished group.
—Max Weber[1]

the state = sovereign political authority; the government

their communion with God. For these believers, the soul is the more central to ethics than the state. (4) For thinkers who accept historical complexity, Christ and culture are in perpetual paradox. Faith and unbelief run side-by-side and interweave in complicated ways. (5) A fifth grouping are those believers who affirm Christ as transforming culture. Christians are to bring God's renewal into the present situation. For H. Richard Niebuhr, much of culture is embodied in the state, and history demonstrates that because of these varied attitudes, Christians have disagreed about how their faith is to function within the state.

The other brother was Reinhold Niebuhr, a professor of practical theology at Union Theological Seminary in New York City and an ordained minister in what is now the United Church of Christ. Starting out his career as a liberal theologian, he grew increasingly convinced that the classic Christian doctrine of original sin told the sad truth about the absolute pervasiveness of sin, and thus any liberal hope for an improved state was a fantasy. In his most famous book, *Moral Man and Immoral Society* (1932), he argued that although humans have a natural impulse to help others, the more pervasive human impulse is the individual will to live, and this selfishly turns into a will to have power over others. Although the state presents itself as working for the common good, the state actually intensifies this will to have power over others and grabs to itself everything that it can. Yet people blindly accept the authority of the state, pretending that the state will function morally, since the realism of the pervasiveness of sin is unpleasant to face. As a Christian theologian, Reinhold Niebuhr urged believers to become politically active, attempting to improve the moral situation of their state. Yet they must always remain skeptical about both their own motives and the state's claims, since sin has distorted it all.

> God, give us grace to accept with serenity the things that cannot be changed, courage to change the things which should changed, and the wisdom to distinguish the one from the other.—the Serenity Prayer, composed by Reinhold Niebuhr[2]

Accompanied by these two brothers, one who outlined the quite different ways that Christians have understood their relationship to culture, and the other who stressed that all these ways are fraught with selfishness, this chapter addresses some of the issues most closely connected with politics and the churches' existence within the state.

What are various Christian postures in relation to the state?

A contemporary understanding of "the state" is only about five hundred years old. Through much of Christian history, theologians accepted the reality of their political situation as if it was their only available world, and most Christians had little or no power to affect its policies. Thus "how to deal with the state" was only another way to say "how to live." Until the revolutions of the modern world, acceptance of the **divine right of kings** guaranteed a relatively passive relationship to the state. Yet the historical record presents examples of at least five different Christian postures in relation to the authority of the government.

divine right of kings = the political theory that God establishes the monarch as the earthly representative of divine authority and power

In some situations, believers have chosen to disobey their government in public witness to their faith. The biblical citation "we must obey God rather than any human authority" (Acts 5:28) has bolstered those Christians who understood disobedience to immoral law as faithfulness to God and who thus undertook civil disobedience. After July 4, 1776, the Anglicans of Philadelphia no longer prayed for the King of England in their Sunday intercessions, crossing out in red ink the petitions for the King and Parliament as printed in their authorized liturgy. Many Anglican congregations went through some years of distress, because although their clergy had vowed submission to the British crown, their more radical parishioners rejected any deference to their governmental homeland. When in 1933 the Nazi regime in Germany altered national policies so as to make the Protestant Church an arm of the anti-Semitic government, about one-sixth of the Protestant pastors refused to grant the state the ultimate authority the law demanded, and instead they established the Confessing Church. Hundreds of these clergy were arrested, and some were executed as a result of their resistance.

An alternate posture that some Christians have advocated is withdrawal from the state. The logic here is that many political leaders are power-hungry and self-serving and that political situations will inevitably demand immoral behavior of their participants. These believers argue that Jesus did not urge political involvement. Rather, the religious goal is inner peace with Christ and heaven after death, not an impossible dream about a moral society. To avoid participation in the evils of the state, a Christian is better off being somehow isolated from political realities.

An example of withdrawal has been the cloistered life in contemplative monasteries and convents. In some of the strict communities, vowed persons never left the monastery for any reason whatsoever, and until the twentieth century they may have heard no news about the outside world. They focused on a life of prayer, not activity in an evil nation. A different example of withdrawal from the state is the contemporary Amish communities. The Old Order Amish do not vote in national elections, do not assert their rights in

Fig. 9.2. These cloistered nuns pray for the government, but live isolated from it.

local governance, and reside in whichever country grants them good farmland and societal isolation.

Another Christian posture is to witness to the faith from within the state. These Christians view themselves as leaven in the dough, breathing the Spirit of God into politics to improve its morals. This attitude was expressed already by Augustine at the time of the decline of the Roman Empire. Augustine wrote about humans as struggling within two cities, the human city guided by selfish love and what he termed "the city of God," characterized by selfless love. Augustine was realistic about perennial human sinfulness, and so he urged Christians to become witnesses to God's way within a world that would never embody God's way. For example, Augustine viewed brothels as a necessary evil. Christians would not frequent them, and clergy would preach against them, but the cities of the world needed to maintain them to preserve social order.

The idea that Christians witness to their faith from within the state has been the dominant practice in the United States. The founding fathers, some of whom were practicing Christians, were inspired by the Enlightenment ideal of the primacy of the individual. Although according to the Bill of Rights the government can make no laws that suggest an **established** religion, the writings of the intellectuals in the early republic affirmed that when individuals voted for their governmental representatives, they would make their moral preferences known.

an established religion = a religion with state sanction and financial support

Perhaps this hope was at first a naïve idea that Christians would agree with one another on social issues. By the time of Abraham Lincoln and his Second Inaugural Address, Americans knew that Northerners and Southerners "both read the same Bible and pray to the same God, and each invokes His aid against the other."[3] Some of the many Christians who witnessed to their values were the Methodist women picketing at taverns in Ohio as a way to protest the uncontrolled alcoholism of prairie life. Most mainstream Protestant churches currently adopt this posture, urging their members to participate fully in a government that nonetheless cannot be expected to embody fully the will of God. Some American churches speak of the vote as a particularly Christian aspect of government, since it provides believers with a method of witnessing to the state.

A fourth avenue is partnership with the state. According to this way of thinking, Christians should stand hand-in-hand with the state whenever possible. The state will never be fully acceptable to Christians, but Christians do the best they can, trying to garner civic power to assist Christian life and mission. In a democracy, they utilize legislation to promote Christian ethics. The state may view this cooperation as beneficial to everyone, since religion has sometimes been viewed as a stabilizing force in the society.

One early historical example of this cooperation was when the Roman Emperor Constantine, because he saw it politically advantageous for there to be a single theological position in his realm, used his authority to further the Christian religion by building churches and by organizing and financing the early bishops' councils. He also made it illegal for some professions to conduct business on Sunday, although he recognized that for example farmers had to work by tending to their animals each day. In the United States, once Prohibition was the law of the land, some churches praised God for what they saw as the state's cooperation with their religious values. That church property in the United States is tax exempt is an example of churches using whatever is legally possible to make their life easier. Those Christians who work toward laws and a constitutional amendment forbidding abortion exemplify the posture of utilizing the state to criminalize what is other than their own religious belief.

Are we asking government to make criminal what we believe to be sinful because we ourselves can't stop committing the sin? The failure here is not Caesar's. This failure is our failure, the failure of the entire people of God.—Mario Cuomo, Roman Catholic Governor of New York from 1983 to 1994[4]

Some historical examples of such collaboration may strike the contemporary world as far more problematic for Christianity. Peter the Great, the czar of Russia from 1696 to 1725, used his absolute authority to enact several laws that in effect brought the Russian Orthodox Church under the control of the government. For example, he made the choice of bishops not an election by the clergy, but an appointment by the government. Since all Christians do not concur on all moral questions, the use of law to support a certain ethical position may be seen as a blessing to some but not to others. This was the case with Prohibition, since not all Christians agreed that the consumption of alcohol was a sin and ought to be outlawed. Indeed, churches had to seek a legal exemption from Prohibition so that they could continue to serve wine at communion. Many countries with a high percentage of Christians did not in the past provide for legal divorce, and the contemporary legalization of divorce meant that Christians could not rely on the state to enforce a certain understanding of marriage.

A fifth posture is to maintain a Christian state. The word "theocracy" says that God, *theos*, rules, although in such states it is actually the religious authorities who rule according to their religious wisdom. Here Christians make their own religion legally binding, sometimes making all other religious practice criminal activity. The Roman Emperor Theodosius, who reigned from 379 to 395, made Christianity the only legal religion in the empire and destroyed pagan temples and shrines. Queen Elizabeth I of England in the 1559 Act of Uniformity made participation in the Church of England legally required, and even using a variant form of Christian public worship was subject to fine and imprisonment. In reaction against the Church of England, but employing the same posture, the seventeenth-century theocratic colony of Massachusetts Bay made attendance in their Calvinist churches a legal requirement, and Christians of different persuasions were expelled from the colony. A freer colony to which these exiles fled, Rhode Island, was referred to by those opposed to religious liberties as Rogues Island.

The most influential experiment in Christian theocracy was established in Geneva by the Protestant Reformer John Calvin in the sixteenth century. Calvin resisted the idea articulated by both Augustine and Martin Luther that Christians reside within two cities, a secular state and a religious community. His ordered mind wanted a single city, and under his leadership, Geneva became a strict theocracy. Not only was church attendance required, but since he believed that some of the Jewish practices of keeping Sabbath applied to Christians, laws forbade not only all commercial, but also most recreational, activities on Sunday. Some **blue laws** remain on the books in some places of the United States, for example the prohibition against selling liquor on Sunday.

blue law = a law restricting behaviors on a Sunday

In some places, these options are intermingled. Currently, some nations continue to name Christianity as the state religion, such as Orthodoxy in Greece, Roman Catholicism in Costa Rica, Anglicanism in England, and Lutheranism in Norway. Currently, these countries give some privileges to their state church, without imposing restrictions against other religious practice. However, usually these instances are less genuine theocracies than they are the church and state hand-in-hand. For example, some nations that give Roman Catholicism special status have also enacted laws that disregard Catholic Church teaching.

Another example of combined postures is held by some American evangelicals, who demonstrate the withdrawal from the evil society by homeschooling their children. Because they judge that public schools inculcate elementary school children with non-Christian values, such as exposure to moral diversity and the requirement to study contemporary science, they teach their children at home, shielding them from state-supported schools. Yet some of these evangelicals have worked to elect to the state board of education like-minded persons who will ensure only certain history and science textbooks are approved for statewide use. Some evangelicals are now active in national elections, favoring presidential candidates who share their religious views and will work to make alternative views illegal.

What do Christians say about the legal equality of all individuals?

Most Christians throughout history think inside their box, sharing a substantial part of their values with their wider culture. They must then more or less interweave the contradictory principles of supporting the order of the state and embodying countercultural Christian ideals. Many ancient societies practiced slavery of their own lower classes, of conquered peoples, or of darker-skinned persons, with even their most sophisticated and learned thinkers assuming and advocating slavery, and most Christians in slave cultures concurred with this position. Slavery was considered an essential link in the Great Chain of Being. What was higher on the chain was endowed with more Being and had legal authority over everything below, and what was lower on the chain had increasingly less Being and was legally subservient to everything above. Most Christians believed that at creation God had set up this Great Chain of Being, and their task was to maintain and support it, expressing contentment with their placement on the chain.

Many twenty-first-century Christians think of Jesus in the opposite way, as having advocated for the legal rights of each individual and rejecting all forms of slavery. But this is another example of the power of the contemporary social situation to provide the framework into which religious faith is set, the box within which citizens think. The Bible does not include a single sentence set in the mouth of Jesus dealing explicitly with the economic system of slavery, and he used examples from the slave society in his parables without any indication of censure. The epistles include contradictory advice. Although Paul's letter to the Galatians includes the manifesto that in Christ there is neither Jew nor Greek, slave nor free, male nor female (3:28), Paul's letter to Philemon

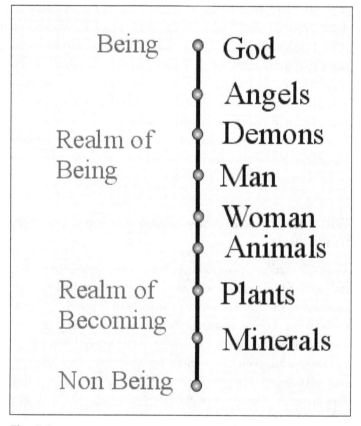

Fig. 9.3.

discusses the situation of Onesimus, a runaway slave, whom Paul is sending back to his master: perhaps Paul hoped that Philemon would free Onesimus. Moreover, the late first-century biblical household codes (Eph. 5:22–6:9; Col. 3:18–4:1) Christianize the ethical structure of the Roman Empire, which includes masters bearing authority over their slaves. With the exception of Gregory of Nyssa in the fourth century, all Fathers of the church assumed the condition of slavery as a given when, for example, they condoned severe beating of disobedient slaves.

One Christian who came to defend the rights of slaves was the sixteenth-century Roman Catholic Dominican friar Bartolomé de las Casas. Sent from Spain to evangelize the natives of modern-day Haiti and the Dominican Republic, he reacted against the widespread practice of the Europeans' atrocities against the native peoples, who, even when Christian, were considered by many colonists as subhuman and were thus legally enslaved. Las Casas worked for fifty years to change the practices of the Spanish court and to institute new laws that outlawed the brutalizing of the natives, and he is sometimes named as one of the first advocates for universal human rights. Yet Las Casas himself at one point suggested that slavery could continue by the importation of captives from Africa to the Indies. He died back in Spain, threatened with accusations of heresy and treason, and having failed to change the legal policy that was maintained by Christians, which made of the native people an enslaved workforce.

> The situation of a slave, under a human master, insures to him food, raiment, and dwelling, together with a variety of little comforts; it relieves him from the apprehensions of neglect in sickness, from all solicitude for the support of his family, and in return, all that is required is fidelity and moderate labour. I have known many freedmen who regretted their manumission.—John England, Episcopalian bishop of South Carolina, 1840[5]

Until the nineteenth century, many Christians accepted slavery as the politically necessary economic system, indeed, as the ethical social condition divinely ordained since the Fall. Sermons preached in the South during the Civil War defended the institution of slavery as God's method of organizing society, albeit urging Christian slaveholders toward restraint in their methods of punishment. Although slaves were catechized to obedience, some Christians in southern states advocated against the baptism of slaves, since baptism suggested equality before God. The religious debate during the Civil War led to several Protestant denominations splitting into two opposing organizations, the northern church denouncing slavery and the southern one supporting it.

In the twentieth century, with slavery outlawed in most nations, the discussion moved to equal rights for previously enslaved populations. In the United States, the Jim Crow laws supported by many Christians in some southern

Nothing can be more certain than that man was formed by his Maker for freedom, and that all men have a right to be free. Nothing can be more certain than that God has implanted in the human soul a desire of liberty which is a fair expression of what he intends shall be the settled condition of things in the world.—Albert Barnes, pastor of First Presbyterian Church in Philadelphia, 1857[6]

states enforced racial prejudice, while the Baptist minister Martin Luther King Jr. is honored for his efforts to eradicate legal discrimination. His "Letter from Birmingham Jail" advocated that if the law of the land is unjust, Christians are required to disobey the law, albeit with nonviolent methods of protest. In South Africa, the revered Anglican archbishop Desmond Tutu not only served as a national leader to end the apartheid system that had been established by immigrant white European Christians, but also since the end of apartheid he has advocated for the government to proceed with patterns of restorative justice. He is known also for promoting the Truth and Reconciliation program that adapted Christian practices of confession for use by the state.

One step removed from the question of slavery is the economic system in many countries that allows or even encourages a lower class to serve as a minimally paid labor force. Some northern European countries with majority Christian leadership have a kind of democratically established state socialism by which taxes keep the upper class from extreme wealth and the lower class from genuine poverty. Many Christians in these countries defend this economic system as the most Christian way to maintain a nation. Yet the United States includes many Christians who lobby against any legal attempts to shorten the distance between the rich and the poor, arguing that the maintenance of individual rights is a more Christian obligation of government than is the enforced alleviation of poverty.

encyclical = a papal letter to worldwide Roman Catholic bishops

Social Gospel = early twentieth-century movement that identified the good news of the gospel as addressing the needs of the poor

Another instance of Christian support for the poor was the 1894 papal **encyclical** *Rerum Novarum*, which spoke for the economic rights of the laboring class and defended the organization of labor unions. The Baptist minister Walter Rauschenbusch (1861-1918) is identified with the Protestant movement called the **Social Gospel**, which advocated for various laws to assist the lives of the urban poor. According to Rauschenbusch, Jesus preached the coming of the just reign of God, not merely individual salvation. The twentieth-century theological movement called liberation theology, arising from the poor in Central and South America, strongly condemned all structures of the state that allow the rich to benefit from the near-slavery of the poor. Liberation theologians criticized

Fig. 9.4. Raised a Quaker, Laura Haviland joined Methodist abolitionists to lecture against slavery, displaying slave irons in her presentations.

a Christian understanding that took comfort in a heavenly reward while ignoring the plight of the poor. The twentieth-century Brazilian Roman Catholic archbishop Dom Hélder Câmara embodied this belief when he chose to reside not in the bishop's palace, but among the poor of his diocese. About this question of political ways to lessen poverty there remains considerable disagreement among Christians.

What do Christians say about war?

The authors of the Old Testament wrote about ancient Israelite war as having been commanded by God and its victories as God's gifts to the chosen people. When later both Judah and Israel were conquered by neighboring nations, the prophets' position was that God used the enemy's military to punish the chosen people because of their unfaithfulness to the covenant. The same ambivalence about the military might of the state is found in the New Testament, in which various passages suggest that God uses the military power of the state for both the good and the ill of believers.

Although during the early centuries of Christianity the Roman army served largely as a police force, there is some evidence that Christians were discouraged from serving as soldiers, since not only were they required to swear allegiance to the emperor as to a god, they might be ordered to kill, and killing was a sin. Being a soldier seemed far from following Christ. This **pacifist** opinion is maintained in the present by what are called the Peace churches, for example Mennonites and Amish, whose members will not serve in the armed forces. When Christian pacifists are challenged concerning the impracticality of their position, they respond with a statement of faith that places their lives in the hands of God and that understands Christian belief as something other than practical politics.

pacifism = the rejection of all forms of violence

The opposite position is held by some Christians, who maintain an obedient support of their nation state. Many American Christian churches introduced a national flag into their worship space during the world wars, and this suggests that believers are to support their nation's governmental policy. Christians have also engaged in Holy War, for example when the Western Church engaged in the Crusades. Here the idea was that God blesses a specific war as a way to further the goals of the faith. In a Holy War, the death of the soldier is a blessed religious sacrifice, rather than a sad, or perhaps even meaningless, tragedy. Granting the complexity of the Bible, all these positions can be supported with scriptural citations.

With Emperor Constantine having legalized Christianity, the commander-in-chief of the Roman armies might be Christian. It was left to the thinker Augustine to consider when war could be justified. Augustine proposed a set of criteria that allowed for a justified war: war had to be conducted for a just cause by a legitimate legal authority; all peaceful means of negotiations must have been tried and have failed; there must be a reasonable hope of success, to balance against the massive miseries that war inflicts; the combatants must use

Fig. 9.5. The Jerusalem Cross is also called the Crusaders' Cross, with Christianity reaching the four corners of the earth from its origin in Jerusalem.

proportional means, not, for example, bombs against spears; and, least likely to be possible in modern war, noncombatants are not to be harmed. During the twentieth century, when the United States has undertaken military action, whether termed "war" or not, Christian ethicists discuss the morality of the engagement, often assisted by Augustine's theory. However, some Christians maintain that Augustine would judge all modern warfare as unjust, and then contemporary Christians must decide whether to accede to Augustine's demands.

It was not until the sixteenth century, with Protestantism accentuating the idea of the individual standing alone before God, that Christians addressed the issue of whether an individual citizen, who was not a pacifist, could ever refuse to serve in the military. During medieval warfare, returning soldiers were given penances to atone for their military activities. However, with no functioning system of penance, Protestant individuals became morally responsible for what they might view as reprehensible actions. In the twentieth century, Christians

After much prayer, thought, and personal struggle, I have decided to withhold 50 percent of my income taxes as a means of protesting our nation's continuing involvement in the race for nuclear arms supremacy. In conscience I cannot support or acquiesce in a nuclear arms buildup which I consider a grave moral evil.—Raymond G. Hunthausen, Roman Catholic archbishop of Seattle[7]

debated about the morality of specific wars, the most socially and religiously wrenching example seen in the decade-long argument over the war in Vietnam. Members of the Peace churches were granted release from the military draft, and draft boards, comprised of citizens, some of whom were Christian, reviewed the petitions of citizens who were not religious pacifists to determine whether to grant them Conscientious Objector status and to assign them alternative service.

What are some other political issues that Christians debate?

One political issue is equal rights for women. Both the classical Great Chain of Being and the biblical household codes have been cited in support of the legal maintenance of male authority. The "rule of thumb" referred to a British law that allowed a husband to beat his wife so long as the stick had a smaller circumference than his thumb. Even in the nineteenth century, most countries with a majority Christian population considered a married couple a single legal unit, which was held by the husband: a wife was not a recognized legal unit and could not address the law on her own. In most democracies with a high Christian population, it was not until the late nineteenth century that women were granted the vote, and in the United States, not until 1913. Yet, similar to the question of slavery, occasional and exceptional Christian voices spoke out for the equality of men and women, and from the seventeenth century on, some Christians argued for women's rights by citing biblical passages, especially the New Testament stories of women who spread the gospel. Historians debate whether the political move to grant women legal equality occurred independent of Christian witness or whether Christians, for example those Protestants who ordained women years before women could vote, helped to bring about this social change.

Another issue is the death penalty. An enduring disagreement among Christians is whether any position presented in the Bible is to be considered the divinely inspired view for all times or is only the historical record of how previous believers thought and acted. Thus, as with other issues discussed here, Christians do not agree about whether the state ought to exercise the right of capital punishment. Those Christians and church bodies that support capital punishment present biblical passages in which God advocates that the ruling authorities execute criminals. Other Christians and church bodies argue that the state ought not kill people as punishment for murders, citing Jesus' call to forgiveness. No contemporary church argues for a full implementation of capital punishment, which in the Old Testament includes the crime of adultery and Sabbath breaking.

Another issue is abortion rights. As with other issues discussed here, Christians do not agree about the legality of abortion. For some Christians, abortion is essentially murder, and thus the biblical commandment not to murder would demand that Christians under no circumstances could condone it. For these Christians, outlawing abortion is no different than outlawing murder, and largely because of the political pressure enacted by these Christians, various laws have greatly limited the availability of abortion in the United States. Other Christians judge abortion as a sorrow, rather than a crime, and encourage a sexual ethic within which the call for an abortion would be extremely rare, for example, a young teenager raped by her father. These Christians argue that were abortion illegal, only the poor would suffer, as the rich could travel to a locale where abortions are readily available. As well, forcing women to bear

Fig. 9.6. In the sixteenth century, third-wave Protestants were executed by the state authority in both Protestant and Roman Catholic jurisdictions.

It is one thing to say that Jesus wants us to do more than our fair share for the poor. It is another thing to say that He wants us to use the fist of government to distribute those benefits. Let the government get out of the charity business, and let the family, churches, and communities be free to take care of the less fortunate.—D. James Kennedy, *How Would Jesus Vote?*[8]

unwanted children causes immeasurable harm to many. These Christians argue that the churches ought not attempt to criminalize abortion, just as those who judge birth control immoral ought not attempt to criminalize its distribution. There are also liberal Christians who view a woman's pregnancy as her own judgment, and they argue that a woman need consult only God as to whether she should bring a pregnancy to term.

Another issue is the legal definition of marriage. Christians do not speak with one voice concerning the question of whether the state should sanction same-sex marriage. Some Christians quote words that the New Testament sets in the mouth of Jesus that describe marriage as between a man and a woman (Matt. 19:4-5). Others refer to the biblical stories of creation of the first man and woman as proof of God's intention for marriage (Gen. 2:24). However, other Christians believe that the opposition to homosexuality and the desire to prohibit equal rights to homosexuals are no different from other moral issues, such as divorce, about which contemporary Christians make different judgments than did the authors of the Bible, and over which the secular state ought not maintain a specific traditional religious position. This question is currently in legal flux, and the final legal situation in the United States, as well as in other countries, will please some Christians and not others, in spite of the fact that marriage legalized is different from marriage blessed by a Christian community.

The single largest problem facing those single mothers who work is the limited availability and high cost of child care. Any poverty-reduction package must include substantial increases in funding for child care.— Jim Wallis[9]

Christians do not agree about whether the state should enforce laws that define precisely the moments of the beginning and the ending of life. For example, some Christians argue that any relaxation of the legal requirements to care for the dying would introduce policies of euthanasia and sanction death of the infirm. Meanwhile, other churches have designed prayer rituals to be held at the bedside of the dying, at which the ordained minister and the family pray together before life-support machines are turned off and the patient is allowed to die. For some Christians, God has designed technology so that society can maintain life at all costs. For other Christians, not everything medically possible is also morally acceptable.

It is important to state that these conflicting Christian ethical positions are not lightly made or easily affirmed. National churches maintain committees of ethicists, theologians, and politicians who study contemporary issues in great depth, propose position papers to their churches, and in some cases require national church assemblies to vote on the controversial opinions. The issues confronted in this chapter demonstrate several ongoing disagreements: Is Augustine or Calvin more correct? That is, are there two cities, or ought Christians strive to make one city the law of the land? Are biblical positions on moral issues valid for Christians of all times and in all the nations of the world? How ought Christians to live within a state that is more or less congruent with their beliefs?

Suggestions

1. Review the chapter's vocabulary: blue laws, divine right of kings, encyclical, established, pacifist, routinized, Social Gospel, state.
2. Max Weber wrote that Calvinist Christianity had sanctioned and encouraged capitalism as the state's economy. Draw up some Christian objections to capitalism.
3. Present arguments for and against the social benefits of laws that support the religious positions of a majority of citizens.
4. Discuss the current laws that deal with the treatment of animals. Should there be a distinctively Christian position on this?
5. Write a personal essay in which you propose a situation for which the government reestablishes a military draft and within which you would be willing to be drafted.
6. Discuss the differences between Romans 13, in which Paul urges Christians to be subject to the ruling authorities as having been established by God, and Revelation 17, in which the visionary describes the Roman Empire as a whore riding on a beast that will be conquered by the Lamb, who is Christ.
7. Read and discuss the short story "Voyage Four: 1661" (1978) by the well-known American author of historical sagas, James A. Michener. Set in colonial Boston, the story narrates the trial, imprisonment, whipping, and hanging of the Quaker Thomas Kenworth by the Puritan authorities.
8. For a major project, read and write a report on the 1969 novel *Silence* by the Japanese Christian author Shusaku Endo. Endo narrates the horrific situation in the seventeenth century when Japan outlawed Christianity: the Jesuit missionaries were not themselves tortured, but rather had to witness the torture of Christian peasants. To "apostasize" is to publicly deny the faith.

9. Two films depict the opposite situations: one in which a Christian uses the governmental structures to further godly aims, and another in which the churches ignored the crimes of the state. View and discuss the film *Amazing Grace*, based on the life of William Wilberforce, a devout Christian who chose to serve God as a member of the British Parliament rather than as an ordained Anglican priest, and who is credited with ending the slave trade. John Newton, the author of the hymn "Amazing Grace," is a character in the film. View and discuss the 2002 film *Amen.*, based on the life of the devout Protestant Kurt Gerstein, a member of the Nazi S.S. who tried unsuccessfully to urge Protestant and Roman Catholic officials to condemn the extermination of the Jews.

For Further Reading

Haugen, David, ed. *Religion in America: Opposing Viewpoints*. San Diego: Greenhaven, 2010.

Smith, Lacey Baldwin. *Fools, Martyrs, Traitors: The Story of Martyrdom in the Western World*. New York: Alfred A. Knopf, 1997.

Yoder, John Howard. *Christian Attitudes to War, Peace, and Revolution*, edited by Theodore J. Koontz and Andy Alexis-Baker. Grand Rapids: Brazos, 2009.

What do Christians say about sexual issues?

| **10**

Fig. 10.1. Edwina Sandys wrote of her 1974 crucifix titled *Christa*: "I did think about women's sacrifice. . . . I'm a woman, and I'm portraying Christ as a woman," said Sandys.[1]

◈ An answer from a scholar

Mary Douglas (1921–2007) was a British social anthropologist whose work dealt with the symbolic role that the human body plays in maintaining communal values and boundaries. Douglas proposed that the male and female bodies are microcosms of both the constructive and the destructive powers in human society. In her 1966 study *Purity and Danger*, Douglas described how the need for communities to protect themselves from disorder and from all forms of **pollution** leads them to attempt to maintain personal bodily purity and to regulate all sexual behaviors. She used the word **dirt** to refer to any matter that such communities judge to be out of place and thus would disrupt the social order. What is not dirt helps to uphold social order. Using anthropological data from many parts of the world, she demonstrated that what is deemed dirt to one culture may not be dirt in others. Each culture establishes and tries to enforce sanctions that reinforce regulations about protection from pollution, thus urging everyone to conform to the authorized social order. Especially matter or behavior that is anomalous, that is, not obviously clean or unclean, must be arbitrated so that the community knows how to evaluate its potential for good or ill.

pollution = Douglas's term for the disruption of the social order

dirt = Douglas's term for any matter that is out of place

Douglas was particularly interested in how religions sanction some matter and some behavior as clean and others as dirt. She wrote that according to monotheism, God created order and beauty, and thus monotheistic religions attempt to honor and maintain that divinely ordained order. Since human bodies contain potential to be either socially positive or negative, religion will maintain regulations that include both the physical—thus dealing with what goes into and out of the body—and the moral—thus promulgating a certain sexual ethic. During her career, Douglas analyzed biblical rules about food, bodily emissions, and sexual ethics as examples of religion's role in keeping dirt out and divine order in.

A grave act of pollution is regarded as a religious offense. Persons who transgress rules about the body must be marginalized, since their body symbolically introduces dirt and their activities upset communal order. Since in actual life such offenses regularly occur, religions must maintain rituals that establish or reinstate purity. Because humans are usually categorized as either male or female, persons with anomalous sexuality are likely to be ostracized as embodying dirt that disrupts the religiously ordained order. The term "holiness" originally referred to this divinely instituted order. However, Douglas maintained that the rules about dirt change over time, and what was dirt in the past may not be judged dirt by the same religious system at a later time.

Fig. 10.2. The clothing of Amish women emphasizes their community's rejection of the pollution of individualist culture and the dirt of sexual allure outside of marriage.

Douglas wrote that when persons in religious authority act wrongly, they lose the spiritual power vested in the office, since they have introduced dirt, rather than symbolizing a rejection of dirt.

Using Douglas, one can say that Christian authorities will be expected to uphold both a certain understanding of the human body that prohibits dirt from diminishing societal cleanliness and a sexual ethic that strives to maintain God's original order for human sexuality. The two biblical stories of creation in Genesis will be central to Christian discussions about God's intentions for the human body. Christian communities will maintain definitions of sexuality, regulations about nakedness and bodily functions, rules for sexual behaviors, and punishments for those who introduce dirt into the community. Polluting actions constitute much of what Christianity calls sin. Christianity substituted a weekly gathering around bread and wine for the Jewish attention to purity through correct eating, and the church largely abandoned ancient prohibitions dealing with menstruation. But the proclamation of a new society of justice and love inaugurated by Christ required considerable attention to sexual ethics. Rituals of confession and forgiveness and rites of penance become common,

Holiness means keeping distinct the categories of creation. It therefore involves correct definition, discrimination and order. Under this head all the rules of sexual morality exemplify the holy. Incest and adultery (Leviticus 18:6-20) are against holiness, in the simple sense of right order. Holiness is more a matter of separating that which should be separated than of protecting the rights of husbands and brothers.—Mary Douglas[2]

since there will be a continual need to reestablish purity when dirt has marred communal wholeness. However, the implications about sexuality in Genesis 1 and Genesis 2–3 differ from each other, and the Bible stipulates severe punishments for inappropriate sexual behaviors—rules that the Bible itself indicates were not enacted. Thus we can expect that over time and around the world Christians will disagree about sexuality and about what constitutes dirt. Such differences can be extremely disruptive within the wider Christian community, because communities rely on stable notions about dirt for their well-being.

◇ Answers from the churches

Conversation about sexual issues is filled with ambiguous vocabulary. The noun "sex" can mean a biological differentiation in some species that effects reproduction, but colloquially it means sexual intercourse. "To sleep with" is an odd colloquialism for sexual intercourse. The noun "gender" refers to the behavioral and psychological traits by which a society understands the differentiation between the sexes, and it also refers to a grammatical category present in some languages by which objects that have no sexuality are deemed masculine, feminine, or neuter. Some women welcome being called "feminine," and others reject the social implications of the term. "Man" can mean either humankind or male. Readers must be aware that texts about sexual issues that were written or translated in previous centuries may be cast in vocabulary that is no longer standard in contemporary American English: the reader must determine, for example, what in any text the word "man" means.

What do Christians say about sexual identity?

Christian assertions about sexuality begin with the doctrine that God created a good world. The human body is essentially good, since God did not make mistakes in creation. Sexual differentiation is good. Furthermore, that God became incarnate in a human body demonstrates the goodness of the bodily creation. Christian believers are expected to thank God for their good bodies and to use that body in a morally appropriate way.

In Christianity's earliest years, some Christians offered the further idea that the two sexes were equally good. God intended the sexes to be parallel.

Although in Judaism the obligatory practice of male circumcision gave a priority to men in the religion, sexual parity can be seen in that Christian baptism is available equally to men and women. Paul wrote that in Christ, there is no male and female (Gal. 3:28). Paul calls the woman Junia "prominent among the apostles" (Rom. 16:7), although for centuries biblical translators assumed this female name was an error in the Greek text, and they altered Junia into a male form, the supposed name Junias. Indeed, one historical theory proposes that the surprisingly rapid growth of Christianity was due in part to its openness to women, in contrast to the androcentrism, the male-centeredness, of some religions in the Roman Empire.

However, later books in the New Testament demonstrate the power of Greco-Roman culture to influence the developing churches. Patriarchy, the authority of the father or oldest male, had been the dominant social pattern in the Mediterranean world for some two thousand years and thus was assumed by many people to be the correct, if not the only, way to live. According to the androcentric Greek philosophy, the male was characterized as having more mind, more reasoning ability, than the female, and the female as having more body, more matter, than the male. Thus for social stability and in the opinions of most people, male identity was preferred. This assumption of male dominance is apparent in the New Testament's household codes, which command the wife to be subject to her husband (Eph. 5:22-28; Col. 3:18-19). Passages in the pastoral epistles that proscribe the activities of Christian women and restrict their clothing, jewelry, and hair styles indicate to contemporary readers that certain behaviors were in fact going on, and historical records do not indicate to what degree these regulations were heeded (e.g., 2 Tim. 2:9-10). In the thirteenth century, Thomas Aquinas relied on Greek philosophical categories to affirm that in creation God gave males a higher intellect than females, and although the souls of males and females are equal before God, their roles on earth and in the church were to be based on their God-given identifying characteristics. Medieval scholars taught that God had given males more will and intellect, and females more memory and imagination. This male dominance has characterized much of church teaching throughout history.

Despite the assumption of male dominance, the primary theologians, such as Augustine and Thomas Aquinas, affirmed the goodness of women in God's creation and their equality with men before God. Furthermore, Aquinas disagreed with Aristotle in one important matter: he wrote that the human soul comes, not from the male, as Greek philosophy taught, but rather from God. Yet the idea that women were more like Eve than like Mary prevailed, and at times male misogyny, a hatred of women, was intense in the church. Especially

Fig. 10.3. Da Vinci's famous depiction of the Last Supper suggests an all-male leadership within the church.

in Europe during the fourteenth and fifteenth centuries, the witchcraft craze demonstrated an extreme fear of women's identity. *Malleus Maleficarum*, a book written in 1486 by two Dominican priests, condemns women who, having been formed from Adam's bent rib, are by nature intellectually childlike, always deceptive, and marked by insatiable lust, infidelity, and illicit ambition. This text, which includes stories of the power of some females to effect male impotence, served as a manual for church leaders for the examination, detention, and execution of women who the authorities decided were dangerous to church and society.

In the nineteenth century, the popular belief in what is called the Cult of True Womanhood encouraged some Christians to maintain the opposite worldview: that males were more inclined to aggression and selfishness than were females. This position claimed that women could serve as images of Christ more readily than could men. Christians are accustomed to feminized depictions of Jesus with long curling hair and floor-length robes, not at all a macho savior. Some feminists urged that churches promote at least female equality, if not a preference for female identity. For some nineteenth-century theologians, notably Friedrich Schleiermacher, women were more innocent than men because they continued to resemble children, who are closest of all to God. For twentieth-century feminists, the connection with childhood was rejected, but some authors suggested that female hormones made women more readily into Christian beings than men. Wherever a number count was made, women have constituted a solid majority of practicing Christians. In the United States, women have consistently constituted about two-thirds of church members, and in some churches around the world the majority of women is higher.

The twentieth century witnessed a Christian reexamination of the identity of homosexuals and transgendered persons. Historically, most church teaching claimed that the very state of being homosexual was sinful. Many churches have maintained a silence that suggested that Christian homosexuality did not exist. During his reign, King James I of England, who commissioned what is called the King James Bible, was infamous for his homosexuality, but most contemporary Christians who revere the translation that bears his name are not aware of this. What ought to be the appropriate Christian response to the gay rights movement is one of the most contested arguments in current church life. Some churches welcome homosexuals and transgendered persons as equal before God, arguing that gender was misunderstood by Christians in the past and that sexual identity is innate in the human person, thus given by God. One international denomination, the Metropolitan Community Church, has a particular outreach to all homosexual, bisexual, and transgendered persons. Other more socially conservative churches, especially many churches in Africa, deny that there is such a thing as homosexual identity, and they remain steadfastly opposed to homosexual and transgendered inclinations as in any way pleasing to God.

> The critical principle of feminist theology is the promotion of the full humanity of women. Theologically speaking, whatever diminishes or denies the full humanity of women must be presumed not to reflect the divine or an authentic relation to the divine, or to reflect the authentic nature of things, or to be the message or work of an authentic redeemer or a community of redemption.—Rosemary Radford Ruether[3]

What about gender roles in the church?

For most Christian practice over the centuries, males have held the dominant positions of authority in the church. Many Christian philosophers have defended this practice by claiming that God intended male superiority in the creation of humankind, and many Christian preachers have cited the curse on Eve (Gen. 3:16), the lists of Jesus' twelve male disciples (Matt. 10:2-4; Luke 6:13-16), and the rule that women keep silent in church (1 Cor. 14:34b-35) as scriptural warrants for the subordination of women in the church and as reasons for ordaining only males. Thomas Aquinas argued that although women's souls were equal to men's before God, women had deficient rational ability to be leaders in the community and thus could not be ordained. Currently, the Eastern Orthodox churches, Roman Catholicism, and some Protestant churches continue the historic practice of ordaining only males as bishops, priests, and ministers. Because historically it was usually only males who were granted authority to teach and write, theology and catechesis over the ages have maintained male dominance in both open and hidden ways.

Throughout Christian history, most women served in the church under male authority. In recent centuries, some women traveled to mission fields where they enjoyed more independence from the male hierarchy. Some women in the religious orders evaded male dominance. In these single-sex communities, women assigned authority among themselves, with bishops sometimes distant from their daily life. In many places, the church's blessing of the celibate life through the religious orders presented to women the only socially acceptable option to the societal expectation of marriage and childbearing. Some nuns understood their bond with Christ as a **spiritual/mystical marriage**. Although certainly some convents served as dumping grounds for unwanted daughters or unmarriageable or widowed women, many vowed women excelled in various fields of thought and service, and history shows that women in religious orders were of incalculable value especially as nurses and teachers over the centuries and around the world.

spiritual/mystical marriage = the intimate experience of a believer bonded to Christ likened to marriage

Nearly all the churches of the Reformation abolished the religious orders. Protestant women served in the church especially as mothers and as teachers of children under the authority of males. Yet exemplified by the publication in 1666 of Margaret Fell's essay *Womens Speaking Justified*, some Protestant women argued from the Bible that God created women equal to men, Jesus was open to the ministry of women, and women were the first witnesses to Christ's resurrection, and thus women ought to have authority in the church equal to that of males. The nineteenth century saw the beginning of women's ordination, when in 1853 Antoinette Brown Blackwell was ordained a minister in a Congregationalist church. Many women traveled around as itinerant preachers or served in ministerial roles in foreign mission fields, with or without the sanction of males. A recurring pattern was that a denomination established an intermediary status between clergy and lay, such as sister, deaconess, or evangelist, in which women could serve, with more than lay authority but without full ordination. Several Protestant denominations were started by women. Especially the writings of Phoebe Palmer inspired the

I told Rev. Richard Allen that the Lord had revealed it to me, that I must preach the gospel. He replied that a Mrs. Cook, a Methodist lady, had also some time before requested the same privilege; who, it was believed, had done much good in the way of exhortation, and holding prayer meetings. But as to women preaching, he said that our Discipline knew nothing at all about it.— Jarena Lee, 1836[4]

nineteenth-century Holiness movement, which has been embodied in various denominations.

Many contemporary Protestant denominations ordain women to their ministry. Some denominations maintain the policy that women cannot become bishops, in which case they would have authority over male clergy. In another move that strives for gender parity, many churches of the twentieth century emended the texts of their hymns and prayers to eliminate sexist language, for example by replacing "brothers" with "brothers and sisters" and by rejecting the noun "man" as a designator of humanity. Some African American Christian women identified themselves as womanists, and Latina women as Mujeristas, and their advocacy is changing their churches. Asian American Christian women too are finding in their group identity a prod to church leadership to open to women more avenues for authority. The movement called Women-Church has answered the desire of some women for a single-sex worshiping community.

Recently, some churches have ordained openly gay candidates to their ministry. Some churches expect gay and lesbian clergy to remain celibate, while others allow that, as with heterosexuals, sexual fidelity between partners is sanctioned. The acceptability of sexually partnered gay and lesbian clergy is currently an extremely controversial issue among Christian churches around the world.

What about the morality of sexual practices?

In considering Christian ethics, it is important to distinguish among several types of ethical statements. Some points of Christian morality express an ethical ideal. For example, that Christians are not to hate one another is an idealistic virtue, one that inspires conduct but cannot be enforced or its infringement punished. Other Christian ethical goals are genuine obligations, for example, that Christians are not to murder others, and these ethical regulations may even become part of society's legal code. Some of each of these may be presented as divine commands, although not all Christians will agree that a certain behavior has been forbidden by God. When teaching, preaching, or writing about sexual ethics, churches may be engaged in describing ideals, obligations, or divine commands, and these variations complicate the discussion of Christian sexual ethics.

One difference among Christian churches is the amount and quality of religious instruction that is conducted on explicitly sexual issues. Many churches instruct youth about sexual abstinence, or at least continence, and some local churches conduct conversation about sexuality with adult members, both via pastoral counseling and in retreat settings. Other churches seldom mention sexual issues, perhaps relying on past centuries of regulations to remain authoritative. However, Christian ethicists have written extensive and thoughtful books that address not only the age-old problem of **adultery**, but also many sexual behaviors from masturbation to in-vitro fertilization. The early twentieth-century theories of Sigmund Freud broadened sexuality from a focus on specific acts that involve the sexual organs to the entire existence of the sexual human person, and this new way to think about sexuality is engaging some contemporary Christian ethicists.

adultery = sexual intercourse of married persons with persons to whom they are not married; in the Bible, sexual intercourse between any man and a woman who is married to another man

Some denominations have relied on committees to write ethical statements that are first considered by the membership and then submitted for approval at conventions. In other churches, the hierarchy retains the responsibility of issuing statements about sexuality. Once again, as with the sections in the pastoral epistles about women's clothing, church pronouncements about sexual conduct indicate which behaviors are in fact going on, and cannot be used as a description of the actual conduct of Christians. An ongoing issue across Christian denominations is who has the authority to speak for the membership and who can be trusted to express correctly God's will on any particular issue.

Because sexuality plays such an immense actual and symbolic role in communal life, churches through the ages have attempted to maintain a more disciplined sexual ethic than did the wider culture. Christians recognized that the exercise of one's sexuality was one of the primary powers that most individuals have, and preachers offered their wisdom as to how to exercise this power in a Christian manner. Paul, who assumed that the end of the world was imminent, suggested that Christians be celibate. Yet in a set of surprising admonitions (1 Cor. 7:1-16), Paul described the wife and husband as both having equal sexual authority in a marriage that is marked by mutuality, and he allowed for divorce and remarriage. However, in the Gospels written several decades later, Jesus is quoted as rejecting divorce when he recommended marriage, on the model of the first woman and man (Mark 10:2-12). The urban society in which Christianity arose increasingly necessitated monogamy, and this has been the dominant Christian pattern. However, especially in Africa with its tradition of polygamy, some Christian communities continue to allow for polygamous marriages.

The dominant Christian sexual ethic reflected agreement about the goodness of heterosexual marriage. Before the availability of reliable birth control, intercourse could lead to pregnancy, and every society needs to attend to the care of its children. Thus not surprisingly, the church taught that sexual intercourse be restricted to married persons. Since it is the woman who gets pregnant, concern for premarital or extramarital abstinence was stronger for women than for men. At some times in history, for example in colonial Massachusetts, sexual intercourse outside of marriage was a crime and was prosecuted in the courts. In some Christian communities, censure against pregnant unmarried women was intense, as if the community meted out the punishment so that the church or civic authorities need not. However, for centuries, social precautions against intercourse outside of marriage were pronounced mostly for the women in the upper classes, where inheritance issues complicated the birth of children.

For at least the first thousand years, the church did not conduct marriage services of any kind. Local rituals arose as part of the communal feasting that celebrated the marriage. For example, the priest blessed the bed on which the couple lay, albeit fully clothed, or the couple stood with the priest at the church doorway to receive a blessing toward procreation. It became standard in late medieval times for the woman publicly to say her Yes to the marriage as part of the ritual of the wedding. Although it is likely that many women were forced into compliance, at least the church attempted to grant women also an equal role in agreeing to marriage. Increasingly the pattern of parents arranging the marriage of their children—thus the ritual at weddings of the father giving his daughter away to her husband—was replaced by individual choice, and Shakespeare's play *Romeo and Juliet* illumines the problems even for the clergy when young persons wished privately to make vows with their chosen marriage partners.

Among Roman Catholics, it was in 1430 that marriage was described as a sacrament and the ritual expected of all couples. Currently in many countries, marriage is understood as a legal contract that actually takes place in the courthouse. If a Christian couple wishes to have the marriage blessed, there is then also a church service. In the United States, churches have been granted the right to perform the legal ceremony of marriage, although a state license is still required. In some especially European Christian populations, marriage is becoming rare, and cohabitation increasingly the normal social situation.

Although clergy advocated that intercourse remain within marriage, history shows that this admonition was widely ignored. For example, an extensive log

> The question is often raised, "Is oral sex sex?" The question received prominence when Bill Clinton as president of the United States equivocated upon being asked by the grand jury in 1998 if he had had sex with Monica Lewinski. . . . Though young people frequently view oral sex as a casual physical expression, the very nature of the act is highly intimate. . . . Oral sex is sex and belongs in the intimacy of a marriage, not in the exploration of physical intimacy outside of marriage.—Dennis P. Hollinger[5]

kept by a midwife who worked in New England from 1785 to 1812 indicates that 31 percent of the 814 births she recorded took place less than nine months after marriage, and 9 percent more outside of marriage.[6] These high numbers of premarital sexual encounters suggest that the actual pattern among those Christians was that once a woman was pregnant, the couple married. In the twenty-first century, few churches in the United States convey any censure or punishment on sexually active unmarried persons. This raises the question of whether church leaders still consider premarital sexual intercourse to be sinful.

Since the 1960s, when reliable birth control became socially acceptable and readily available in first-world countries, Christian ethicists have disagreed about whether the new situation also changes Christian morality. Some Christians have concluded that medieval regulations were based on both the lack of birth control and the marriage of women at puberty, which rendered premarital sexual engagement as essentially child abuse. These ethicists argue that the new situations of available birth control and of sexual maturity long before childrearing begins suggest that Christians need to consider premarital sexual activity in new ways.

To develop these positions about marriage, Christian ethicists over the centuries debated the purpose and meaning of sexual intercourse. Although some

Fig. 10.4. In the Orthodox marriage ritual, the groom and bride are crowned as if God has made them king and queen in the kingdom of their home.

religious teachings in the Roman Empire viewed sexual practices as demeaning and best avoided, Augustine entered the ethical conversation with what became the most influential Christian position. After his conversion to Christianity Augustine left his common-law wife, the mother of his son, with whom he had cohabited for thirteen years, and he lived a celibate life in a kind of monastery. Yet he taught that marriage was good, established by God. Philosophically, Augustine maintained that the things of God's creation each had a primary purpose and that the primary purpose of human sexuality was the procreation of children. The sin of Eve was described as **lust**. Theologians had debated whether there had been intercourse in the Garden of Eden before the Fall, and Augustine's answer was Yes: God had intended humans to be sexual beings. Indeed, before the Fall intercourse was even better than now, since it was not tarnished by lust.

lust = inappropriate or excessive sexual desire

From Augustine's thought developed the official sexual ethic of medieval Roman Catholicism: intercourse belongs solely within marriage; any use of sexual organs not for the purpose of procreation misuses God's creation; and all sexual desire is akin to sin. The phrase "the missionary position" points to the teaching by some Protestant missionaries that intercourse was ethical only with the man on top. Oral and anal intercourse, masturbation, and all homosexual activities were examples of the sinful misuse of sexual organs. As always, the critical historian questions to what degree this strict morality was actually enacted within Christian marriages. In some Christian communities, even orgasm in the marriage bed was viewed as a sign of sinful lust, rather than as a gracious component of God's gift of sexuality. Some recent Christian ethicists have argued that women's having no heat cycle and experiencing orgasm suggest that God intended humans to enjoy sexual intercourse for other than procreative reasons.

The morality of contraception is another ethical question about which Christians disagree. Following Augustine, the official medieval Western position was that all efforts at contraception were attempts to frustrate God's design for procreation, and thus were sinful. This position has been muted in contemporary Roman Catholic teaching, which is open to the **rhythm method** and acknowledges a secondary intention of marital intercourse, the nurturing of the bond between husband and wife. The 1930 papal encyclical *Casti Connubii* reaffirmed that the wife is subordinate to her husband and that her primary purpose in marriage is childbearing. In 1968, the papal encyclical *Humanae Vitae*, issued in the

rhythm method = sexual intercourse scheduled during a woman's menstrual cycle when she is least likely to conceive wake of the social acceptance of the birth control pill, reaffirmed that all forms of birth control, except for the rhythm method, were sinful. However, this mandate is widely ignored among Catholics. During the twentieth century, some Protestant churches came to advocate the use of contraceptives, as allowing married couples to show mutual love without engendering more children than the family could rear with care. Currently, most practicing Christians in first-world countries, no matter what their church teaches, do not consider the use of contraception immoral.

to ensoul = to receive from God a human soul

The stakes are higher when considering abortion. For Augustine, abortion was a radical form of contraception and thus was forbidden. Thomas Aquinas considered when the fetus became human, in his language, **ensoul**ed. He theorized that male fetuses receive their human soul from God at the sixth week of gestation, and female fetuses at twelve weeks. Thus by the end of the first trimester, the fetus would be considered human and could not be aborted. Recently, however, the point at which a fertilized egg is to be considered a human is under considerable contentious medical and religious discussion. Some Christians teach that all abortions are tantamount to murder, and in a strict position that mirrors their condemnation of all contraception, the Roman Catholic hierarchy teaches an absolute proscription against abortion. For other Christians, granting the high percentage of naturally occurring spontaneous abortions, the choice of abortion may be better than the tragedy of an unwanted birth. For these ethicists, attention to the living is greater than that to those who may be brought to life.

It follows from Augustine's writings that all homosexual actions, even homosexual thoughts, were historically deemed sinful. Monasteries established regulations that kept the monks from any activity that might encourage homosexual practices, and convents prohibited the sisters from developing **particular friendships**. A thirteenth-century illustrated Bible, in depicting parallels between scriptural stories and current realities, compared the sin of Adam and Eve with that of two monks embracing and two nuns embracing. Historically, all Christian churches prohibited homosexual activity.

particular friendship = an intense personal relationship between two members of a religious order

The twentieth century witnessed Christians arguing about the morality of sexual behaviors between consenting Christian homosexual adults. Currently, some churches continue the traditional teaching that even homosexual desires are sinful. Some churches maintain a middle position: being born a homosexual is not a sinful condition, but enacting that homosexuality with any overt behavior is a sin. Yet other churches teach that God makes some persons to be homosexual, and that since sexual activities can nurture love and commitment between persons, Christian homosexuals should be encouraged to live sexually in fidelity with a partner. Several church bodies have authorized rites of commitment between gay and lesbian persons, some referring to this as marriage and some not, and there is a growing body of **queer theology**.

Christian tradition has shown diversity also over the issue of divorce. Some denominations, such as the Amish, absolutely prohibit divorce. Roman Catholicism, wishing to maintain the absolute tie between intercourse and marriage and fiercely resisting the accommodation of divorce, developed the practice of **annulling** marriages. Here a diocesan court decides whether the couple entered into marriage in a mature manner, understanding what Christian marriage is and entails. If not, the church can judge that the marriage vow is null and void, as if the marriage had never existed. Medieval history is laden with stories of which persons of high social status received annulments and which did not and why. In Orthodox churches, divorce is discouraged, but there is a rite for second marriage that includes a confession of sin for the errors within the first marriage. During the twentieth century, mainstream Protestant denominations came to allow for divorce and remarriage in the church with increasingly less censure on the people involved.

In all these conflicted issues, from monogamy to masturbation, from divorce to homosexuality, Christians in various times and places both participate in and criticize the culturally dominant sexual mores. Thus, for example, in cultures where birth control is acceptable, a high percentage of Christians find its use ethical. Yet in locales where infanticide as a form of birth control is common, all Christians have preached against this practice. Although contemporary Christians do not agree on many points of sexual morality, there continues to be universal Christian consensus that adultery is sinful. The biblical passage that likens the relationship of husband and wife to that of Christ and the church (Eph. 5:21-33) has supported the teaching that sexual intercourse of married persons with other partners cannot be appropriate Christian living.

queer theology = theology arising from within and dealing positively with Christians who are lesbian, gay, bisexual, or transgendered

annulment = judgment rendering a marriage as being invalid, as never having genuinely occurred

Tragically, women, more than men, are expected in Christian teaching never to take their own well-being as a moral consideration. I believe, deeply, that moral right is on the side of the struggle for the freedom and self-respect of women, especially poor and nonwhite women, and on the side of developing social policy which assures that every child born can be certain to be a wanted child.—Beverly Wildung Harrison[7]

celibacy = lifelong, vowed sexual abstinence

Another topic important to consider is Christian **celibacy**. To trace the historical importance of the celibate life, one can begin with the Church Father Jerome. It was Jerome's severe criticism of sexual activity that Augustine was countering when he wrote about the goods of marriage. Jerome was deeply influenced by the Greek philosophical position that the higher a creature is on the Great Chain of Being, the less any sexuality ought to function. Jerome argued that the Virgin Mary, Jesus himself, the angels, and God were celibate or altogether nonsexual. Thus the more serious Christians would be sexually abstinent for periods of prayer, or better yet, altogether celibate. Jerome viewed sexual activity as incited by sinful women, and the fact that celibate clergy could focus their energies on church work, rather than on spouse and children, figured in the hierarchy of the West in advocating for the preference for the celibate life.

Today in the Orthodox churches, bishops are chosen from among the celibate clergy, but other clergy are expected to marry. From Jerome's time on, some authorities in the Western church urged clerical celibacy. It was mandated in the eleventh century, in part to prohibit the children of clergy from inheriting what the church considered its own property. For subsequent centuries, people vowed to life in the religious orders were held up as models of Christian virtue, who dedicated their life to the care for others, rather than to the sexual fulfillment of the self. History demonstrates, however, that many of the clergy and religious did not live celibate lives, and in the late Middle Ages the sexual misconduct of clergy was a social scandal. That the priest and friar Martin Luther married a nun who had left a convent marked a radical alteration in the Western church, and nearly all Protestant churches have continued Luther's emphasis of giving the highest value to the married state. Currently, the most liberal Protestant churches allow homosexual clergy to live openly with a vowed partner. During the Second Vatican Council, the Roman Catholic Church spoke in positive terms about the Christian married state, although clerical celibacy is still strongly defended by the Vatican.

What about sexual language and imagery used in descriptions of God?

Beginning already in the fifth century, but especially an issue in the twentieth and twenty-first centuries, are the issues that arise from describing God with human categories. Theologians who were occupied in developing Christian doctrine stressed that God is not literally a father; that is, the triune God does not function sexually as did the gods and goddesses in paganism. In the fourth century, Gregory of Nazianzus wrote that the terms Father and Son are metaphors that illumined the relationship within the triune God; Jesus is not literally the son of God, and the conception of Jesus came about from a miracle, not from sexual intercourse between God and Mary. Thomas Aquinas considered that "He Who Is" is a better name for God than Father, which is too human a term to apply perfectly for God. Yet because Father and Son are universal human categories of experience and affection, the language has often been literalized in the minds of believers, and it remains beloved Christian speech.

Many Christians agree that how one thinks about a gender within God will affect how one thinks about human sexuality. In the current time, some churches find that masculine language and imagery for God correctly points to the male dominance in things human and divine that God desires. God is truly like a Father, and God intends Christians to emulate patriarchy in their families. Some Christians teach that all prayers are to be addressed to God as Father, and some cite the feminist scholar Mary Daly, originally a Roman Catholic nun and at her death no longer a Christian, as epitomizing the inevitable trajectory of those who criticize church patriarchy. However, in recent decades, other churches have worked to lessen this maleness by interspersing "Father, Son, and Holy Spirit" with other titles and metaphors, both from the Bible and from Christian imagination. These Christians deny that God desires patriarchy, and they point to many narratives in the Bible in which God blesses the youngest son or the poor young woman.

The issue of divine sexuality includes consideration of the masculine pronoun. The Hebrew and Greek of the Bible write as if God is a "he," although not functioning as a sexual male, and Christians affirm that God became incarnate in the male Jesus of Nazareth. Thus traditionally the church spoke as if God is "he." In the twentieth century some Christians analyzed the power that even masculine pronouns have on Christian practice and believers' imagination. They argued that if God is masculine, then masculinity is better than femininity, and men are more like God than are women. The outcomes of this contentious debate are varied, with some Christians maintaining the masculine language for God as being obedient to the Bible, and other Christians diminishing masculine references to God in hopes to correct the ancient idea that men are higher on the Great Chain of Being than women. In an influential theological work *She Who Is*, Elizabeth A. Johnson, a Roman Catholic theologian who is a Sister of Saint Joseph, amended Thomas Aquinas's description of God as "he who is" by proposing the pronoun "she" as more appropriate than "he" in conveying the mystery of the triune God. Some Christian denominations

Fig. 10.5. *The Holy Trinity* by Fridolin Leiber (1853–1912), depicts God as three males, with each person of the Trinity identified by a symbolic image on his chest.

and individual authors have provided worship resources that radically reduce or entirely eliminate masculine pronouns for God, believing that a nongendered God is more faithful to Christian doctrine than a male deity and that lessening the connection between God and men will be good news for both male and female believers.

In conclusion, it can be seen that in the basics, most Christian churches in most times and places have agreed that human sexuality is God's good gift, and Christians are expected to live sexually moral lives. No Christian theologians or churches have taught that Christians are free to do whatever they choose with their sexuality. Since much sexual misconduct has public negative consequences, what were deemed sexual sins often received considerable censure from church authorities. Yet in many issues that touch on human sexuality, Christians have not agreed with one another, nor is there agreement about who has the authority to frame the sexual ethic of Christians. Ought the church to quote the Bible, obey the hierarchy, decide official documents through a democratic process, or heed the culture? How serious a sin is sexual misconduct? In the twenty-first century, there is little sign that Christian denominations, and even members of the same denomination, will come to speedy agreement on these sexual issues.

Suggestions

1. Review the chapter's vocabulary: adultery, annulment, celibacy, dirt, ensoul, lust, particular friendship, pollution, queer theology, rhythm method, spiritual/mystical marriage.

2. Some Africans maintain the traditional understanding that the male foreskin and the female clitoris are a kind of sexual dirt that must be removed so that the sexes can be distinct. Apply Mary Douglas's proposal to a discussion of circumcisions and clitoridectomies and whether it is Christian to perform them.

3. Present arguments for and against allowing partnered homosexuals from being ordained.

4. Differentiate between the following words: *woman, womanly, female, femaleness, lady, ladylike, feminine, femininity, effeminate, girl, girlish, bitch, sexist.*

5. Research one the following Christian women: Hilda of Whitby, Hildegard of Bingen, Angela of Foligno, Margery Kempe, Catherine of Siena, Teresa of Avila, Anne Hutchinson, Sarah Grimké, Elizabeth Ann Seton, Aimee Semple McPherson, Carter Heyward, or Ada Isasi-Diaz.

6. In the Bible, Luke's account in Acts 8:26-40 suggests that what was religiously unacceptable in Judaism—being a eunuch—is acceptable within Christianity. Discuss what this story might mean for contemporary Christians.

7. Read and discuss Walker Percy's "The Promiscuous Self,"[8] a short story in which several people, including John Calvin, are interviewed about sexual issues.

8. For a major project, read and write a report on Nathaniel Hawthorne's masterpiece *The Scarlet Letter*. Trace the meaning of Hester Prynne's

"A" throughout the novel to the conclusion, with its suggestion of the coming of a female savior.

9. The 2010 film *Vision* dramatizes the life of the twelfth-century nun Hildegard of Bingen, visionary, abbess, healer, composer, artist, and author of a morality play, as well as works on theology, spirituality, biology, medicine, and herbal uses. The film touches on many issues relating to human sexuality, including male dominance, illicit sex, abortion, the female role in conception, and latent lesbianism.

For Further Reading

Clark, Elizabeth A., and Herbert Richardson, ed. *Women and Religion: The Original Sourcebook of Women in Christian Thought*. Rev. ed. San Francisco: Harper, 1996.

Duck, Ruth C. *Gender and the Name of God: The Trinitarian Baptismal Formula*. New York: Pilgrim, 1991.

Hollinger, Dennis P. *The Meaning of Sex: Christian Ethics and the Moral Life*. Grand Rapids: Baker Academic, 2009.

Pagels, Elaine. *Adam, Eve, and the Serpent: Sex and Politics in Early Christianity*. New York: Random House, 1988.

What do Christians say about science? | 11

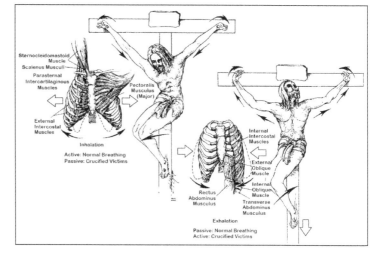

Fig. 11.1. An anatomical drawing of the effect of crucifixion upon the human respiration. The loincloth is inaccurate: victims were crucified naked.

◇ An answer from a scholar

Usually descriptions of nature, whether by means of cosmology, geology, archeology, ecology, physics, anthropology, biology, or psychology, are partial, expressing only one method of scientific investigation. Alfred North Whitehead (1861–1947), a mathematician and cosmologist who has been judged one of the twentieth century's most creative scientific thinkers, considered not discrete parts of the universe, but the interrelationship of the whole. The search for ultimate meaning, he said, requires a single coherent system. His vast scientific learning and his complex prose meant that his writings are difficult to master, but even his bald thesis contradicts the simplistic views that most people have of how the natural world functions. Whitehead said that, granting Albert Einstein's **theory** of relativity and the data about quantum physics, the universe can no longer be pictured like a medieval hierarchical kingdom, nor, as Isaac Newton proposed in the eighteenth century, like a complex machine. Rather, reality must be regarded as one interrelated organism, a dynamic and evolving process that has continued for thirteen billion years. In such "process thinking," statements about what exists are replaced with openness to what is in process of becoming.

theory = in science, a set of principles devised to explain a group of facts that has been repeatedly tested and that can predict natural phenomena

Scientists have separated nonliving matter from living matter; most people distinguish humans from the rest of nature; and theologians have taught that the **supernatural** is other than the natural. Whitehead asserted that all reality is a continuum: living matter proceeds from nonliving matter, and the human from the nonhuman. There is no supernatural, no eternal that is other than what develops from the temporal. Because humanity is continuous with the rest of interrelated nature, religion must develop more credible proposals about human life and its meaning than was acceptable in the past.

supernatural = a realm of reality that is beyond and outside the natural world of experience

Whitehead called on religion to develop **process theology**. For Whitehead, even God is part of the process of the evolving interrelated cosmos. God is the source of both the order of the universe and the newness that arises within it. Part of the process, God participates in the evolving organism of the universe by persuasion. God is not before all creation, but with all creation. Evil is understood as God's self-limitation within the eons of the evolving universe.

process theology = a way to understand God as being a participant in the processes of the evolving universe

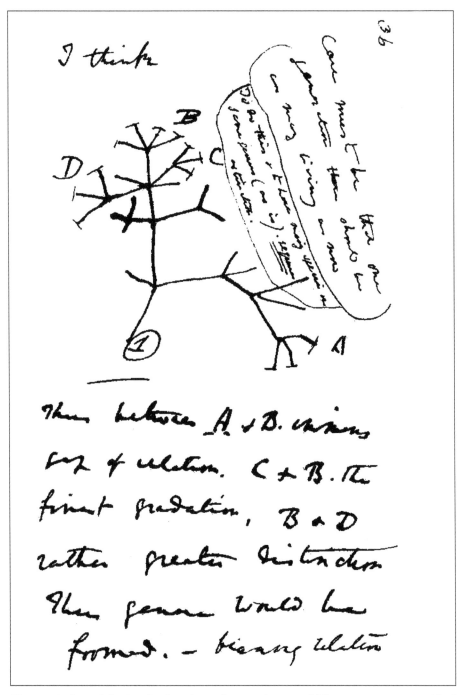

Fig. 11.2. Darwin's simple drawing of nature's tree of life encourages a unified approach to understanding the universe.

In the early medieval times, Heaven was in the sky, and Hell was underground; volcanoes were the jaws of Hell. I do not assert that these beliefs entered into the official formulations: but they did enter into the popular understanding of the general doctrines of Heaven and Hell, and they entered into the explanations of the influential exponents of Christian belief. But whatever be the right doctrine, in this instance the clash between religion and science, which has relegated the earth to the position of a second-rate planet attached to a second-rate sun, has been greatly to the benefit of the spirituality of religion by dispersing these medieval fancies.—Alfred North Whitehead[1]

In his 1925 lectures titled *Science and the Modern World*, Whitehead traced the historical development of scientific thought from its origins in the sixteenth century into quantum theory in the twentieth. Christian doctrine maintained the rationality of God, and so Western thinkers assumed the rational ordering of the universe. This doctrine supported scientific exploration. Taught by science, Christian theology has gradually altered many of its understandings about the universe, and it must continue to do so. Religion, Whitehead wrote, "is not a research after comfort, but . . . is the vision of something which stands beyond, behind, and within, the passing flux of immediate things; something that gives meaning to all that passes, and yet eludes apprehension."[2] But religion as something "beyond the passing flux of immediate things" cannot mean what people historically thought of as the supernatural. Whitehead suggested that religion will continue to decay unless it takes scientific knowledge seriously and works to reject prescientific notions of God as some kind of Being who is outside reality. Religion must reimagine God as part of reality, a participant in a universe that is becoming.

Informed by Whitehead, one can say that over the centuries, Christian theologians have altered much ancient understanding about the world, and they must continue to do so. Perhaps because of the extreme erudition of recent scientific discussions, there remains in church and society simplistic and unscientific notions about the universe. Some Christians must master contemporary science and use that knowledge to render their religious beliefs compatible with the evolving process that constitutes the universe. Only in this way can the God Christians worship be the God of reality, rather than a God of archaic imaginings.

◇ Answers from the churches

Before examining the historic and contemporary responses that Christians give to science, it is important first to look at the several different presuppositions important within the churches that influence how scientific knowledge is received. One vocabulary issue: colloquially in the United States, it is common to speak of those who "believe in evolution." Here "believe" means to give intellectual assent to a proposition. However, throughout Christian history, **belief** in God meant, not intellectual assent to a proposal, but trust in God's power and mercy. Many American eighteenth-century Deists gave intellectual assent to God's existence, but did not trust in God for salvation. Conversation on scientific and religious topics would be helped were speakers clear about their use of the word "believe."

belief = trust in God's salvation

What are various Christian presuppositions about science?

First, there is a wide range of scientific knowledge within the churches. Granting new discoveries and complex scientific theories, the scientific understanding held by many religious authorities is outdated. Much Christian discussion of the topics addressed in this chapter is conducted by immensely learned Christian university professors who may or may not be instructing their own clergy about the latest in science. Some Christian denominations maintain committees that address the complex questions relating to science as preparation for the church's issuing statements of belief and practice, and some denominations do not. Some such statements may shock conservative or minimally educated believers. Some Christians do not know that such position papers exist. Current media have popularized the views of some atheist scientists who argue

Analyze the view of nature expressed in this popular nineteenth-century Christian hymn by Carl G. Boberg:

> When through the woods and forest glades I wander,
> I hear the birds sing sweetly in the trees;
> When I look down from lofty mountain grandeur
> And hear the brook and feel the gentle breeze:
>> Then sings my soul, my Savior God, to Thee,
>> How great Thou art! How great Thou art![3]

that educated persons can no longer be Christian, even though many reputable scientists are practicing Christians. This atheist position has influenced some Christians to ignore science as being detrimental to their faith in God.

Most Christians know little about contemporary science, with their worldview grounded in the nineteenth century. Their attitudes about the relationship between their faith and natural science function largely as personal comfort, not as intellectual proposal. Many people know something of history's two famous trials, that in 1633 of Galileo Galilei (1564–1642) who was accused by a Vatican committee of advocating for a sun-centered universe, and that in 1925 of John Thomas Scopes who was accused in state court of teaching evolution in a Tennessee public school. Yet much of what is popularly assumed about these trials is so oversimplified and the persons involved so caricatured as to be misleading when applied to the wider discussion.

A second influence concerns the various Christian pieties. Some believers accept life as it comes and teach that suffering is inevitable. Pain is God's punishment for sin, and Christians must accept and endure pain, rather than work to eliminate it. For these Christians, scientific investigation is not welcomed, since they see no need for it. For example, it was usual until the mid-nineteenth century that Christian physicians refused to give pain medication to women in labor, since labor pains were viewed as the price women had to pay for the sin of Eve. Such believers may dismiss any promise of medical advances, since they view science merely as a method of trying to play God. However, other Christians view scientific advances as led by a God who hopes to save humans, not only from sin, but also from disease and other forms of misery. Some recent theologians and hymn writers have described humans as **co-creators** with God. This difference in Christian pieties affects how believers respond to scientific discoveries or proposals.

co-creator = the human sharing with God in the ability to create

Fig. 11.3.

Thirdly, Christians interpret the Bible in different ways, and these differences affect discussions of Christian responses to science. For example, one story in the Old Testament about Israelite warfare reports that the leader Joshua needed more time to win the fray, and so he prayed to God to cause the sun to stand still: the added daylight ensured Israelite victory (Josh. 10:12-14). Five hundred years ago, many Christians interpreted this account as proving that the sun traveled around the earth and that God could manipulate the cosmos in answer to prayer. It is usual now for Christians to reject the first claim, but many hold in some degree to the second.

Some conservative Christian groups maintain as much as possible of the biblical worldview, while liberal Christian groups consider that many biblical descriptions of the world are no longer tenable. Most denominations maintain a middle position, saying "no" to God sitting on a throne in the sky, but "yes" to God being able to answer prayer. For some Christians, biblical accounts of miracles are treasured facts. They affirm that Jesus both walked on water

Fig. 11.4. A 1445 painting by Giovanni di Paolo of creation and the expulsion from paradise. Christians do not agree whether to continue to perpetuate this imagery.

and rose from the dead. The accounts of miracles are essential to their belief system, since they argue that one must accept all the Bible's supernatural claims, or none. For other Christians, an early Christian tradition that described Jesus as conquering nature by stilling a storm meant to connect Jesus with the power of God, not to restrict contemporary scientific knowledge of the faithful. It is likely that these different Christians will respond in opposite ways to science.

What was the Christian involvement with science for the first 1600 years?

Both Judaism and Christianity are religions more of history than of nature. By this is meant that according to the Old and New Testaments, God acted most decisively through historical circumstances to save people who were in distressful social situations. However, both religions built upon earlier nature religions. For example, at Christmas Christians celebrate the historical birth of Jesus, but the date was fixed at the winter solstice because earlier religious practices had honored the lengthening of sunlight that begins towards the end of December. Yet especially biblical poetry celebrates a positive view of nature, and Judaism, in claiming the complete sovereignty of the one God, praised God as creator of the world. Because God is good, God's creation is also good.

Christians inherited this view of God's good creation. Historians of science view the basic Christian appreciation for nature as one essential impetus to the rise of science in the Western Christian lands. Furthermore, influenced also by Greek philosophy which described the creator, called the Unmoved Mover, as utterly rational, Christian theology accepted that the universe itself reflects God's rationality. The processes of the earth were not random, but showed forth the order and beauty of the Creator, and to learn more about the rational universe was to discover more about God. Christians were to use their God-given rationality to investigate the God-given rationality of the universe. Until the emergence in the nineteenth century of full-time scholars, nearly all study in the West of what was then termed "natural philosophy" was conducted by Christian clergy or members of the religious orders, and it was fully sponsored by church authorities.

Once again Augustine shines forth. Augustine believed in one God, who can be known through one truth. Any conflicts that believers encountered, any inconsistencies in matters of faith, needed to be systematically addressed using God's gift of reason. Augustine taught that God had established two methods of disclosure: nature and Scripture. These two had to agree, since there is only one God and God's one ultimate truth. In addressing this issue, Augustine proposed a "principle of accommodation": God's word conveyed the truth of salvation in the language and mental categories of those to whom it was spoken. That is, God accommodated revelation to the worldview of the hearers.

Thus, according to Augustine, whenever one's interpretation of the Bible conflicted with scientific knowledge, it is most likely the biblical interpretation that is wrong, since God is leading humans more and more into knowledge of divine truth through their study of science. Augustine was probably encouraged in this conviction by his personal experience. It was not until he encountered the metaphoric preaching of Ambrose that he was willing to accept Christianity, since his previous experience of listening to sermons that interpreted the Bible literally struck him as intellectually indefensible. Augustine wanted to ensure that Christianity could not be ridiculed as being unlearned. Faith was enhanced by rationality, which he considered to be God's unique gift to the human species. Augustine thus agreed with earlier theologians that Christians could not interpret the six days described in the first creation story as what we mean by "day." What is "a day," prior to the creation of the sun on "the fourth day"? Augustine speculated that God actually created the universe in one instant, and that the Scriptures accommodated this truth to the worldview of the ancient Israelites by means of the poetic order and beauty of Genesis 1.

> Now who is there possessed of understanding, that will regard the statement as appropriate, that the first day, and the second, and the third, in which also both evening and morning are mentioned, existed without the sun, and moon, and stars—the first day even without a sky?— Origen, c. 250[4]

Augustine's pattern of applying human reason to the study of science and the interpretation of the Bible was solidified in the massive life-work of Thomas Aquinas. The format that Aquinas used in his *Summa Theologiae* demonstrated human reason grappling with questions of faith, especially as these matters were complicated by scientific knowledge or contradicted by Greek philosophy. Aquinas laid out each position, and then offered his solution and its rationale. Aquinas affirmed that the Scriptures "deliver spiritual things to us beneath metaphors taken from bodily things. . . . The uneducated may then lay hold of them, those, that is to say, who are not ready to take intellectual truths neat with nothing else."[5] Theologians apply their reasoning to each matter under investigation, in seeking the coordinated single truth of the one God.

In summary, before 1600, Christian doctrine asserted the unity of knowledge in both Scripture and nature as revelations of God. Theologians assumed that rationality was God's gift to humankind and was to be used to reason out any perceived conflicts between science and faith; and the church of the West, especially through the educated religious orders, encouraged and sponsored scientific investigation of all kinds. However, after around 1600, the situation changed, and over the past four hundred years Christians have developed several different approaches to their encounter with science. Here is space to consider four current Christian positions on science and faith and several different responses that Christians give to those who reject the possibility of religious belief.

Since 1600, what have been four different Christian positions?

One position sees it as good that science corrects the erroneous worldview of earlier believers. According to this position, which follows Augustine's principle of accommodation, Christians align themselves with the religious faith of believers of previous centuries, but they say that the Scriptures did not speak in scientific categories to persons who could not understand such language. The Bible did not intend to teach science, and it cannot be approached as if it did. As Cardinal Baronius famously said in 1615, "The Bible teaches us how to go to heaven, not how the heavens go."[6] These Christians gladly accept scientific discoveries and substitute this knowledge for biblical descriptions of the universe, which were not and could not have been scientifically accurate.

One historical example of this position can be seen in the career of Galileo, whose use of the new technology of the telescope allowed him to see aspects of the cosmos unavailable to previous Christians. One of Galileo's arguments, modeled after Augustine, was that the Bible describes the universe as geocentric because that was how ancient peoples experienced the earth. They were not wrong in their faith in God, but they were in error concerning the heliocentric universe. His conflicts with some members of the Roman Catholic hierarchy concerning his scientific proposals were exacerbated by the situation brought about by the rise of Protestantism, during which time Roman Catholic authorities resisted or rejected claims made by any individual that conflicted with the church's official teachings. It took about a century for some church authorities in both Roman Catholicism and Protestantism to understand and accept the universe as heliocentric. This position, albeit practiced unsuccessfully by Galileo, is held by many of the world's contemporary Christians.

A second position holds that scientific discoveries actually strengthen Christian faith by showing believers more about God. This position is an intensely religious one. Seeing the universe as one of God's primary modes of revelation, these believers welcome any fact about the universe as demonstrating more of God's power and mercy. In the Book of Job, Job's doubts about divine justice are silenced when he encounters the magnificent wonders of the created universe (Job 38–41). Such believers see a mandate to study the nature of the universe, since such study shows forth more of the nature of God.

A historical example of this attitude is seen in the career of Johannes Kepler (1571–1630). A devout Lutheran, Kepler is renowned especially for having discovered that the orbits of the planets around the sun are elliptical, rather than circular. This discovery eliminated many mathematical quandaries experienced by other astronomers of his time. For Kepler, scientific discoveries were profound religious experiences, manifestations of the majesty of God. Despite numerous conflicts he experienced with both Protestant and Roman Catholic authorities, his study of what he termed the harmonies of the universe confirmed his faith in God. Using traditional Trinitarian language, he placed God the Father in the center of the universe, from whom all things have their being, God the Son on the surface of the sphere, and God the Spirit as its radii, connecting all with one another.[7]

One twentieth-century theologian who, like Kepler, recognized in scientific knowledge an ever-unfolding revelation of God, was the Jesuit priest Pierre Teilhard de Chardin (1881–1954). Teilhard's use of the idea of the Omega point, that to which the entire universe is headed, gave him a way to connect classic Christian eschatology with his study of paleontology. Teilhard wrote of "Christogenesis" as a step in human evolution. Teilhardian-minded Christians not only welcome scientific study and discovery, but encourage it, as a way to delve further into the mysteries of God.

A third position holds that because of the serious challenges that science poses to Christian doctrine, even basic Christian doctrines must be recast. Primary focus has been on the doctrine of creation. In the midst of the Romantic movement of the mid-nineteenth century, when especially poets wrote about nature in totally positive and even sentimental fashion, came Charles Darwin (1809–1882), who in 1859 published *On the Origin of Species*, and in 1871, *The Descent of Man*. Darwin's discoveries about species specialization and his suggestions about natural selection have become part of scientific theories concerning the evolution of the universe and the origins of the human species.

What particularly upset Darwin was the fact of the perpetual violence required within the natural world, since this contradicted the usual Christian teaching that God created earth as a paradise. An idea held by many nineteenth-century Christians, now called **Christian vegetarianism**, held that in God's original creation of paradise all species were vegetarian,

Christian vegetarianism = a belief that God created all animal species to eat only plants, with thus no deaths in paradise with the violence that arises with meat-eating a result of the human fall (Gen. 1:29-30). As a result of studying animal life, Darwin dismissed any such claims, asking instead how Christian faith could account for the immense amount of death that is necessary for the preservation of life within the evolving universe. Could the church continue to teach that God had created the earth as a paradise? Increasingly over his years of study, Darwin grew away from the scientifically conservative church and found Christian faith more difficult to accept.

On the most elementary level, many Christians know themselves to live within an evolving universe. Flu shots are annual events, since the flu virus evolves from year to year. This suggests that the world is not stable, conceived of and delivered whole from the mind of God. Many practicing Christians and theologians dealing with science now combine the discoveries about the evolution of the universe and humankind with their Christian faith, and sometimes this requires a change in Christian teachings. Currently, for example, the Roman Catholic Church teaches an acceptance of the evolution of the human species, granting only that God does give to each human a unique soul. Serious Christian proposals that recast Christian doctrine in accord with current scientific knowledge are found, usually not in regular preaching nor the secular media, but in the writings of Christian theologians, whose consideration of contemporary science may be beyond the knowledge-base of most Christian laypeople. Only gradually over the decades do these proposals enter into more accessible Christian conversation or finally church-sponsored statements of belief and practice.

The two thorniest challenges to Christianity posed by evolution are theological. The first is that an evolutionary process that began thirteen billion years ago and continues through the present into the future seems to minimize, if not nearly eliminate, the role of a beneficent Creator. The process of evolution might suggest that only chance and mutation are responsible for the universe, rather than the guiding hand of a good God. The second, and perhaps the one most psychologically troubling for many believers, is that the evolution of the human from earlier life forms replaces the biblical stories about humans as proceeding from a special act of creation. Thus the unique origin of the first humans can no longer be accepted as fact, and the hope for a supernatural life after death is seriously challenged.

Another example of a scientific proposal that poses serious challenges to Christian doctrine was the work of Sigmund Freud (1856–1939). His descriptions of the human as, like other animals, living with primal natural instincts, the strongest of which is sexual, have led some theologians to rethink how sin is described. Christians who accept to some degree the Freudian description of the evolved human must ask whether, as the Bible says, anger is a sin, or whether, as nature suggests, anger is a natural instinct necessary for survival. Is sexual desire sinful lust, or natural instinctual behavior?

The theological proposal called **panentheism** exemplifies the Christian pursuit of the complementarity of science and doctrine. According to panentheism, Christians need to mature beyond the idea of God residing somewhere outside the universe, on another level of reality. Instead, they might consider that the world is in God, but God is also more than the world. All that is not God has its existence within God. Such theologians have described the Trinity, Father, Son, and Spirit, as Transcendent, Incarnate, and Immanent.

panentheism = the religious view that sees the divine both in and beyond all things

A fourth position is held by those Christians who reject science. This reaction against the scientific discoveries of the last four hundred years can be seen in the Old Order Amish, who refuse to study science and who live without much that modern technology provides. In this way, their community need not address the challenges that science poses, since it attempts to reside only within the biblical worldview.

Yet it is not the steady doubling of the Amish population that is of increasing cultural interest. During the second half of the nineteenth century, many conservative Christians became alarmed by the proposals of critical biblical studies, which claimed that for example the Old Testament was not dictated by God or written by named authors, but was anonymously compiled in later centuries with those religious attitudes contemporary to the compilation. Largely in reaction to this type of biblical interpretation arose the movement now called fundamentalism. The term comes from *The Fundamentals*, the title of a series of pamphlets published from 1910 to 1915, which expressed conservative versions of traditional Christian doctrine. One of the primary fundamentalist claims is for biblical inerrancy, according to which the Genesis stories of creation are to be received as historical fact without any error. Other "fundamentals" of the faith include acceptance of the physical resurrection of Jesus, the virgin birth, and other biblical miracles. Fundamentalists reject the position of Augustine and Thomas Aquinas that reason is God's gift and must be used in considering religious matters, teaching instead that Christian truths are other than, and even opposed to, human reason.

Although this literalist method of biblical interpretation had never before been formally espoused by Christian theologians, it perhaps had been widely popularly believed, and it became and remains a primary framework for many

The Western classical concept of God as Creator has placed too much stress on the externality of the process—God is regarded as creating rather in the way the male fertilizes the female from outside. But mammalian females nurture new life within themselves and this provides a much-needed corrective to the purely masculine image of divine creation. God, according to panentheism, creates a world other than Godself and "within herself" (we find ourselves saying for the most appropriate image).—Arthur Peacocke[8]

contemporary Christians. The more fully this interpretative model is used, the more completely science must be rejected. Some fundamentalist theologians work to reconcile any apparent problems in the biblical text. Many Christians find that these explanations prove the truth of the Scripture, thus ensuring that their religious belief is the correct one, and their acceptance of it will indeed grant them salvation. Some fundamentalist Christians refuse to teach their children advanced science, and they work to define how science is taught in public schools.

How do Christians defend the Bible in view of scientific discoveries?

For some readers of the Bible, the ancient text is believable only to the extent that it is factual. Here scientific method, which seeks to discover and prove the factual nature of all things, is applied also to religious texts. The Deist Thomas Jefferson edited out of his version of the New Testament all supernatural events, all angels, all miracles, and Christ's resurrection. Jefferson saw Jesus as a teacher of morals, and everything else said about him in the Bible was unbelievable superstition that all enlightened persons should reject. In the opposite example of the application of this scientific method, radical fundamentalists believe that every biblical account is factually true. Historical accuracy is possible since God inspired the authors of Scripture.

All Christians have asserted that some of the Bible is factually true, for example, the life story of Jesus. However, since the second century, many theologians recognized that some parts of the Scripture are written in highly metaphoric language. The book of Psalms is a collection of poems, and early biblical exegetes saw lines such as "the Lord has established the world; it shall never be moved" (Ps. 93:1) as poetic statements of faith in divine providence, not as claims that there would never be earthquakes. Yet this passage was cited during the seventeenth century as biblical warrant to deny the movement of the earth around the sun. Christians thus have disagreed about which biblical statements are factual reporting, and which are metaphoric.

Many Christian denominations stand somewhere in the middle of this continuum. Most biblical exegetes see no religious difficulty in identifying some scriptural passages as factual and others as metaphoric. New Testament

Fig. 11.5. An anti-Darwin cartoon published in 1874

authors inherited traditions of poetic imagery from both their Jewish and Greco-Roman ancestors. In these literary traditions, a reference for example to a mountain may be a literal placement on a historic map, or it may be a metaphor for the human reach toward the divine. Biblical interpreters must judge when a biblical mountain refers to an actual mountain and when it denotes "a mountaintop experience." For some Christians, the poetic meaning is not less real than the factual. Indeed, it may be more existentially important for believers than would be factual reporting.

Genesis 6:15 gives the dimensions of the ark as 300 cubits by 50 cubits by 30 cubits, and the cubit was at least 18 inches long. On this basis, the volumetric carrying capacity of the ark can be calculated as at least the equivalent of that of 522 standard railroad stock cars. A standard stock car can transport 240 sheep, so that the ark could have carried at least 125,500 sheep. . . . The ark had to transport only land animals, of course, so that the mammals, birds and reptiles were essentially all that needed accommodations. . . . The Lord caused them to "come unto" Noah and the place of safety from the gathering storm. Once they were safely on board, lodged in their stalls, and properly fed, most of them very likely settled down for a long period of dormancy, or hibernation.—Henry M. Morris[9]

For some Christians, reading Genesis 1 as a poem written in about the sixth century before Christ causes them little or no religious dissonance. However, they must now clarify what is meant by praising God as Creator of a universe of both beauty and natural violence. For many Christians, Jesus' virgin birth is a central religious doctrine that they cannot imagine discarding, while other Christians consider the virginal conception and birth of Jesus as metaphor, borrowed from Greco-Roman religious legends. If the imagery of a miraculous birth indicates the unique connection between Jesus and God, the virgin birth can be seen, not as a gynecological fact, but as religious imagery about Jesus' relationship with God.

Some persons claim that religion requires faith, although science provides proof. Yet other persons counter that science itself is a belief system. Scientists engage in endless searches to expand knowledge, correct errors, and test propositions, and they rely on metaphoric language, for example "black holes," to express their discoveries. Scientists can carry on their tasks only because they "believe" in facts that cannot be proved and matter that cannot be seen. Christian theologians utilize the same mental exercises in a parallel search for truth. Thus, say some Christians, there is more similarity than difference between the two fields of human endeavor.

John Polkinghorne (b. 1930) is a prominent British theoretical physicist and respected Anglican priest whose prolific publications and many presentations describe religion and

If we and everything else that exists in the universe are matter, are body, then can we also speak of "the body of God"? What would it mean to extend the model to God, the creator and redeemer of the universe? . . . In this body model, God would not be transcendent over the universe in the sense of external to or apart from, but would be the source, power, and goal—the spirit—that enlivens (and loves) the entire process and its material forms.—Sallie McFague[10]

science as two avenues toward truth. Religious doctrine and scientific theory focus on two different aspects of the same reality. Polkinghorne is among the Christian scientists interested in the **anthropic principle**. The anthropic principle focuses on the extreme and absolute precision within the initial conditions of the universe that was required for human life to develop and thrive. Either, Polkinghorne says, there are countless other universes in which human life did not develop, or the astonishing coincidences in the evolution of this universe leads one to imagine a creator who foresaw the development of a species such as ours. Similar conditions conducive to life may exist on other planets. Polkinghorne advocates continual conversations between scientists and theologians, in what he considers their mutual search for truth.

What are some current controversial issues?

To indicate the complexity of the conversation between science and Christian doctrine and practice, here are some of the questions that currently engage Christian thinkers. Most Christian discussions of these matters are available through religious publishing houses, which tend to print those books that cohere with their own religious viewpoint. Thus the more one knows about the world of religious publishers, the more one can anticipate the content and direction of each argument.

Concerning cosmology: How did God create the universe? Does God control the universe? Is God still continuing to create? Where is God? (What does that question mean?!) What is the Christian interpretation of the Big Bang thirteen billion years ago? Would a universe thirteen billion years old suggest a greater or a lesser Creator?

Concerning geology: How old is the earth? For Christians, does it matter? What can Christians learn about God from the findings of archaeologists? What do hominid bones that are two million years old suggest about a God of majesty and mercy? How ought Christians to interpret all the dating that is found in the Old Testament? What do Christians mean by the Bible being the word of God? Is it appropriate that Christians

In most of Christian history, Adam was assumed to be both an actual individual and a representation of humanity. In the light of evolutionary biology, we can retain the latter but not the former. We must take this story seriously but not literally. Adam's story is Everyman's journey from innocence to responsibility and sin.—Ian G. Barbour[11]

anthropic principle = the precise combination of elements and timing required for the universe to accommodate conscious life

It is likewise this vision of God and the human person that makes Orthodox bioethics fundamentally different from all forms of profane or secular moral teaching. Orthodox bioethics has as its chief end to indicate the pathway that leads through the vicissitudes and temptations, the sufferings and joys of daily life, and into eternal participation in the life and glory of the Risen Christ.— John Breck[12]

who have different answers to these questions separate themselves out into their own denominations?

Concerning ecology: What are the facts about climate change? Are Christian ecofeminists correct in blaming male patterns of behavior for global climate change? What ought Christians to do about current ecological issues? Can there be a Green Christianity? What does it mean for Christians to experience God as present in water, bread, and wine? Is God also in rivers, trees, and alcohol? How ought contemporary Christians to interpret Genesis 1:28?

Concerning anthropology: When did the human species originate? What do contemporary Christians mean by "soul"? What is meant by humans having "the image of God"? Do only *Homo sapiens* have it? What is the relationship between humans and the rest of animate life? Will humans have some kind of life after their death? What kind? Where or when? What is a scientifically credible understanding of the two natures of Christ?

> Then we say that prayer which the Saviour delivered to his own disciples, saying, "Our Father, which art in heaven." They also are a heaven who bear the image of the heavenly, in whom God is dwelling and walking in them.—Cyril of Jerusalem[13]

Concerning biology: Ought every occasion of sexual intercourse be open to conception? When is contraception moral? Is it ever obligatory? Is in-vitro fertilization an appropriate recourse for infertile Christians? Can lesbian Christians undertake artificial insemination? Is surrogate motherhood open to Christians? Does choice concerning pregnancy and childbirth diminish or enhance Christian values about God's gift of life? At what point in fetal development ought a spontaneous miscarriage be treated as human death? When is elective abortion a Christian option? Are all organ transplants ethical for Christians? What about assisted suicide? When can physicians withhold treatment? Is disconnecting a life-support machine murder? For how long ought Christians keep alive a person who requires a ventilator? Can Christians ever welcome death, or must death always be fought against? Are some burial practices more Christian than others?

Concerning medical advances: When are medical interventions inappropriate for Christians? When if ever is genetic engineering supportable by Christians? What about stem cell research? Should Christians be vaccinated? Should the government require everyone to be vaccinated?

Concerning public policy: When can the government require of Christians participation in a health-related practice of which they disapprove? Who should pay for expensive medical care? How do other societies with either a large or a small Christian population handle these matters? Should Christian children be required to study science in school? What about the many teachers who, to avoid controversy, skip certain chapters in science textbooks? How ought differing groups of Christians treat one another in the course of such public debates?

Let these many questions function as the summary of a chapter about the complexities of the centuries-old and ongoing conversation between science and Christian faith.

Suggestions

1. Review the chapter's vocabulary: anthropic principle, belief, Christian vegetarianism, co-creator, panentheism, process theology, supernatural, theory.

2. According to Whitehead's process theology, there is no supernatural. Lay out the parameters of religion if there is no supernatural.

3. Present arguments for and against stem cell research as a Christian-approved method of medical research. In preparation, consult the current published positions of several different churches.

4. Choose one of the questions listed in the final section of the chapter, and compare the positions of at least three different Christian authors, for example, a Roman Catholic, a liberal mainstream Protestant, and a conservative evangelical Protestant. Who is authorized to determine the Christian response to science?

5. Write a personal essay about the traditional Christian doctrine that humans have "the image of God." What do you think this means? Did Neanderthals have it? Do trained service-dogs have it? Do you have it?

6. Discuss the following miracles as recorded in the Gospel of Mark, written in about 70 CE: Jesus heals a man who has an unclean spirit (Mark 1:21-28); Jesus stills a storm at sea (4:35-41); Jesus raises a dead girl to life (5:21-24, 35-43); Jesus feeds five thousand people with five loaves and two fish (6:30-44); Jesus appears with Moses and Elijah (9:2-8); and Jesus is raised from the dead (16:1-8). How might Christians interpret these stories?

7. Read and discuss William Hoffman's short story "The Question of Rain,"[14] in which a liberal Protestant minister is pressured during a drought to lead Sunday prayers for rain.

8. For a major project, read and write a report on Mark Salzman's novel *Lying Awake*,[15] in which a contemporary contemplative nun discovers

that her extraordinary spiritual visions are arising out of her epileptic condition, and she must decide what medical route to follow.

9. View the 2009 film *Agora*, a historical drama based on the antagonism in the fourth and fifth centuries between the Christians of Alexandria, Egypt, and the pagan mathematician and astronomer Hypatia. The conflicts led to her murder in 415. Consult historians concerning the involvement of Bishop Cyril of Alexandria in the events depicted.

For Further Reading

Armstrong, Karen. *The Case for God.* New York: Anchor Books, 2009.

Barbour, Ian G. *Religion and Science: Historical and Contemporary Issues.* Rev. ed. San Francisco: HarperOne, 1997.

Ward, Keith. *The Big Questions in Science and Religion.* 2nd ed. W. Conshohocken, PA: Templeton Foundation Press, 2008.

What do Christians say about religious truth?

12

Fig. 12.1. Feathers adorn the cross that marks a Christian First Nations grave in Canada. In many tribes of Native Americans, the eagle is the animal most closely associated with the wisdom and power of the Creator. Eagle feathers are treasured, given as signs of accomplishment and long important in traditional Indian religion.

◇ An answer from a scholar

British-born philosopher John Hick (b. 1922) has been acclaimed one of the most eminent philosophers of religion of the twentieth century. Conversant with various forms of Christianity and learned in other **world religions**, Hick faced the philosophical dilemma of religious truth in the current time: How can devout persons of all the different world religions claim that their religion is true? How can people take seriously the claim that their own religion is the only true one? Is the only solution that all religions are false? But how then could one account for the vast realms of religious experience and their effects on human life? Hick judged that most attempts to make world religions mutually compatible are intellectually shallow, since religions in Eastern and in Western traditions do not agree about even what religion is. In his many influential publications and his participation in **interfaith** dialogues, Hick proposed a philosophically oriented vocabulary to assist conversation about religion in the current time.

world religions = religions that are present throughout the world, usually listed as Indigenous Religion, Hinduism, Buddhism, Confucianism, Taoism, Judaism, Christianity, and Islam

interfaith/interreligious = including different world religions

The daily lives of humans are filled with concerns that are not of the deepest significance or the most enduring value, that is, are not ultimate concerns. But religions seek to encounter and describe the mystery of what is ultimate, what transcends that which is regular or transitory. To designate this ultimate reality, Hick proposed the term the **Real**. Religions are different ways to represent the Real. However, each of the primary world religions includes the acknowledgment that what religion describes is beyond human language and beyond human thought. Thus all descriptions of the Real are partial and inadequate, and, says Hick, equally close to and equally far away from the Real.

Real = for Hick, a philosophical term for ultimate reality, for what is of greatest importance

Truth claims are personally significant ways to describe one's encounter with the Real, and these encounters are historically determined and culturally influenced. Most people have been born into a religious culture, and its categories have shaped their minds and affections. In Western religions, the Real is experienced as a personal deity, called by various names, such as God, the Trinity, YHWH, and Allah. In Eastern religions, the Real is described as nonpersonal, for example as Brahman or Tao. To explain his position, Hick likened any absolutist religious claims to the ancient idea that all the universe revolved around the earth. He proposed instead that each religion, like each planet in a sun-centered universe, has its own journey, and its journey does not negate the path of other planets. Hick suggested that the authenticity of religious experience should be judged by the extent to which its adherents are transformed from natural self-centeredness to a new orientation centered in what is transcendent.

For Hick, the Real is transcategorical, that is, beyond our categories. But all experience, including the Real, is expressed by means of our categories. Thus some Christian theologians have taught that "God in Godself" is far beyond "God for us," that is, God as humans are capable of encountering. Yet the experience of "God for us" is genuine, even monumental within human life. Since humans cannot express the totality of the Real, religions employ metaphors for it. Hick, remaining a Christian, suggested that Jesus is a metaphor for one's experience of transcendent reality. Religious metaphors, even if literally false, are existentially true because they express the Real in pictures accessible to humans and capable of determining human behavior.

Using Hick, one can say that granting a world with competing religious claims, and granting the goal of religion marked by intellectual integrity, Christians ought to engage with other religions in conversation about their varied experiences of the Real. Christians can adhere to their faith while also acknowledging that Christianity is, like other world religions, only a partial picture of what is of ultimate value. Indeed, depending on the specifics of time and place, culture and language, Christians themselves have differed with one another, sometimes violently, in their descriptions of the Real.

> A mountain is experienced visually as smaller the further we are from it and larger the nearer we are. But the mountain itself cannot be said to be either large or small—these are relational terms. It is what it is, and it is experienced differently from the point of view of different perceivers. And the Real is what it is, but is experienced from the distinctively human point of view as benign or serendipitous. But friendly or hostile, benign or dangerous, are relational terms which do not apply to the Real an sich.—John Hick[1]

◈ Answers from the churches

If religion is a communal worldview about ultimate reality enacted in rituals and expressed through ethics, it is not surprising that many religious persons will hope, even demand, that their religion be true, or at least be true enough to be worth the effort. Here, the adjective "true" means totally consistent with reality, without error, basically correct, able to grant what it promises. The idea that one's own religion is true gives psychological comfort to millions of persons and has granted many communities social stability. Yet not all world religions make competing truth claims. Some religious traditions are not engaged in the kind of thought processes that lead to truth claims, and are contented to be **henotheist**. An example is evident in the original meaning of

henotheism = belief in one's own religion, without denying the validity of other religions the biblical first commandment: "You shall have no other gods before me" implies that despite the competition presented by Baal, Asherah, and other deities of neighboring tribes, the Israelites are to worship YHWH, rather than the other gods and goddesses.

In the twentieth century, some philosophers adopted a postmodern philosophical position. Although the modern world trusted that human reason would lead the species to a fuller acceptance of truth, postmodernism distrusts human reason, doubts that there is such a thing as a single truth toward which to aspire, and judges all values as being socially determined. According to postmodern thought, everything depends on one's point of view, and all knowledge and opinion are no more than interpretations that serve someone's desire for power. About religion, the postmodern says that if someone accepts Christ as the Savior, then that person is saved by this belief. However, Christ's salvation cannot be imagined as some ultimate truth that must be shared with others. Christ is not Truth for everyone since there is no such thing as truth for everyone.

However, historically, particularly adherents of monotheisms have indeed made competing truth claims, by asserting that their religion is truer than others. The great prophets of the exilic period of the Old Testament rejected their own people's earlier idea that other deities existed, asserting instead that there is only one God, whom the entire earth is to worship. Following this Jewish understanding, Christianity has historically asserted its own truth. Christian leaders have even authorized the executions of persons of other religions, deeming their very presence in society as dangerous to the public order and threatening for the faithful. This chapter surveys the current situation of Christianity's claims concerning religious truth, its own and that of other world religions.

Is Christianity the only true religion?

Over the millennia of human history, it was usually the case that everyone in one locale participated more or less willingly in the single communal religion. In many places in the past and still today in some parts of the world, this can be said also of Christians. People became Christians because they were born into Christian families and communities. Thus it is fair to say that many, perhaps most, of the Christians who have ever lived understood their religion to be the best religion, simply because it was the only religion they were aware of. The religion of their community, and only that one religion, formed their minds and directed their behavior.

As I wrote this book, I fought within myself, trying to make sure I wrote honestly about what was going on in my heart and mind. Parts of what you read here will probably seem somewhat inconclusive. That is because I am still unsettled about certain things myself. My faith journey is not complete, by any stretch of the imagination. Over the years, I have had to change opinions and beliefs that I once held with dogmatic fervor. Now, there are fewer and fewer things about which I am absolutely certain. However, I hold those things with an ever-increasing tenacity. And this one thing I do know, in accord with the apostle Paul, and that is Jesus Christ—crucified, risen, and coming again.—Tony Campolo[2]

Some people do become aware of other religious practices. This might be a medieval person encountering a different world religion in another country, or a contemporary American whose parents practice different religious traditions. Confronted with another pattern of religion, some people remain confirmed in the religion of their childhood, as if saying, This one religion is right, at least for me. The sense that a religion is chosen and maintained by personal preference has been called the **individualist** position. Such a focus on the individual believer has figured prominently in the history of missionary work, when for example a single member of a community accepted the Christian faith without any family or community support.

However, throughout the centuries, the idea that Christ is the truth was not grounded merely on the conviction of individuals who claimed to have achieved this truth. In many times and places, the church itself has taught the **exclusivist** doctrine that only Christians will be saved. Many passages in the Bible have been cited to support the exclusivist position. Two verses commonly quoted are, "Jesus said to him, 'I am the way, and the truth, and the life. No one comes to the Father except through me'" (John 14:6) and "If you confess with your lips that Jesus is Lord and believe in your heart that God raised him from the dead, you will be saved" (Rom. 10:9). What is called the **Great Commission**, "Go therefore and make disciples of all nations" (Matt. 28:19), is presented by one of the evangelists as Jesus' last words, his final instructions to his followers, and

> **individualism** = a position maintained by some Christians that salvation is granted to individual believers who are saved as a result of personal choice

> **exclusivism** = a position held by some Christians that only Christians will be saved

> **Great Commission** = from Matt. 28:19, a command for Christians to evangelize the whole world

As soon as you embark at the said islands you may summon the chiefs and Indians thereof . . . by all the ways and means you may be able to devise, that they should come into the knowledge of Our Catholic Faith. . . . And if after the aforesaid they do not wish to obey what is contained in the said summon, you can make war and seize them and carry them away for slaves.— King Ferdinand of Spain's instructions to the explorer Ponce de León, 1514[3]

Paul's letters and Luke's narratives in Acts urge that what was understood as the truth of salvation in Christ be shared with all peoples of the world. For exclusivists, religious practice that is not centered in Christ will not grant forgiveness of sins and reconciliation with God, and thus non-Christian religion cannot lead to salvation.

The epitome of the exclusivist position can be seen in the third-century theological claim, which in the thirteenth century became an official pronouncement from the Western church: *Extra ecclesiam nulla salus*, Outside the church there is no salvation. Only people convinced of the absolute truth of the faith can maintain this position. Such confidence led to the pattern of making Christianity the state religion, sometimes mandating that all persons living in the nation be baptized. The exclusivist position remains a core doctrine for some denominations, and it has been the fundamental underpinning to the missionary movement that works to convert all peoples to the truth of the Christian faith. Sponsored by home churches, countless missionaries, clergy and lay, teachers and health workers, have dedicated their lives to the task

Fig. 12.2. In Johann Valentin Haidt's 1747 painting, the native peoples of North America, newly converted to Christianity, are welcomed into heaven.

of preaching the gospel somewhere in the world, with the intent that those inhabitants will accept baptism and believe in the truth of Christ. Some contemporary Christians assert that only after everyone on earth has heard the gospel of Christ will God bring about the end of this world, after which a perfect existence in heaven will be enjoyed only by believers.

Some exclusivists refuse to participate in any interfaith prayer, since by their understanding only prayer that is offered in the name of Christ will be heard by God. Some fundamentalist Christian clergy discourage their members even from table-prayer with Christians of other denominations, whose theology is viewed as erroneous. No matter how salvation has been understood—eternal life of the immortal soul in heaven, resurrection from the dead at the end of time, a communal existence of shared purpose, a personal life freed from guilt—the exclusivist claims that Christ is the only truth towards these religious goals. For countless Christians over the ages, the primary reason to hold to the truth of Christianity has been the promise of a final reward in heaven. Increasingly, however, many Christians report that they do not fear hell. Many practicing Christians doubt that hell exists. Thus for these believers, one foundational reason for maintaining trust in Christ has been removed.

What is the inclusivist position?

Over recent centuries, an alternate position has developed. For some theologians, the ultimate truth of Christ's salvation embraces the lesser truths found in other religions. This is called the **inclusivist** position. For these people, it is inconceivable that God intends to save only Christians, who are a small minority of all humans. Especially when considering the tens of thousands of years of human life before even the development of monotheistic Judaism, the idea of inclusivism understands that the grace of God made manifest in the life, death, and resurrection of Jesus Christ is broad enough that it can include billions of people who have never heard of Christ.

inclusivism = a position held by some Christians that Christ's salvation can include also non-Christians

Thus, for example, when another religion offers persons a method of reconciliation, the inclusivist says that it is Christ who has activated this religious practice, even if the ritual and its symbols seem alien and do not mention Christ. It is almost as if these persons are Christian anonymously. This idea has been helpful to some believers. It gives Christian sanction for the pattern in many cultures of religious tolerance. According to inclusivism, Christians

Let us pray for those who
do not share our faith in
Jesus Christ: Almighty and
eternal God, gather into
your embrace all those
who call out to you under
different names. Bring an
end to interreligious strife,
and make us more faithful
witnesses of the love made
known to us in your Son—
part of a prayer for Good
Friday published in 2006[4]

Abrahamic = the three monotheistic   religions—Judaism,
Christianity, and   Islam—that
claim descent from Abraham,
who lived in the ancient Near
East perhaps in about 1800 BCE

can harmoniously live alongside non-Christians since the church can trust that Christ's mercy already is reaching out to all people. Inclusivist Christians need not argue the truth of their faith over against that of their non-Christian neighbors. However, inclusivism has been rejected by some members of other world religions, for whom this idea seems to suggest that they are to be considered somehow Christian without their consent or even despite their beliefs.

What about the other Abrahamic religions?

It might seem that the world religions that are most likely candidates for such inclusivism are the other **Abrahamic** religions, Judaism and Islam. Churches acknowledge that Christianity is directly descendant from Judaism and that Jesus was Jewish. Judaism and Christianity share many fundamental religious tenets: there is one good creator God; this God cares for earth and its people; God expects exemplary behavior, and yet offers sinners forgiveness; God speaks through a holy book; people ought to assemble regularly for worship; and despite human troubles, God promises a good end to all things. Yet often it is siblings or cousins who, because they are so close, can quarrel most fiercely over those issues that distinguish them. Indeed, the history of Christian relationship with the Jews has been fraught with difficulties from the beginning.

Around 50 CE, Paul wrote that those Gentiles who believe in Christ are grafted onto the tree of Judaism. Here Paul is assuming that the primary

When we have to keep in mind both the necessity of Christian faith and the universal salvific will of God's love and omnipotence, we can only reconcile them by saying that somehow all men must be capable of being members of the Church; then it must be possible to be not only an anonymous "theist," but also an anonymous Christian. The expressly Christian revelation becomes the explicit statement of the revelation of grace which man always experiences implicitly in the depths of his being.—Karl Rahner, SJ[5]

community that is saved by God is Jewish, but through Christ, Gentiles can become attached to the chosen people of the Jews. If this attitude had been maintained, Christians would have proceeded in deepest respect for Jews and for their historic connection with God. But already the New Testament demonstrates that the Jews who accepted Jesus as the Messiah grew increasingly antagonistic against those Jews who did not. By 80 CE, Matthew describes the Jews as being guilty for the execution of Jesus, and by the year 100, the Gospel of John shows an attitude far different from that of Paul. "The Jews" is the

Fig. 12.3. A book by three women, one a Muslim, one a Christian, and one a Jew, inspired others to undertake interfaith conversation.

phrase repeatedly used by the fourth evangelist to label those who are enemies of Christian believers.

In the second century, Christian theologians who argued the truth of their faith contrasted their beliefs with those of other religions, and in so doing they castigated both pagans and Jews for their refusal to accept Christ. Over the centuries, condemnation of the Jews grew more and more virulent. Perhaps one contributing factor was that after the fourth century, pagans no longer presented a religiously viable option in the areas where the theologians lived, and so it was the Jews who remained.

Several social conditions contributed to the intensification of Christian prejudice against the Jews. Christians accepted for themselves the regulation in the Old Testament that believers ought not charge one another interest in a loan, and thus the Jews became the European bankers and were despised for their financial success. Jewish attempts to maintain their own distinctive lifestyle was repellent to many medieval people who had little experience in dealing with diversity of any kind. Jews were not considered full citizens of those European countries that maintained Christianity as a state religion. Psychologists have suggested that humans find it convenient to blame someone beyond themselves for their troubles, and Jews got the blame for events such as the Black Plague. A particularly anti-Semitic prayer, which became standard in the Latin liturgy for Holy Week, referred to the Jews as "perfidious." The Holocaust Museum in Washington, D.C., presents evidence of those Christian attitudes and actions toward the Jews during the early part of the twentieth century that could accommodate, even plan and execute, the murder of millions of Jews, and this within ostensibly Christian countries.

In the decades since World War II, many theologians and churches, regardless of their opinions about religious truth, have attempted a new way forward toward reconciliation between Christians and Jews. Some theologians rediscovered Paul's understanding that the faithful God continues to honor the biblical covenant with the Jews. Interfaith conversation between Christians and Jews is growing. Some Christians are encouraging occasions for interfaith prayer, since inclusivists suggest that Judaism provides the best example of another world religion that is included in God's grace. Joint prayer sessions between Christians and Jews often utilize texts from the Psalms, the religious poems from the Tanakh which Christians are accustomed to using in their own worship.

One politically controversial connection between some Jews and some Christians concerns the State of Israel. Some conservative evangelical Christians, because of their interpretation of the Book of Revelation, enthusiastically

Fig. 12.4. Some Jews remain Jewish, by keeping Sabbath and maintaining kosher, yet also believe in Jesus as their messiah.

support the expansionist land claims of the State of Israel, because they believe that the return of the Jews to Jerusalem is a precondition for the return of Christ to earth, which these Christians gladly anticipate. Part of this proposal anticipates that a majority of Jews will convert to Christianity to await the coming of Christ. Yet other Christians reject this interpretation of Revelation and speak against any policies of the State of Israel that have harmed the Palestinian people. Christians worldwide do not agree on how to distinguish Judaism as a religion and the State of Israel as a nation. Indeed, any conversation between Christians and Jews needs to clarify whether the noun "Jew" is referring to a person practicing the religion of Judaism, a person who is ethnically Jewish, or a resident or supporter of the State of Israel.

The interfaith relationship between Christians and Muslims has been nearly as problematic as that between Christians and Jews. Developing historically as the third great monotheistic world religion, Islam shares many of its basic religious ideas with Judaism and Christianity. The Qur'an of Muslims includes narratives of ancient characters that are found also in the Jewish Tanakh and the Christian Bible. Yet because of the history of Muslim nation-states, some Muslim leaders and some Christian rulers have engaged in horrific military conquests of each other, a situation that has no parallel with the Jews, since until 1948 there was no Jewish state. Because of periodic wars and crusades, benign relationship between the two religions has been minimal. However, as more and more Muslim people immigrate to predominantly Christian countries, interaction between the two religions is increasing.

During the nineteenth century arose the notion that religion was fading away from human concern. This naïve secularist suggestion has been exploded by the fierce dedication to one's own religious truth that is evident in the rise of fundamentalisms. Fundamentalist religious movements maintain that theirs is the only true religion, some asserting that the world would be better off if other religions were expunged. The late twentieth century saw in Islam the same intensification of a fundamentalist spirit as was evident in Christianity. Some Muslim fundamentalists have expressed themselves in small groups who, without the overt support of any state, undertake terrorist attacks on Christians. Thus the twenty-first century presents new situations of misunderstanding and conflict between Christians and Muslims, over against which some Christian theologians are attempting to encourage peaceful interfaith conversation.

What is the pluralist position?

Granting a smaller world, in which persons of many persuasions live as neighbors and deal with each other across the globe as fellow consumers, yet another Christian position is marked by the claim of **pluralism**. According to this idea, even though there have been and are in the present some religions that do more harm than good, that promulgate more nonsense than truth, with some groups not even deserving to be classed as religion, at least the major world religions all offer equally valid paths toward salvation.

pluralism = a position held by some Christians that many religions can be true

The Parliament of the World's Religions, which met in Chicago in 1893, was the first formal gathering of representatives of both Eastern and Western religious traditions. It awakened many people to the earth's religious diversity, and it provided an impetus to pluralists to see their way as the only way forward.

The pluralist position is the more accessible when less is made of life after death, since with some world religions claiming individual life after death and others not, both cannot be true. Yet to the extent that religion seeks more profound and wholesome life for human communities, pluralists see that quite different religions can effectively meet these goals. Each religion must be examined, not from outside, from the standpoint of a different religion, but rather from within itself. Pluralists stress the differences, not the similarities, among world religions, and thus reject the notion that religions compete with one another. The world religions are irreconcilable with another. Each religion is unique, and people must beware of facile comparisons that are based on inadequate or faulty knowledge. To encourage interfaith dialogue, some

Fig. 12.5. This fourteenth-century painting by Giotto depicts the legend of Francis of Assisi coming in peace to visit Sultan Malik al-Kamil during the Crusades in 1219.

Christian preachers have cited the odd biblical narrative in which Jesus stands corrected by a non-Jewish Canaanite woman (Matt. 15:21-28).[6] If Jesus benefited by correction from a nonbeliever, so might everyone else.

Some Christians hesitate to support interfaith overtures because the efforts seem to diminish the urgency to evangelize for their own faith. However, Christians convinced by the pluralist position strongly advocate for interfaith dialogue. They maintain that persons of faith need to listen to those of other faiths, one result of which will be a more profound religious understanding for each participating faith. The twentieth-century American Cistercian monk Thomas Merton was an influential early promoter of interfaith dialogue, in his case through the world's monastic communities. Merton said that Christianity and Buddhism did not compete with one another, but instead offered totally

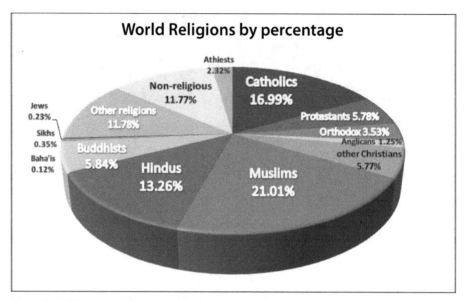

Fig. 12.6. The term "primal faiths" groups those indigenous religions practiced in their original geographical area and ethnic situation.

different ways of being religious, and so he suggested that some Christians practice not only their own faith, but also Buddhism. Merton asserted that his Christianity was deepened by his years of careful attention to the monasticism of other world religions.

The political scientists Robert Putnam and David Campbell have recently written that the United States is marked by a high degree of religious plural-ism.[8] All the major religions and countless minor ones flourish among its residents, and there is both a high degree of religious practice and a high degree of religious tolerance. Putnam and Campbell suggest that this climate of plu-ralism, in which many, if not most, Americans avoid any overt criticism of other religions, has come about in part because of the high rate of interfaith marriages and a high rate of persons switching from one denomination or reli-gion to another. These data indicate that even a majority of members of those Christian denominations whose clergy assert exclusive truth are themselves personally pluralists. It is as if the pluralist situation in the United States has brought about a pluralist answer to the question about Christian truth.

What is the syncretist position?

One more variant in the inquiry about Christian truth is espoused by syncretism. For the syncretist Christian, beliefs, symbols, and rituals from other religions can blend together with those of historic Christianity. The result, far from causing any intellectual or spiritual difficulty, births a religion of greater truth. The most fully developed example of religious syncretism has been Bahá'i, a religion arising in 1844 that intentionally combines beliefs and practices of other world religions, with the express hope of presenting a religion that could encompass all the world's peoples and thus bring an end to competing religious claims. Living in a pluralist world has encouraged some Christians along this path. Many syncretist Americans, for example, in families in which one partner is Jewish and the other Christian, celebrate both Hanukkah and Christmas. Probably in some such situations, the questions of religious truth are not addressed; instead, the values of various religious symbols and rituals are practiced.

Yet syncretism among Christians is not only a result of interfaith marriages. Throughout Christian history, in some situations in which Christianity was introduced, the existing indigenous religion was brutally stamped out. Yet in other situations, the traditional religion was blended into the faith brought by the missionaries. For example, some Christians of Native American descent include a Corn Ceremony in their liturgical year. "We're Catholics because Mary is the Corn Mother," said a young Native American guide to visiting tourists, in a clear expression of syncretism. The Hispanic Christians for whom a **Quinceañera** includes a celebration of Christian Eucharist is another example. Some vibrant forms of African Christianity include so many non-Christian beliefs and practices that their status as Christian has been contested.

Certainly the majority of people who practice a religion are not engaged in the intellectual pursuit of religious truth. However, a serious academic study of Christianity must attend to this question, since by its very definition, monotheism raises the issue of truth. Is there one God? Who says? What does this belief imply for its adherents as well as for the outsiders? However, as with many other issues, Christians disagree with one another both about the truth of their faith and about the very existence of religious truth. For some Christians who think about these questions, Christ is Truth, the only Truth that saves. For inclusivists, Christ saves even non-Christians. For pluralists, Christ is one of many ways toward truth. For syncretists, truth combines different

> Pluralism is not the kind of radical openness to anything and everything that drains meaning from particularly. It is, however, radical openness to Truth—to God—that seeks to enlarge understanding through dialogue. Unless all of us can encounter one another's religious visions and cultural forms and understand them through dialogue, both critically and self-critically, we cannot begin to live with maturity and integrity in the world house.—Diana Eck[7]

Quinceañera = celebration of a girl's fifteenth birthday, historically including a blessing of her future fertility

Fig. 12.7. Among the Yaqui Christians of Mexico and Arizona, the deer dancer from the people's traditional nature religion celebrates the risen Christ at Easter.

religious proposals in a greater search for truth. For postmodern Christians, there is no truth toward which to search.

Suggestions

1. Review the chapter's vocabulary: Abrahamic, exclusivism, Great Commission, henotheism, inclusivism, individualism, interfaith/interreligious, pluralism, Quinceañera, Real, world religions.

2. Hick proposes that the validity of a religion can be tested by whether its adherents demonstrate a transformation from self-centeredness to concern for others. Propose examples of the difficulty of this as a religious test.

3. Present arguments for and against the proposal that truth is an outmoded concept that is no longer useful in the world.

4. Examine the origin, beliefs, and practices of the Church of Jesus Christ of Latter-Day Saints, also called the Mormons.

5. Write a personal essay in which you present your philosophical preference for one of the Christian positions described in this chapter.

6. In the Bible, contrast 1 John 4:1-6 with Acts 17:16-32, concerning Christian attitudes and approaches to other religions.

7. Read and discuss the short story "The Man to Send Rain Clouds" by Leslie Marmon Silko,[9] in which a burial on a reservation demonstrates the syncretistic practices of some Native American Roman Catholics.

8. For a major project, read and write a report on the 1994 novel *Knowledge of Angels* by Jill Paton Walsh.[10] In Walsh's narrative, a man from a society with freedom of religion who espouses no religion is being judged by medieval Christian theologians. A wild child—a girl who was raised by wolves—is used to test the theory that knowledge of God is inherent in humans, and thus atheism could rightly be considered a capital crime.

9. View and discuss the 2010 film *Of Gods and Men*, about the 1996 murder by Islamic terrorists of seven Cistercian monks who ministered to a Muslim community in Algeria. Cistercians vow never to leave their original community: Ought these monks to move away from danger? One monk who finally was martyred said to his superior about his Christian faith, "I don't know if it is true anymore. I pray, and I hear nothing."

For Further Reading

Eck, Diana L. *Encountering God: A Spiritual Journey from Bozeman to Banaras.* Boston: Beacon, 1993.

Numrich, Paul D. *The Faith Next Door: American Christians and Their New Religious Neighbors.* New York: Oxford University Press, 2009.

Smith, James K. *Who's Afraid of Postmodernism? Taking Derrida, Lyotard, and Foucault to Church.* Grand Rapids: Baker Academic, 2006.

Conclusion: Why continue studying Christianity?

Fig. Concl. 1. In Jean Bellegambe's 1520 *Mystical Bath*, believers are bathing in a font filled with the blood of the crucified Christ.

What more is there to learn about Christianity?

What Is Christianity? has been only a foundational study of Christianity. For some students, it serves as a springboard from which to dive into deeper study of the Christian religion. This conclusion suggests ways to pursue more knowledge about Christianity.

In the present time, when images are recognized as fundamental to human cognition, there is much to learn about and from Christian images. For example, one might ask why a sixteenth-century artist would show believers at the foot of the cross romping in a Jacuzzi filled with Christ's blood, and whether the artist's sponsors were pleased with this depiction of the crucifix. There are countless unique depictions of the crucifix, which is only one of many images with religious meaning for Christians. Courses in art history and art appreciation can have lifelong value.

Each chapter began with attention to the field of the phenomenology of religion. Many phenomenologists consider not only Christianity, but also other world religions. Courses in this field of study might be offered by the undergraduate philosophy or the religious studies department.

Having studied chapter 1, students may wish to learn more about the Bible: how it was written, how it has been translated, how it is interpreted by various Christian preachers, what it means to individual believers, and how it is used by different Christian groups. Courses in Bible abound.

Having studied chapter 2, students may want to learn more of what Christianity says about God, how the teachings developed, what contemporary theologians are writing, and how theology relates to what is popularly believed. For this study, theology courses are available.

Having studied chapter 3, students may be interested in Christology. What did each century of Christian theology add to the accumulated understanding of Jesus of Nazareth? What do contemporary theologians say about who Jesus was? Is Jesus the same as Christ?

Having studied chapter 4, students might want to understand more fully how the church functions, since the Spirit usually pushes believers into community. Can an individual be Christian without participation in the church? Courses in ecclesiology and the sociology of religion may be available.

Having studied chapter 5, students may take a course in the psychology department about how various spiritualities become central in the lives of different Christians. What accounts for the choice of one's denomination? Why do people change denominations?

Having studied chapter 6, students may wish to attend some Christian worship services, in order to compare and contrast what happens in churches with what the textbook says. Live worship can be contrasted with the Christian worship events that are televised every Sunday morning. Since worship involves attention to symbol, students may wish to take a humanities course that examines how symbols function for individuals and communities.

Having studied chapter 7, students may wish to take more history courses. Very little occurs within human history without some small or great connections with religion. Most students have insufficient understanding of the role religion has played in American history. Recent publications deal with women as much as with men, the average people as well as with the famous names, social history as well as political history.

Having studied chapter 8, students may be interested in reading some of the great spiritual classics that were penned by eminent Christians. A course in Christian classics might be offered either in the university's religion department or its literature department. Biographies of saints might be characterized by either pious praise or critical judgment.

Having studied chapter 9, students may want to take a political science course that investigates some of the current controversies concerning the role of religion in government. Are any religious issues on the current docket of Supreme Court? How did religion enter national debate during the last presidential election?

Having studied chapter 10, students may wish to address ethical questions about sexuality. Religion courses may consider different denominational beliefs. Biology courses may deal with sexuality issues. More knowledge about Christian attitudes toward sexuality may help when evaluating how believers are depicted in popular novels and films.

Students may choose to investigate any of the questions at the close of the chapter 11. Especially those majoring in one of the sciences or those preparing for a career in healthcare will want to know how Christians of all kinds address these socially divisive questions. An educated person needs to know more about how science and religion interact around the world.

Having studied chapter 12, students may be interested in taking a philosophy of religion course that examines the idea of truth. Learning about other of the world's religions will assist anyone interested in pursuing a career in journalism or international relations, or indeed, in getting along with one's neighbors.

What is Christianity? It takes more than one textbook to answer this question.

Fig. Concl. 2. This probably early third-century graffiti, found inscribed on a wall in Rome, ridicules Christianity with the words "Alexamenos worshiping his God."

Suggestions

1. Interview three people who had some affiliation with Christianity but no longer practice the religion. Ask why. Analyze their comments in light of what you have learned.
2. Interview three people who are devout practicing Christians. Ask them what they get out of their faith and what they put into it.
3. Visit Sunday worship services of three different Christian denominations. Describe what you encounter using correct vocabulary. Compare and contrast the experiences.

4. Attend worship services at a synagogue or a mosque, or visit a Hindu temple or a Buddhist meditation center. Compare and contrast this event with Christian worship.

5. Read more of the Bible. Use a study Bible that includes helpful annotations.

6. Read any book listed in the Bibliography, and write a report in which you cite something in this textbook.

7. Watch all the suggested films. Chapter 8 includes a number of suggestions. Here are more films to add to the list: *A Month in the Country, Chocolat, Edges of the Lord, Elmer Gantry, The Gospel of John, Green Pastures, Higher Ground, Jesus Christ Superstar, Les Misérables, The Mission, Places in the Heart, Second Chance, Shadowlands, Tender Mercies, We Have A Pope,* and *Winter Light.* Several worthwhile documentaries are: *Into Great Silence* (2007), *Jesus Camp* (2006), *Let the Church Say Amen* (2002), *Mine Eyes Have Seen the Glory* (2006), *The Monastery: Mr. Vig and the Nun* (2006), and *Weapons of the Spirit* (1987).

8. A recent book delineated what many American youth understand their Christian faith to be, a belief that has been called Moralistic Therapeutic Deism:[1] (a) A god exists who created and orders the world and watches over life on earth; (b) God wants people to be good, nice, and fair to each other, as taught in the Bible and by most world religions; (c) the central goal of life is to be happy and feel good about yourself; (d) God is not involved in my life except when I need God to solve a problem; and (e) good people go to heaven when they die. Comment on this creed in light of this textbook.

CHRONOLOGY: WHAT ARE SOME SIGNIFICANT DATES IN CHRISTIAN HISTORY?

BCE	(Before the Common Era)
c. 1800	life of Abraham
c. 1250	covenant at Sinai and Israelite settlements in Palestine
1000	kingdom of Israel under King David
750–540	the preaching of the prophets
587	Babylon conquers Jerusalem and destroys the temple
537	the exiled Jews return to Jerusalem and repair the temple
470–322	Greek philosophers (Socrates, Plato, Aristotle) active in Athens
63	Roman Empire conquers Palestine and captures Jerusalem
37	the temple rebuilt again by puppet King Herod
c. 4	birth of Jesus of Nazareth
CE	(Common Era)
c. 27	Jesus of Nazareth preaches, heals
c. 30	Jesus executed by crucifixion
c. 36	name "Christian" first used in Antioch in contemporary Syria
46–57	Paul's missionary journeys
46–60s	Paul writes epistles, the earliest New Testament literature
48	Council of Jerusalem decides for Gentile mission
64–68	periodic persecutions begin under Emperor Nero; deaths of Paul and Peter
c. 70	Gospel of Mark written
70	temple destroyed, and church no longer centered in Jerusalem

c. 80	Gospel of Matthew written
c. 90	Gospel of Luke written
90	canon of Jewish Scriptures, the Tanakh, determined
93	persecutions under Emperor Domitian
c. 100	Gospel of John written
100–150	remaining books of New Testament written
100–200	noncanonical gospels written
120–220	the Apologists write reasoned explanations of Christian belief
144	Marcion excommunicated for rejecting Old Testament use
150	Justin writes to Emperor description of Christian worship
190	controversy over the dating of Easter
200–250	refutations of Christian heresies written
258	the deacon Lawrence martyred
285	Antony of Egypt, father of monasticism in East, becomes desert hermit
285	Roman Empire divides into Western and Eastern empires
301	Armenia becomes first Christian state
303–312	Great Persecution under Diocletian, churches destroyed, Scriptures burned
313	Emperor Constantine legalizes Christianity in Edict of Milan
324	Eusebius writes first church history
325	Council of Nicea decides for the divinity of Jesus
335	Emperor's mother Helena founds sacred sites and church buildings in Holy Land
370s	three Cappadocian Fathers further develop doctrine of the Trinity
387	baptism of Augustine, who becomes the preeminent Western theologian
380	Emperor Theodosius I declares Christianity the sole state religion
c. 380	Egeria records pilgrimage to Holy Land
390	Bishop Ambrose of Milan excommunicates the emperor for ordering a massacre
397	Council of Carthage ratifies New Testament canon as we know it
c. 398	Augustine writes *The Confessions*

405	Jerome translates Bible into Latin
431	Council of Ephesus decides title for Mary "mother of God"
432	Patrick arrives in Ireland as missionary
451	Council of Chalcedon decides one person with two natures of Christ
476	end of Roman Empire in the West
527	Constantinople, the Eastern imperial capital, enacts anti-Jewish laws
529	Benedict formulates Rule for Western monasticism
529	Council of Orange condemns Pelagius's teachings
600	Pope Gregory reforms liturgy and begins absolutist claims
632	death of Muhammad
638	Muslim Arabs capture Jerusalem
680	Sixth Council of Constantinople names pope as head of Christianity
726	beginning of iconoclastic controversy in Eastern Orthodox Church
c. 785	Roman Rite for worship established
800	Charlemagne crowned by pope as emperor of Holy Roman Empire
863	Cyril and Methodius translate Bible and liturgy into Slavonic
988	Orthodox Church established in Russia by Vladimir of Kiev
993	first formal canonization of a saint by pope
1054	Great Schism between Orthodox and Roman Catholic churches
1070	Canterbury becomes primary bishopric in England
1098	Anselm of Canterbury constructs the substitutionary theory of atonement
1099	First Crusade captures Jerusalem
c. 1150	Hildegard of Bingen begins her writings
1144	Second Crusade, called for by Bernard of Clairvaux, defeated by Muslims
1163	construction of Cathedral of Notre Dame in Paris begun
1189	Third Crusade

1202–1204	Fourth Crusade sacks the Eastern Christian city Constantinople
1206	Francis of Assisi begins life of poverty
1210	Chartres Cathedral begun
1212	Children's Crusade
1215	Fourth Lateran Council defines transubstantiation
1250–1430	women mystics writing their visions
c. 1263	Thomas Aquinas publishes scholastic theology
1302	Pope Boniface VIII claims universal jurisdiction of papal office
1309–1417	period of rival simultaneous popes
1314	Dante Alighieri writes *The Divine Comedy*
1347–1351	Black Death kills 40 percent of European population
1370	Catherine of Siena appeals for reform in papacy and among clergy
1396	John Wyclif completes translation of Bible into English
1400–1700	period of witch hunts and executions
1415	Council of Constance condemns Wyclif to be burned at the stake
1439	Council of Florence defines seven sacraments for Western church
1454	Gutenberg Bible first book printed in the West
1478–1834	Spanish Inquisition inaugurated to seek out Jews, Muslims, and heretics
1492	Jews and Muslims expelled from Spain
1494	pope divides lands in the Americas between Portugal and Spain
1500s	Roman Catholic mission to non-Western world
1508	Michelangelo paints the ceiling of the Sistine Chapel in Rome
1517	German reformer Martin Luther begins opposition to Western church practices
1519	Ulrich Zwingli begins Swiss Protestant reforms
1521	Emperor holds trial (Diet of Worms) of Luther; Luther is excommunicated
1530	Augsburg Confession agreement signed by some European Protestants
1531	date said to be the Mexican appearance of Mary to Juan Diego
1534	Luther's German translation of Bible published
1534	King Henry VIII breaks with Rome, establishes Church of England
1535	John Calvin establishes Protestant theocracy in Geneva

1536	William Tyndale's English translation of Bible printed; Tyndale burned
1536	Radical Reformation begins in Holland under Menno Simons
1540	Ignatius of Loyola founds Jesuit order to defend Roman Catholicism
1547	Roman Catholic Council of Trent condemns Protestantism
1559	Queen Elizabeth I issues Act of Uniformity in England
1572	Teresa of Avila experiences "spiritual marriage"
1583	Matteo Ricci, Jesuit missionary, arrives in China
1589	Orthodox patriarchy established in Moscow
1597	martyrs of Japan signal attempt to eradicate Christianity from Japan
1611	King James Version translation of Bible published
1618–1648	Thirty Years' War between Roman Catholics and Protestants in Europe
1620	pilgrims bring their Protestantism to Massachusetts Bay Colony
1632	Galileo charged with heresy for supporting Copernicus's theory of universe
1666	John Bunyan writes *The Pilgrim's Progress* (first part) while in prison
1666	Margaret Fell writes *Womens Speaking Justified*
1670	Philip Jacob Spenser founds Pietist movement
1682	Quaker William Penn establishes Pennsylvania with religious tolerance
1692	witch trials and executions in Salem, Massachusetts
1700s	Protestant missions to non-Western world
1721	Russian tsar Peter the Great declares church an arm of the state
1723	beginning of J. S. Bach's musical compositions for worship
1726	First Great Awakening in colonial America begins
1738	John Wesley begins inspired preaching that influences Methodist Church
1789	French Revolution enacts severe anti-church measures
1791	first amendment to U.S. Constitution ensures freedom of religion
1792	Second Great Awakening begins
1793	Jean Astruc publishes documentary hypothesis
1801	Cane Ridge, Kentucky, camp meeting

1843	Phoebe Palmer publishes *The Way of Holiness*
1853	Congregationalist Antoinette Brown first woman ordained into ministry
1854	Roman Catholic doctrine of the Immaculate Conception promulgated
1858	Bernadette Soubirous's visions of Mary in Lourdes
1869	Thomas Welch invents grape juice
1870	Roman Catholic doctrine of papal infallibility promulgated
1900	Boxer Rebellion in China martyrs 50,000 Chinese Christians
1903	Amy Carmichael publishes record of India mission work
1906	Azusa Street revival popularizes Pentecostal movement
1907	Walter Rauschenbusch pioneers the Social Gospel movement
1910	publication of *The Fundamentals* marks beginning of fundamentalism
1910	William Wade Harris establishes first independent African church in Liberia
1915–18	Armenian Christian Church nearly eradicated
1918	Vladimir Lenin attempts to eradicate Orthodox Christianity in Russia
1921	Kimbangu Church of Jesus Christ founded in Zaire
1925	Scopes "Monkey Trial" debates teaching evolution in American schools
1934	creation of Confessing Church in opposition to Nazi-sponsored church
1934–37	Josef Stalin attempts to eradicate Christianity in Soviet Union
1940	founding of Taizé community under Roger Schutz
1948	World Council of Churches established
1950	Roman Catholic doctrine of the Assumption of Mary promulgated
1950s	Billy Graham crusades cover the globe via person, radio, television
1954	"under God" inserted into U.S. pledge of allegiance
1962–65	Roman Catholic Second Vatican Council updates church practice
1966	Mao's Cultural Revolution attempts to eradicate Christianity in China
1968	*Humanae Vitae*, Roman Catholic encyclical denouncing birth control
1971	emergence of liberation theologians in Latin America
1979	Mother Teresa of Calcutta receives Nobel Peace Prize

1980	El Salvador's Archbishop Oscar Romero, advocate for social justice, assassinated
2003	consecration of Gene Robinson, first openly gay bishop in Anglican Communion
2015	university students continue to study Christianity

BOOK LIST: WHAT ARE SOME WORTHWHILE BOOKS WRITTEN BY CHRISTIANS?

The textbook includes quotations from many Christian books and cites others in the Suggestions. This chronological bibliography lists other worthwhile works written by Christians.

Autobiographies and Memoirs

Augustine. *The Confessions*. 398.
Kempe, Margery. *The Book of Margery Kempe*. c. 1435.
Woolman, John. *The Journal of John Woolman*. 1774.
Newman, John Henry. *Apologia Pro Vita Sua*. 1864.
Thérèse of Lisieux. *Story of a Soul*. 1898.
Schweitzer, Albert. *Out of My Life and Thought*. 1933.
Merton, Thomas. *The Seven Storey Mountain*. 1948.
Day, Dorothy. *The Long Loneliness*. 1952.
Wilkerson, David. *The Cross and the Switchblade*. 1962.
Nouwen, Henri. *The Road to Daybreak: A Spiritual Journey*. 1990.
McNamee, John P. *The Diary of a City Priest*. 1993.
Lamott, Anne. *Traveling Mercies: Some Thoughts on Faith*. 1999.
Miles, Sara. *Take This Bread: A Radical Conversion*. 2007.

Poetry and Literature

Romanos the Melodist. *Kontakia*. c. 550.
Dante. *The Divine Comedy*. c. 1320.
Chaucer. *The Canterbury Tales*. c. 1390.
John of the Cross. *The Dark Night of the Soul*. 1579.
Herbert, George. *The Temple*. 1633.

Milton, John. *Paradise Lost*. 1667.

Wesley, Charles. 6000 hymns. 18th century.

Lewis, C. S. *The Chronicles of Narnia*. 1949–1954.

Dillard, Annie. *Holy the Firm*. 1977.

LaHaye, Tim, and Jerry C. Jenkins. The Left Behind series. 1995–2007.

Norris, Kathleen. *Dakota: A Spiritual Geography*. 1993.

Spiritual Classics

anon. *The Cloud of Unknowing*. c. 1375.

Catherine of Siena. *The Dialogue*. 1378.

The Little Flowers of St. Francis. 14th century.

Julian of Norwich. *The Revelations of Divine Love*. c. 1400.

Kempis, Thomas à. *The Imitation of Christ*. c. 1420.

Luther, Martin. *Freedom of a Christian*. 1520.

Ignatius Loyola. *The Spiritual Exercises*. 1524.

Teresa of Avila. *The Interior Castle*. 1577.

Br. Lawrence. *The Practice of the Presence of God*. 1642.

Palmer, Phoebe. *The Way of Holiness*. 1845.

anon. *The Way of a Pilgrim*. 19th century.

Kierkegaard, Søren. *Fear and Trembling*. 1843.

Bonhoeffer, Dietrich. *Life Together*. 1939.

Nee, Watchman (Ni T'o-sheng). *The Normal Christian Life*. 1957.

Schmemann, Alexander. *For the Life of the World*. 1963.

NOTES

Introduction

1. Brian Hayden, *Shamans, Sorcerers, and Saints: A Prehistory of Religion* (Washington, DC: Smithsonian Books, 2003), 21.

2. Adolf von Harnack, *What Is Christianity?* Classic Reprints (Charleston, SC: Forgotten Books, 2009).

Chapter 1

1. Mircea Eliade, *Myth and Reality*, trans. Willard R. Trask (San Francisco: Harper & Row, 1963).

2. Ibid., 13–14.

3. All biblical citations in this text are from the New Revised Standard Version, published 1989.

4. *Sarah Morgan: The Civil War Diary of a Southern Woman*, ed. Charles East (New York: Simon & Schuster, 1991), 269.

5. *The Confessions of St. Augustine*, book 5, chapter 14, paragraph 24.

6. Henry M. Morris and Martin E. Clark, *The Bible Has the Answer*, rev. ed. (Green Forest, AR: Master Books, 1987), 8.

7. Marcus J. Borg, *Reading the Bible Again for the First Time: Taking the Bible Seriously but Not Literally* (San Francisco: Harper, 2001), 17–18.

8. Miriam Adeney, *Kingdom without Borders: The Untold Story of Global Christianity* (Downers Grove, IL: InterVarsity, 2009), 71.

9. Kwame Bediako, "Scripture as the Interpreter of Culture and Tradition," in *Africa Bible Commentary*, ed. Tokunboh Adeyemo (Grand Rapids: Zondervan, 2006), 3.

10. Marjorie Kemper, "God's Goodness," *Faith Stories*, ed. C. Michael Curtis (New York: Houghton Mifflin, 2003), 51–66.

Chapter 2

1. Rudolf Otto, *The Idea of the Holy*, trans. John W. Harvey (New York: Oxford University Press, 1958), 27.

2. Otto, 59.

3. *Meister Eckhart: The Essential Sermons, Commentaries, Treatises, and Defense*, trans. Edmund Colledge, O.S.A. and Bernard McGinn (New York: Paulist, 1981), 187.

4. Augustine, Sermon II on New Testament Lessons, par. 16. A translation available in *A Select Library of the Nicene and Post-Nicene Fathers*, ed. Philip Schaff (New York: Charles Scribner's Sons, 1903), VI, 263.

5. Leonid Ouspensky and Vladimir Lossky, *The Meaning of Icons*, trans. G. E. H. Palmer and E. Kadlowbovsky (Crestwood, NY: St. Vladimir's Seminary Press, 1982), 204.

6. Edward Rothstein, "Abraham's Progeny, and Their Texts," *New York Times*, October 23, 2010.

7. *Pseudo-Dionysius: The Complete Works*, trans. Colm Luibheid (New York: Paulist, 1987), 135.

8. Annie Dillard, *Holy the Firm* (New York: Harper & Row, 1977), 55, 58–59.

9. Catherine of Siena, Prayer 12, *The Prayers of Catherine of Siena*, ed. Suzanne Noffke, OP (New York: Paulist, 1963), 102.

10. Carmen Renee Berry, *The Unauthorized Guide to Choosing a Church* (Grand Rapids: Brazos, 2003), 58.

11. John Calvin, *Institutes of the Christian Religion*, 1, 1, 1.

12. Brian Wren, "How Wonderful the Three-in-One," *Bring Many Names: 35 New Hymns* (Carol Stream, IL: Hope, 1989), #22.

13. Andre Dubus, "A Father's Story," *God Stories*, ed. C. Michael Curtis (New York: Houghton Mifflin, 1998), 35–54.

Chapter 3

1. C. G. Jung, "The Concept of the Collective Unconscious," *The Collected Works of Carl G. Jung*, trans. R. F. C. Hull, vol. 9 (Princeton: Princeton University Press, 1959), 42–53.

2. Jung, "Concerning Rebirth," ibid., 120–21.

3. C. G. Jung, "Archetypes of the Collective Unconscious," ibid., 3–41.

4. Mechthild of Magdeburg, "The Flowing Light of the Godhead," *Beguine Spirituality*, ed. Oliver Davies (New York: Crossroad, 1990), 55.

5. www.jonathan-edwards.org/Sinners.html.

6. Augustine, *The Confessions*, book 1, ch. 6: 7–8.

7. See for example *Jesus at 2000*, ed. Marcus J. Borg (Boulder, CO: Westview , 1997).

8. Gustavo Gutiérrez, *We Drink from Our Own Wells*, trans. Matthew J. O'Connell (Maryknoll, NY: Orbis, 1984), 43, 50.

9. Thérèse of Lisieux, *Story of a Soul: The Autobiography of Saint Thérèse of Lisieux*, trans. John Clarke, OCD (Washington, DC: ICS Publications, 1996), 199.

10. For details about the Christological councils of the fourth and fifth centuries, see David F. Wright, "Councils and Creeds," in *Introduction to the History of Christianity*, ed. Tom Dowley (Minneapolis: Fortress Press, 2002), 164–86.

11. C. S. Lewis, *The Lion, the Witch and the Wardrobe* (New York: Macmillan, 1950), 132–33.

12. Tim LaHaye and Jerry B. Jenkins, *Left Behind: A Novel of the Earth's Last Days* (Wheaton, IL: Tyndale, 1995) and eleven subsequent volumes.

13. Mary Gordon, "The Deacon," *Faith Stories*, ed. C. Michael Curtis (Boston: Houghton Mifflin, 2003), 20–37.

Chapter 4

1. Émile Durkheim, *The Elemental Forms of Religious Life*, trans. Carol Cosman, abridged and ed. Mark S. Cladis (New York: Oxford University Press, 2001), 142.

2. Durkheim, 170–71.

3. Hannah More, *Practical Piety: Or the Influence of the Religion of the Heart on the Conduct of Life* (New York: The American Tract Society, 1811), 12.

4. Ambrose, "The Names of the Holy Spirit," *The Sunday Sermons of the Great Fathers*, ed. M. F. Toal (Chicago: Henry Regnery, 1959), III, 13.

5. John Calvin, *Institutes of the Christian Religion*, 3, 1, 1.

6. Charles Finney, *The Memoirs of Rev. Charles Finney* (New York: A.S. Barnes & Company, 1870), 18.

7. Francis of Assisi, "A Letter to the Entire Order," in *Francis and Clare: The Complete Works*, ed. Regis Armstrong and Ignatius Brady (New York: Paulist, 1982), 61.

8. Randall Balmer, *Mine Eyes Have Seen the Glory: A Journey into the Evangelical Subculture in America* (New York: Oxford University Press, 1993), 66.

9. Edwina Gateley, cited in *Mystics, Visionaries, and Prophets: A Historical Anthology of Women's Spiritual Writings*, ed. Shawn Madigan, C.S.J. (Minneapolis: Fortress Press, 1998), 492.

10. Mary Ward Brown, "A New Life," *God Stories*, ed. C. Michael Curtis (Boston: Houghton Mifflin, 1998), 22–34.

11. Marilynne Robinson, *Gilead* (New York: Farrar, Straus & Giroux, 2004).

Chapter 5

1. Ninian Smart, *Dimensions of the Sacred: An Anatomy of the World's Beliefs* (Berkeley: University of California Press, 1996), 4.

2. Adrian Cunningham, "Obituary: Ninian Smart," *The Independent*, London, February 5, 2001.

3. Smart, *Dimensions*, 4–5.

4. Vigen Guroian, *The Melody of Faith: Theology in an Orthodox Key* (Grand Rapids: Eerdmans, 2010), 5, 7.

5. Dorothy Day, *By Little and By Little*, ed. Robert Ellsberg (New York: Alfred A. Knopf, 1983), 69–70.

6. Gottlieb Mittelberger, "Journey to Pennsylvania," in *Pennsylvania Dutch Folk Spirituality*, ed. Richard E. Wentz (New York: Paulist, 1993), 121.

7. www.ccel.org/ccel/bartleman/los.i.html, "How Pentecost Came to Los Angeles," 57.

8. Flannery O'Connor, "Parker's Back," *The Complete Short Stories of Flannery O'Connor* (New York: Farrar, Straus & Giroux, 1971), 510–30.

9. James Agee, *The Morning Watch* (New York: Ballantine, 1950).

Chapter 6

1. Catherine Bell, *Ritual: Perspectives and Dimensions* (New York: Oxford University Press, 1997), 169.

2. E. D. Neill, *The Episcopal Recorder*, www.infidels.org/library/john_remsburg /six_historic_americans/chapter_3.

3. Peter W. Marty, "Praise in an Awe-Deficient World," *The Lutheran*, January 2011, 3.

4. Anne Lamott, *Traveling Mercies: Some Thoughts on Faith* (New York: Anchor, 2000), 100.

5. Justin, trans. Gordon Lathrop, *Central Things: Worship in Word and Sacrament* (Minneapolis: Augsburg Fortress, 2005), 78–79.

6. Nora Gallagher, *Things Seen and Unseen: A Year Lived in Faith* (New York: Vintage, 1998), 126.

7. Suzanne Strempek Shea, *Sundays in America: A Yearlong Road Trip in Search of Christian Faith* (Boston: Beacon, 2008).

Chapter 7

1. Clifford Geertz, *The Interpretation of Cultures* (Philadelphia: Basic, 1973), 89.

2. Geertz, 94.

3. Geertz, 124–25.

4. Pliny the Younger, www.earlychristianwritings.com/text/pliny.html.

5. *Augustine: Confessions and Enchiridion*, trans. Albert C. Outler, The Library of Christian Classics VII (Philadelphia: Westminster, 1955), 54–55.

6. *Egeria: Diary of a Pilgrimage*, trans. and ed. George E. Gingras, Ancient Christian Writers 38 (New York: Paulist, 1970), 11.

7. www.earlyamerica.com/lives/franklin/chapt10.

8. Jaime Lara, *Christian Texts for Aztecs: Art and Liturgy in Colonial Mexico* (Notre Dame: University of Notre Dame Press, 2008), 141, 143.

9. www.en.wikipedia.org/wiki/List_of_Christian_denominations.

10. "The Martyrdom of Saints Perpetua and Felicitas," *The Acts of the Christian Martyrs*, trans. and ed. Herbert Musurillo (Oxford: Clarendon, 1972), 110.

Chapter 8

1. William James, *The Varieties of Religious Experience* (New York: New American Library, 1958), 55.

2. James, 54.

3. James, 277.

4. Lawrence Cunningham, *The Meaning of Saints* (San Francisco: Harper & Row, 1980), 65.

5. St. Patrick's Breastplate, trans. Juilene Osborne-McKnight, *I Am of Irelaunde* (New York: Tom Doherty Associates, 2000), 154.

6. Justin Catanoso, *My Cousin the Saint: A Search for Faith, Family, and Miracles* (New York: HarperCollins, 2008), 125, 271–72.

7. www.hymnsite.com.

8. Wayne Weible, *Medjugorje: The Message* (Orleans, MA: Paraclete, 1989), 115–17.

9. Sandra Cisneros, "Little Miracles, Kept Promises," in *A Celestial Omnibus: Short Fiction on Faith*, ed. J. P. Maney and Tom Hazuka (Boston: Beacon, 1997), 3–14.

10. Kimberly Cutter, *The Maid* (New York: Bloomsbury, 2011).

Chapter 9

1. Max Weber, *The Sociology of Religion* (Boston: Beacon, 1963), 17.

2. Niebuhr's preferred form, www.wikipedia.com.

3. Abraham Lincoln's *Second Inaugural Address*, www.wikisource.com.

4. Mario Cuomo, "Religious Beliefs and Public Morality," www.archives.nd.edu.

5. *The Works of the Right Reverend John England, First Bishop of Charleston* (Cleveland: Arthur H. Clark Co., 1908), V, 192–94.

6. Albert Barnes, *The Church and Slavery* (Philadelphia: Parry & McMillan, 1857), 34–39.

7. Hunthausen, pastoral letter, cited in *A Documentary History of Religion in America Since 1865*, ed. Edwin S. Gaustad (Grand Rapids: Eerdmans, 1983), 598–99.

8. D. James Kennedy and Jerry Newcombe, *How Would Jesus Vote? A Christian Perspective on the Issues* (Colorado Springs: WaterBrook, 2008), 118.

9. Jim Wallis, *God's Politics: Why the Right Gets It Wrong and the Left Doesn't Get It* (San Francisco: HarperCollins, 2005), 235.

Chapter 10

1. Edwina Sandys, video #1176118-One-Bite-of-the-Apple.

2. Mary Douglas, *Purity and Danger: An Analysis of Concepts of Pollution and Taboo* (Baltimore: Penguin, 1970), 67.

3. Rosemary Radford Ruether, *Sexism and God-Talk: Toward a Feminist Theology* (Boston: Beacon, 1993), 18–19.

4. "The Religious Experience and Journal of Mrs. Jarena Lee," in *Spiritual Narratives*, Introduction by Susan Houchins (New York: Oxford University Press, 1988), 2:11.

5. Dennis P. Hollinger, *The Meaning of Sex: Christian Ethics and the Moral Life* (Grand Rapids: Baker Academic, 2009), 138–39.

6. Lauren Thatcher Ulrich, *A Midwife's Tale: The Life of Martha Ballard, Based on Her Diary, 1785-1812* (New York: Vintage Books, 1990), 152.

7. Beverly Wildung Harrison, "Theology of Pro-Choice: A Feminist Perspective," in *Abortion: The Moral Issues*, ed. Edward Batchelor Jr. (New York: Pilgrim, 1982), 223.

8. Walker Percy, "The Promiscuous Self," in *The Substance of Things Hoped For*, ed. John Breslin, SJ (Garden City, NY: Doubleday, 1987), 231–43.

Chapter 11

1. Alfred North Whitehead, *Science and the Modern World* (New York: Macmillan, 1925), 189.

2. Whitehead, 191.

3. Carl Boberg, "How Great Thou Art," www.wikipedia.com.

4. Origen, *De Principiis*, Book IV, 16.

5. Thomas Aquinas, *Summa Theologiae*, 1a, 9, reply.

6. www.oratoriosanfilippo.org/galileo-baronio-english.pdf.

7. James A. Connor, *Kepler's Witch* (San Francisco: HarperCollins, 2004), 332.

8. Arthur Peacocke, *Paths from Science towards God: The End of All Our Exploring* (Oxford: Oneworld, 2001), 139.

9. Henry M. Morris and Martin E. Clark, *The Bible Has the Answer*, rev. ed. (Green Forest, AR: Master, 1987), 105–6.

10. Sallie McFague, *The Body of God: An Ecological Theology* (Minneapolis: Fortress Press, 1993), 18, 20.

11. Ian G. Barbour, *Religion and Science: Historical and Contemporary Issues*, rev. and expanded ed. (New York: HarperCollins, 1997), 269.

12. John Breck, "Orthodox Bioethics in the Encounter Between Science and Religion," in *Science and the Eastern Orthodox Church*, ed. Daniel Buxhoeveden and Gayle Woloschak (Burlington, VT: Ashgate, 2011), 130.

13. Cyril of Jerusalem, *Lectures on the Christian Sacraments*, ed. F. L. Cross (Crestwood, NY: St. Vladimir's Seminary Press, 1977), 75.

14. William Hoffman, "The Question of Rain," *God Stories*, ed. C. Michael Curtis (New York: Houghton Mifflin, 1998), 95–107.

15. Mark Salzman, *Lying Awake* (New York: Vintage, 2000).

Chapter 12

1. John Hick, *An Interpretation of Religion: Human Responses to the Transcendent*, 2nd ed. (New Haven: Yale University Press, 2004), xxv.

2. Tony Campolo, *Speaking My Mind: The Radical Evangelical Prophet Tackles the Tough Issues Christians Are Afraid to Face* (Nashville: W Publishing Group, 2004), xi–xii.

3. D. B. Quinn, ed., *New American World* (New York: Arno Press and Hector Bye, 1979), 238–39.

4. *Evangelical Lutheran Worship, Leaders Desk Edition* (Minneapolis: Augsburg Fortress, 2006), 637.

5. Karl Rahner, SJ, *Theological Investigations*, vol. VI (Baltimore: Helicon, 1969), 391–94.

6. For one example, see Kathryn M. Lohre, "Upholding common human values and respecting differences," www.wcc-coe.org/wcc/what/interreligious/cd48-02.html.

7. Diana L. Eck, *Encountering God: A Spiritual Journey from Bozeman to Banaras* (Boston: Beacon, 1993), 196.

8. Robert D. Putnam and David E. Campbell, *American Grace: How Religion Divides and Unites Us* (New York: Simon & Schuster, 2010).

9. Leslie Marmon Silko, "The Man to Send Rain Clouds," in *A Celestial Omnibus: Short Fiction on Faith*, ed. J. P. Maney and Tom Hazuka (Boston: Beacon, 1997), 49–53.

10. Jill Paton Walsh, *Knowledge of Angels* (Boston: Houghton Mifflin, 1994).

Conclusion

1. Kenda Creasy Dean, *Almost Christian: What the Faith of Our Teenagers Is Telling the American Church* (New York: Oxford University Press, 2010).

PHOTO CREDITS

Fig. 10.2: Credit: Hemis.fr / SuperStock.

Fig. 10.4: Photo © Jocelyn Mathewes (www.jocelynmathewes.com). Used by permission.

Fig. 11.1: Credit: *Journal of the American Medical Association* (1986).

Fig. 11.3: Calvin and Hobbes © 1996 Watterson. Dist. By Universal Uclick. Reprinted with permission. All rights reserved.

Fig. 12.1: © Andrew Penner / istockphoto.

Fig. 12.3: For more information about The Faith Club visit www.thefaithclub.com.

Fig. 12.4: Photo © Librado Romero / The New York Times. Used by permission of Redux Pictures LLC. All rights reserved.

Fig. 12.7: Credit: Miguel Salgado / Used here under Creative Commons SSA 3.0 license.

The following images are in the public domain: Intro. 2, Intro. 4, 1.1, 1.2, 1.6, 1.7, 2.5, 3.2, 3.4, 3.6, 4.3, 4.4, 6.5, 7.5, 7.6, 7.7, 7.8, 7.10, 7.11, 8.1, 8.2, 8.3, 9.4, 9.5, 9.6, 10.3, 10.5, 11.2, 11.4, 11.5, 12.2, 12.5, 12.6, Concl. 1, Concl. 2.

INDEX

CPSIA information can be obtained
at www.ICGtesting.com
Printed in the USA
BVHW051742021120
592333BV00006B/66